Sport and violence in Europe

Dominique Bodin
Luc Robène
Stéphane Héas

Council of Europe Publishing

French edition:
Sports et violences en Europe
ISBN 92-871-5510-0

The opinions expressed in this work are the responsibility of the authors and do not necessarily reflect the position of the Council of Europe.

All rights reserved. No part of this publication may be translated, reproduced or transmitted, in any form or by any means – electronic (CD-Rom, Internet, etc.) or mechanical, including photocopying, recording or any information storage or retrieval system – without prior permission in writing from the Publishing Division, Communication and Research Directorate (F-67075 Strasbourg Cedex or publishing@coe.int).

Cover photo: Pluriel/Blaise
Cover design: Graphic Design Workshop, Council of Europe
Layout: Desktop Publishing Unit, Council of Europe

Published by Council of Europe Publishing
http://book.coe.int
F-67075 Strasbourg Cedex

ISBN 92-871-5511-9
© Council of Europe, June 2005
Printed at the Council of Europe

Contents

	Page
The authors	7
Foreword	9
The nature of sport	11
The origins of sport	11
Sport and violence	13
Violence in sport: from rude behaviour to bloodbath	15
Is there more to sport than violence?	16
Football grounds and violence	19
Is hooliganism a type of violence particular to modern society?	19
Hooliganism at ancient games	21
Hooliganism and football today	23
Hooligans as ordinary young people	42
How can the development of hooliganism in Europe be assessed?	42
The problem of failure to define hooliganism	43
Just ordinary young people	43
Hooliganism and social disorganisation	45
Social anomie	45
Absence of relationships and a laissez-faire attitude leave room for hooliganism	45
Hooliganism and the line between laissez-faire and collusion	47
The consequences of applying or failing to apply social rules	49
The difficulty of introducing an effective crowd control policy	52
Political ideologies in the football stadium	57
In the beginning: the British skinhead movement	57
Fan culture and political ideologies	58
The nature of ideology in the stadiums	59
Emerging shades of extremism	64
Ought sport to be any better than the rest of society?	66
Disasters – another form of violence	67
Organisational failure or a poor response by police and security staff: Sheffield and Heysel	67
Ill luck	68

    Mercenary motives on the part of those in charge 69
    Dilapidated infrastructure 70

Sport, politics and the violence they have in common 71

How sport is used as a political tool, and the political functions of violence in sport 73

    Sport as a stage for political violence and counter-violence 73
    Sport as a means of retaliation or sanction 78
    Sport as a seedbed for violence in politics 80

Sport and reasons of state 82

    Physical and ideological conditioning 82

The state, and forms of political violence in sport 84

Violence in sport from an economic perspective 89

Money and sport in Europe: strengths and fault lines 91

    Economic portrait of sporting Europe shows considerable disparities ... 91
    Unequal provision of sports infrastructure and equipment 96
    Money in sport, and the imbalances between different types of sport 99
    Budgetary inequalities among European clubs: the example of football 103
    Does the economic domination of sport in Europe inevitably generate inequality? 106

Deregulation of the sport market: business v. ethics 111

    From the Bosman ruling to flexibility 111
    Athletes subject to influence 114
    Marketing sporting prowess and managing the trade in athletes and players 119
    The dehumanisation of sport 124
    Sponsorship, and athletes as human billboards 127

Sports scandals in Europe 129

    Mafia-type interests at work 129
    Corruption as a form of regulation 131
    The interface between business and terrorism 133
    Sport and business: a voyage through troubled waters 135

Media violence and manipulation through sport 141

Sport, the media and propaganda 141

Inequalities in the allocation of airtime 144

Sport, business and the media: the emergence of a "product" 146

Disenchantment 151

Human bodies and violence 155
Difficulties of approach and angles of interpretation 155
How Europeans approach sport and other forms of physical exercise .. 156

Physical injuries and accidents in sport: media images and reality 159
The mass media and the violence associated with sport: are these forms of violence emphasised or overlooked, prevented or intended? 159
    Does violence invite further violence? 159
    Sport as the "opium of the people": a modern version of the circus? 163
Sports accidents do happen – and are even documented 166
    Alarming data on sudden death among athletes 166
    Accidentology: a convincing body of data 169

Addiction, sport and human bodies: strong political and social implications for Europe 179
Looking beyond addiction as a medical problem 180
    Addiction or a personalised biochemical approach to human beings 181
    Are we trying to make physical activity too "reasonable"? 185
Doping as a behaviour pattern: alien or familiar? 188
    Are both sport and doping modern imperatives? 188
    Finding an approach to doping between control and negotiation ... 191

Violence directed at minority groups 197
Work and reason over-valued 197
    Early and intensive training, and the power of dominant social and cultural thinking 199
    Demystifying sport and enforcing laws and rights 202
    What values ought to be rehabilitated? 204
Real violence and symbolic violence: the gender factor 207
    Where and when are women involved in the practice of sport? 209
    How violence in different forms excludes sportsmen as well as sportswomen: from gynophobia to homophobia 215

Conclusion 221
Is there nothing more to sport in Europe than violence? 221

Bibliography 229

The authors

Dominique Bodin

Lecturer in Sociology at the Department of Science and Technology for Physical Education and Sports, University of Rennes 2, and member of the university's Research Unit for Teaching Methods, Skills and Technology in Physical Education and Sports. Associate of the Education and Training Social Research Unit at the University of Bordeaux 2.

Luc Robène

Lecturer in History at the Department of Science and Technology for Physical Education and Sports, University of Rennes 2, and member of the university's Research Unit for Teaching Methods, Skills and Technology in Physical Education and Sports.

Stéphane Héas

Lecturer in Sociology at the Department of Science and Technology for Physical Education and Sports, University of Rennes 2. Member of the university's Research Unit for Teaching Methods, Skills and Technology in Physical Education and Sports and associate of the Social Development Research Unit, an arm of its Sociological Analysis Unit.

Foreword

In setting out to write a book entitled *Sport and violence in Europe* we realised that we faced many pitfalls. First there was the danger of merely painting the same grim picture as we so often find in press coverage of sports events at all levels – a picture of corruption, doping, wheeler-dealing, cheating and violence in various forms. All this, of course, cannot be entirely avoided, for sport is much more than organised play. It involves issues, desires and objectives, success and failure, validation and identity-building and is thus a social activity within a competitive system.

Another danger was that we might limit our analysis of sport (or sports) to the perspective of sociological criticism, arguing in effect that if there seemed at times, or indeed frequently, to be little distinction between violence and sport, it was because sport had political functions: external functions in helping to promote an established political system, or internal functions as a simple "opium of the people", helping to place society in soft focus, blurring class divisions and social problems as part of a "bread and circuses" approach.

Then there was the opposite pitfall of simply echoing the praise too often heaped on sport as a world apart, less stressful than ordinary civil society and one that lends itself to the promotion of education, inclusion, integration and the prevention of violence both in society generally and among young people – not to mention good health and countless other benefits, to the point that sport is seen as a universal solution, a miracle cure for social ills and individuals' problems and shortcomings.

Yet another danger was that it might not prove possible to illustrate our themes with examples from the whole of Europe, for such examples serve not only to promote understanding but also to extend the reader's awareness beyond the national context to the European one. Drawing examples from all over Europe also helps to spread the reference base and thus to avoid castigating certain countries more than others. We decided to take on all these challenges at once, postulating that the pleasure and passion of involvement in sport can sometimes bring with it mechanisms of exclusion or domination, manifestations of nationalism or xenophobia, and forms of violence both physical and non-physical. It may be that sport (like a modern version of market-square entertainment) simply mirrors our societies, their complexities, functions and dysfunctions, as well as their cultural, economic and social development. Far from aiming for an exhaustive treatment of the subject – an unrealistic aim in any case – we chose to address a number of themes selected for specific reasons. On the one hand we aim to highlight, through an exploration of some familiar territory, both the ambiguous relationship between sport and violence and the emergence of European regulations and directives, as well as sports programmes that set out to promote intercultural exchanges in the broad sense (whether within nations or internationally) as a means of preventing violence. On the other hand, by looking at different forms of violence in sport and offering readers a number of essential, up-to-date references to stimulate their appetite for further study, we invite them to make their own intellectual journey.

The word "Europe" features in our title, but what Europe do we mean? Are we talking about the countries that currently form the European Union? Do we include those waiting to join it? Or do we mean a somewhat broader entity, embracing "non-European" countries that are nonetheless – by virtue of their proximity to Europe, their political links or their ongoing economic exchanges with it – our "partners": countries like the Russian Federation, for example, our relations with which necessarily influence our choices and decisions?

It was this last approach that we decided to adopt, on the basis that, just as policies (including sporting policies) may be intertwined, peoples, cultures and ethnic groups frequently exist and move across borders, and such movement may result either in forms of violence apparently based on ancient cultural antagonisms or, on the contrary, in the development and further promotion of intercultural exchanges and closer ties between peoples.

Ultimately the book aims to pull together the main themes relevant to the relationship between sport and violence, drawing in a balanced way on information from the media, from court reports and the law and from statistics and research. Because the subject is too big for a single book – and to imagine otherwise would be unrealistic – we have also tried to supply a bibliography that will offer readers a wide range of contemporary references, enabling them to explore the field further in the light of their own interests.

The nature of sport

The origins of sport

This book is not intended as a history of sport and violence. Many such histories have been written over the years and it is unlikely that we could improve upon them. To attempt it would not only be beyond our resources, but would also be a dubious venture in terms of methodology if it assumed a linear pattern of events – a pattern long refuted by the majority of historians. Instead, our aim will be to observe and analyse the close and complicated connections that exist today between sports and violence. We use the plural here advisedly for while "sport" and "violence" are intimately connected concepts, they are each in their own right complex and multifaceted.

Some authors consider that sport had its origins in violence, in ancient rituals or in wars marking out milestones in the life of societies (Jeu, 1975). Much television airtime continues to be devoted to interviews or programmes on themes such as "Sport? It's war!" or "Sport as a substitute for war". Suffice it to note that, since ancient times, there has been a continuing association between violence and what was to become "sport" – although it began as a range of specific physical practices. The ancient games (Corinthian, Isthmian, Nemean and Olympic) offered, at least to some extent, a respite from conflict. They really did represent a substitute for, or an alternative form of, warmaking, a means of affirming the supremacy of a city state over its rivals. Physical practices such as *pancratium* (Graeco-Roman wrestling) were extremely violent, resulting on occasions in the death of the combatants (Jeu, 1987). Doping was already practised although it relied more on religious and folk beliefs than on the range of products (chiefly synthetic but also biological) in use today. Beliefs were as powerful then as now and they served to augment the effects, specific and general, of various substances that were rubbed in, ingested or inhaled. Some athletes, for example, ate different meats according to their speciality: fatty pork for wrestlers who wanted to develop their body mass, goat to improve jumping ability and bull meat for fist fighters (De Mondenard, 2000, p. 7). Historians and philosophers have also left us records of crowd behaviour, collapsing amphitheatres and clashes between rival groups of fans that strongly resemble events which have occurred at modern-day soccer matches.

We intend to concentrate, however, on the relationship between modern sports, which developed in England in the late eighteenth century, and violence.

Despite the similarities between modern sport and the ancient games (the competitive aspect and the importance of fair play etc.), four key factors make today's sports distinct: they are widespread, they are highly organised, the element of physical violence within them has been reduced, and they have a specific social function.

The most obvious difference is the way in which sports have spread throughout society and around the world. Whereas only a small number of individuals physically participated in the ancient games, modern sports are potentially accessible to everyone. That is not to say that there is no inequality. People in less advanced countries are less likely to practise a sport, and in moderately wealthy or industrialised countries sports are obviously practised differently, in different contexts and for different purposes, depending on the social, cultural and national backgrounds of the participants. The most striking factor, however, is the fact that sports have largely gone global. Very few people now can avoid seeing sports played. Despite glaring inequalities between developed and developing countries and between inhabitants of developed countries in terms of income levels and leisure time, more and more sports facilities are being built and so many sporting events are broadcast on television that it sometimes seems there can be no escape from sport. It has become, to all intents and purposes, a universal phenomenon.

The second distinction lies in organisation. Unlike ancient games (such as the French *soule*) modern sports do not have an explicitly ritualistic or ceremonial function, and are not tied to a religious calendar (Bourdieu, 1979; Chartier and Vigarello, 1982; Elias and Dunning, 1986). As sport established itself, it created its own calendar separate from that of ordinary community life, it gradually standardised local practices (in terms of numbers of players, rules and pitch sizes, for example), and it facilitated social mixing among its practitioners.

The third factor is the clear decrease in physical violence among competitors. Sport in its modern form has been "sanitised". The violence played out on pitches and in arenas is symbolic (Jeu, 1975, 1987) – when a commentator declares that a beaten team is "dead" it is not to be taken literally – and in the rare cases where death does result it is at a later stage as a consequence of injuries sustained or illness contracted. In a nutshell, sport no longer serves the same purpose. Whereas the ancient games were essentially a preparation or substitute for war, sport in the twentieth century has gradually come to reflect different aims and values, such as education, the pursuit of hedonism, fitness and body-building, an appetite for competition and spectacle, social or occupational integration, a sense of belonging and social cohesion. There are also other reasons, however, for the decline in violence. As society has become more peaceful, individuals have become less tolerant of violence.

The same process has taken place within sport, so much so that participation in the most violent sports, such as boxing, has declined sharply in the space of 100 years as people have turned instead to new forms of physical activity (like rhythmic gymnastics, climbing and surfing) where the emphasis is on aestheticism or contact with the natural world. Sport thus holds up a mirror to our societies and the changes affecting them, our different cultures and the way they manage and interpret the emotions that individuals experience. Elias and Dunning went so far as to assert that "knowledge about sport was knowledge about society" (1986, p.19).

The clearest difference between modern sports and the ancient games, however, is their function in society, for modern sports play a role in controlling violence. In his study of the "civilising process" Elias (1969a/b) shows how modern societies based themselves on the condemnation of violence and the state monopoly of it and how, in this process, warriors were turned into agents of the sovereign authority,[1] standards of civility, cleanliness and respect were introduced, violence was "euphemised"[2] and individuals were trained to curb their impulses.

Invented originally to round off the education of young members of the "English upper classes, the landed aristocracy and gentry", sport gradually spread to the rest of society as people began to have leisure time: it offered not only a means of learning to accept control and to exercise self-control (through observance of the rules and respect for one's opponents and the referee or umpire, through the training process and through co-operation between team members) but also a place where emotions had a physical outlet and spectators could yell encouragement or vent their anger. The title and subtitle of Elias's and Dunning's book, *The quest for excitement: sport and leisure in the civilizing process,* is a good indicator of the role they ascribe to sport in society.

Sport and violence

Here, however, we find the first ambiguity inherent in modern sport. It is indeed a codified, or euphemised, area of society in which violence is not like the violence of the ancient games, being more symbolic than real, yet it is also an area unlike any other in contemporary society, one in which people can express passion, despair, fervour, discontent and violence, and can be released from them.

---
1. Elias (1985) uses the word "courtization" in this context to describe the gradual transformation of the mediaeval warrior nobles of feudal times into a courtly nobility grouped together around a sovereign, a process that was repeated more or less everywhere in Europe.
2. Reduction in the incidence and severity of violence.

But how should we define violence? Elias can describe sport as helping to channel violence because his definition of violence is limited to its physical manifestations. In this he takes the same line as Chesnais, who denies that violence can also assume moral and symbolic forms and asserts that to speak of violence in that sense is a misuse of language on the part of certain western intellectuals (Chesnais, 1981, p. 13).

To accept such a narrow definition is to overlook the extent of the violence that exists in sport in different forms, and to change how we interpret it. It also means focusing exclusively on visible – and thus "standardised" – violence. But such an approach is surely unrealistic. As Skogan (1990), Roché (1996, 2001) and Debarbieux (1996, 2002) have shown in relation to other areas where antagonisms exist, it is impossible to conceive of violence merely in its most abrupt manifestation, that of assault and battery whether deliberate or not, still less in terms of crime, premeditated or otherwise. The fact is that the most minor occurrences, the least manifestations of rudeness, can generate a spiral of violence within which people's perceptions of violence differ – depending on whether their viewpoint is that of aggressor or victim, of the weaker or the stronger party, of an inhabitant of western Europe or someone whose country is at war, or on whether they live on a tough housing estate or in a fashionable suburb, on whether they are male or female, young or old and whether or not they have already experienced violence. So significant are these differences that perceptions of violence may reasonably be classed as objective or subjective (Wieviorka, 1999). Bodin has made the point that what we call violence, or at least what is regarded as violence in our modern western societies, would certainly not have the same significance in other places or in other eras. The perpetration and perception of violence are thus conditioned by its social, spatial and temporal context (Bodin, 2001, p. 11).

And if we accept only the limited definition, how do we classify verbal violence? How do we classify demonstrations of racism and xenophobia that stop short of racist attacks? How do we address the role of women in sport at both competitive and management levels? Or the role of people with disabilities? How do we discuss doping or the suspected links between some sports and criminal, indeed mafia, milieus? How can we interpret hooliganism if we do not attempt to understand and identify the multiple incidents of rudeness, harmless "fun" or provocation that lead up to it?

The definition proposed by Héritier would seem better suited to describing and understanding what goes on in the realm of sport, and it is that definition we have chosen to follow in exploring the relationship between sport and violence. She takes the view that the word "violence" may be applied in all sorts of contexts where situations occur that are marked by violence: not only violent acts, hatred, rage, massacre, cruelty or collective atrocities, but also the "softer" forms of violence perpetrated by economic domination, by the capital/labour relationship or the north/south divide, not to mention the "everyday" violence meted out to people in vulnerable positions such as women, children and the socially marginalised (Héritier,1996, p. 13).

After all, it is important in describing modern sport not to overlook the essential. As it was gradually organised into an institutional system of predominantly physical competitive practices, each delimited, codified and governed by an agreed set of rules, for the declared purpose of comparing performances, exploits, achievements or physical prowess in order to designate a champion or set a record (Brohm, 1992, p. 89), sport became a "total social phenomenon" which could thus animate society and its institutions in their entirety (Mauss, 1923, p. 274). While sport certainly has a celebratory aspect and an aspect of challenge before an assembled crowd (Jeu, 1993), it also provides an occasion, medium or backdrop for many violent acts. Violence of different kinds results not only from the clashes between individual trajectories, but also from the ways in which these are used for political or economic ends. Sport needs to be seen not merely as something virtuous and praiseworthy (promoting education, health, a sense of belonging, integration and social cohesion) but rather as a more complex social reality.

Violence in sport: from rude behaviour to bloodbath

Examples of rude behaviour[3] (arguing with a referee or goading opponents) occur regularly, and verbal and symbolic violence (insults directed at players or referees, or the provocation of rival fans) are commonplace. Female athletes are frequently harassed, sexually and otherwise, although such cases are often deliberately forgotten or hushed up.[4] Exclusion in one form or another affects many sportspeople: female players who have to put up with unsuitable training or match schedules and second-rate coaching, and the women who find themselves denied posts in sports management,[5] as well as people with disabilities, the less gifted, and even highly talented athletes if they are out of favour with the powers-that-be. It is reasonable to use the term "institutional violence" in such cases. Of course, the most familiar forms of violence are physical: athletes sustain injury in competition or through over-

---

3. Minor non-punishable incidents that are not in themselves reprehensible but that ultimately have the effect of harming social relations.
4. Female athletes also need a great deal of courage and patience in order to establish that they have suffered physical or psychological harm. This was evident in 1993 in a case where four members of the French Athletics Federation were charged with raping a female colleague.
5. It is instructive to look at the number of national sports federations in Europe that are headed by women or the number of women with nationwide responsibility for different sports.

training and sometimes careers are ended as a result, as in the case of gymnast Elodie Lussac, who was forced to go on competing when injured; there are cases of doping and deaths of athletes; there are violent clashes between fans; stadium stands have collapsed, killing and injuring large numbers of people; and on occasions incidents between fans have been bloodily suppressed, as in 1984 in Moscow, when 340 deaths resulted. Sport also provides an occasion for, and re-ignites, local, national and international antagonisms. There is opposition in every country between provincial regions and the capital. Sporting encounters between France and Germany are highly partisan, and the levels of ticket sales and airtime for the United States v. Iran match in the 1998 World Cup were out of all proportion to the soccer skills of the two teams involved.

All this being so, it would be hard to deny the existence of the "domestic and external political functions" underlying sporting activities (Brohm, 1992). The evidence is not hard to find. There are extremist movements that have no scruples about parading their ideologies at sports stadiums, which thus become the scene of manifestations of racism and xenophobia. Sports venues can also be turned into arenas for ethnic, cultural or religious conflict. The clashes between Croat and Serb supporters at the European Water Polo Championships in 2003 are one example. At international level, the east-west sporting rivalry of the cold war was surely war-making of another kind, or at least a means of promoting and asserting the supremacy of a political and economic system. The many boycotts of Olympic Games were indicators of these political tensions. Only in such a context can we understand the reaction of General de Gaulle, when he declared, after the debacle of the Rome Olympic Games, "Never again!" or the statement by former East German Chancellor Erich Honecker at a press conference to launch the 1984 Olympics: "Sport is not an end in itself; it is a means of achieving other ends."

Since the fall of the Berlin Wall, however, politics has taken second place to economics. Not all aspects of the commercialisation of modern sport are negative, of course. Top athletes in certain sports have been the first to reap real benefits from the change. But sport has also been affected by corruption (involving, for example, the International Olympic Committee and more recently the President of the Portuguese Professional Football League) and there have been examples of shady ties being forged with mafia-type or terrorist organisations.

Is there more to sport than violence?

There is, of course, more to sport than violence. In the end it is probably no more than what people make it. While it can sometimes be a theatre of insanity, it is also an outlet for huge numbers of enthusiasts. It is the stuff of our children's dreams, as they identify with the champions, mimic their moves and dream of one day becoming champions themselves. It is also a powerful engine of integration and social inclusion. In France, for example, no one cares a jot whether Zidane or Platini before him are second-generation immigrants or simply French citizens. Sport is a celebration that brings people together and allows them to relate to one another. The opening and closing ceremonies of the Olympic Games are there to remind us that sport is more than opposition and confrontation between individuals and nations; it also brings nations together in one place, where people can meet, pit themselves and measure themselves against one another and thus get to know one another, accept one another and appreciate their differences. In addition, sport is a means of "rehabilitation" for individuals. This is evident, for example, in prisons, where the centuries-old policy of surveillance and punishment (Foucault, 1975), reflecting a utilitarian penal logic, has been replaced by the aim of educating prisoners, with sport as part of the process, not merely as occupational therapy but rather as one means of enabling inmates to socialise through recreational activity. A similar approach can be seen in countries at war – a good example being the work of the "Sports sans frontières" organisation in Kosovo in fostering co-operation between children from different communities.

Thus it is not sport itself that is on trial, but rather what people make or seek to make of it. It is important that those involved at all levels in sport, as participants or decision makers, should bear this in mind, so that the sports field can continue to be a place of fusion, a place of communion among individuals who might well be diametrically opposed in terms of culture, politics or religion, and a place where they can achieve what politicians so often fail to achieve, namely a certain form of humanism (Bodin, 2001, p. 202).

Football grounds and violence

Is hooliganism a type of violence particular to modern society?

If there is one specific form of violence commonly associated with sport, or at least with sports fans, it is hooliganism. One could almost say that, in everyday conversation, hooliganism is the only form of violence actually recognised as such, apart from the violence that athletes inflict on one another and themselves either as part of a culture of excessive effort or on the field of play. This focus on hooliganism probably reflects the fact that certain violent events are blown up by the media, or it may be that most people find hooliganism particularly hard to reconcile with the traditionally celebratory image of sport.

In order to understand hooliganism, however, we need to look beyond the common definitions and collective perceptions of the problem, and the prevailing stereotypes and prejudices. A hooligan in the popular imagination is a young English male who has difficulty fitting into society, a delinquent in everyday life, who gets drunk and uses football matches as pretext for going on the rampage in the stadium. But events have shown that the social reality of the phenomenon is much more complex than we might imagine from this simplistic picture. Examples abound: police officers beaten up in the Boulogne stand at Parc des Princes on 28 August 1993 during a match between Paris Saint-Germain (PSG) and Caen; the attack on Gendarme Daniel Nivel by four hooligans in the vicinity of the Bollaert ground in Lens on 21 June 1998 during the World Cup tournament; the manifestations in recent years of racism and xenophobia in stadiums virtually everywhere in Europe, from the grounds of Rome and Parma in Italy to those of Atletico and Real Madrid in Spain, PSG in France, and Red Star Belgrade in the former Yugoslavia; or the clashes between rival fans at the PSG-Galatasaray Champions League match on 13 March 2001, which left fifty-six people hurt. Hooliganism takes many forms and exists everywhere in Europe. The distorted perception of the reality may have its roots in the tragic events seen on television in 1985, when thirty-one spectators died at the Heysel stadium during the UEFA Champions League final between Liverpool and Juventus of Turin, in the way the tragedy was interpreted and in the sanctions subsequently imposed on English clubs and their fans. Yet Heysel was not an isolated case in the history of soccer or sport generally. Nor was it an archetypal case of hooliganism. These are forms of violence that affect soccer throughout the world but they are not all attributable to English fans nor indeed to ordinary law-breakers.

In order to understand hooliganism it is not enough to observe what are often events of extreme physical violence; instead, we need to situate the events within a historical and social process so that we can attempt to interpret them. All too frequently hooliganism is characterised by its ultimate expression: physical violence or damage to property and infrastructure. The violence may be the work of groups of fans inside a football ground or, given the crowd control measures commonly taken nowadays (a security ring around the ground, use of stewards inside the stadium, police presence, video surveillance and same-day court appearances for offenders), it may occur some distance away. It may be directed against the police force or against passers-by who have no connection with the match, or the aim may be to wreck cars, break shop windows or stone buses transporting rival fans. Clearly the violence practised by hooligans takes many forms but to list them like this provides no insight whatever into the way in which individuals – often quite unremarkable individuals – come to behave in such a manner. Rather, it encourages us to think of violence merely in terms of its active manifestation or the transgression of established social norms and the punitive measures taken in response, so that our awareness of it goes no further than a sociological definition of the criminal acts involved (Durkheim, 1895). Instead, we need to look at sequences of individually quite petty incidents (the theft of insignia, for example, exchanges of insults or provocations) in order to identify the root causes of much more serious and disturbing events. The types of violence described above are, in fact, merely the "practical accomplishment" (Garfinkel, 1967) of a long process of subtle and complex social interactions between different groups with a stake in a given sports event (supporters, managers, police officers and journalists). The process can involve sporting rivalry, acts of provocation or vendettas, reflecting the way in which the history of soccer and soccer clubs, at both "micro" and "macro" levels, helps to forge identities and cultures. It is simply not feasible to limit our perception of soccer fans' violence to sudden dramatic events such as the stabbing of a British fan in an alleyway in early 1998.

In many cases we find hooliganism lumped together with other unrelated phenomena: was the Heysel stadium tragedy a result of hooliganism, for example, or was it not due at least in part to shortcomings in passive security measures (crowd checking and surveillance, evacuation procedures or arrangements for segregating rival fans), shortcomings which subsequently led to the adoption of a European convention on the subject? Similarly, the media – in responding to breaking news, seeking to sensationalise and to offer the type of coverage that boosts ratings – have a tendency to ascribe to hooliganism events such as those that occurred in Sheffield in 1989, when ninety-five people were crushed to death as crowds tried to get into the Hillsborough stadium without tickets for the FA Cup semi-final between Liverpool and Nottingham Forest. Yet incidents like this may have more to do with police incompetence or (as in the case of the Furiani disaster in Bastia, Corsica, on 5 May 1992) with mercenary motives on the part of managers who attempt to sell more tickets than there are places in a stadium.

Hooliganism at ancient games

While hooliganism is associated mainly, if not exclusively, with modern-day soccer, clashes did occur on the occasion of physical contests in ancient times, just as they continue to occur at other types of sports events today.

The fact is that violent behaviour by crowds of sports fans is nothing new. Obviously, as indicated in the foreword, we are not attempting to place modern sport in a continuum stretching all the way back to the ancient games; we are simply making the point that at other periods of history, in other places and in connection with other contests, certain types of collective behaviour had much in common with present-day hooliganism. On occasions, indeed, the response to such incidents was to implement specific control measures that seem quite disturbingly modern: tightening the enforcement of order, barring individuals from an arena, restricting what people were permitted to bring in.

Without embarking on an entire historiography, it is instructive to look at a number of examples from different periods, which indicate an apparently recurrent pattern in the way in which crowds relate to the spectacle of competition and the violence it can engender.

One of the earliest records of clashes between rival fans is supplied by Tacitus (*Annals*, 14.17), who recounts a brawl in Pompeii in AD 59. During a gladiatorial contest organised in the city by Livenius Regulus, groups of spectators from Nuceria and Pompeii began trading insults and throwing stones and ended up in armed conflict. So many people were killed or injured in the clash that it resulted in a ten-year ban on Pompeians attending sports events and in the dissolution of "supporters' clubs". The parallels with English hooliganism in the 1980s and the banning of certain clubs from European competition is striking.

Thuillier (1996), in his study of *Le sport dans la Rome antique* [Sport in Ancient Rome], describes spectacles involving forms of sport that had a quite particular function: while, on the one hand, they constituted a type of military training, they were also recreational "treats" laid on for the public by civic councillors at ruinous expense. Although such activities, which took place in circuses and amphitheatres, were certainly intended as an "opium of the people", they nonetheless occasioned many incidents. There are records of several Heysel-style disasters when large numbers of people were crushed by crowds in the great circus in Rome, which had a capacity of more than 150 000. During the same period the amphitheatre at Fidenae, not far from Rome, (which was hastily built to accommodate large numbers of spectators) collapsed, killing and injuring hundreds.

Somewhat closer to our own day, the mediaeval game of *soule* – played in rural areas of France and involving two teams competing for possession of a pig's bladder, which they tried to bring home to hang on the belfry of their village church – occasioned so many passionate outbursts and brawls between spectators (sometimes settling private scores) that the Church officially banned it on the grounds that it provoked social unrest (Mendiague, 1993). English folk football of the same period, which shared only its name with the modern sport, involved similar incidents and was likewise banned on many occasions.

From the same era we have a singularly modern picture of the types of violence associated with chivalric tournaments and involving both participants and spectators. It was not uncommon for objects of all kinds to be thrown at the contestants, and laws were enacted repeatedly forbidding spectators to carry weapons, the fear being that rival groups would identify to such an extent with their respective champions' causes that they would end up fighting among themselves in the arena (Jusserand, 1901).

Bredekamp (1998) provides a description of various measures for keeping order among spectators (separation of rival groups of fans, a ban on pitch invasions, low tolerance of incidents, and maintenance of a police presence). Were he not writing about *calcio fiorentino*, a form of football played in Florence between the sixteenth and eighteenth centuries, one could be forgiven for assuming that the measures described were among those used to control football crowds in the Europe of the 1970s and 1980s!

In the late eighteenth century, the first ascents by balloonists were the scene of popular protests on a regular basis, occasioning angry unrest, extreme violence and vandalism to such an extent that in Bordeaux two troublemaking spectators were sentenced to death and hanged (Robène, 2001).

More recently again – in the late nineteenth century – Tranter (1995) describes the Cappielow riot of 8 April 1899, which involved 200 fans during a cup semi-final between Greenock Morton and Port Glasgow Athletic Club. He not only writes of a police crackdown but also describes how the level of violence in British football was on the increase at the time. All the incidents recounted are surprisingly modern, with parallels in the behaviour of today's hooligans and in the types of control measures put in place to prevent incidents or restore order.

These examples are enough to demonstrate – were any demonstration necessary – that what we refer to as "crowd violence" is not exclusively a phenomenon of contemporary sport or contemporary society.

In 1997 the French sports paper *L'Equipe* listed a global total of more than 1 300 deaths caused by hooliganism at football matches, the incidents having occurred more or less all over the world. Certain events even more tragic than the Heysel disaster were covered up for many years. In Moscow in 1982, for example, after a UEFA cup tie between Spartak and Haarlem (Netherlands), 340 people were killed in a police crackdown on unruly Spartak fans. One could continue in the same vein with a litany of incidents that have marred various games and sports, in particular soccer.

This brief chronological overview shows how violence associated with large gatherings of people and involving an element of competition and spectacle would seem to be a recurring fact of life, albeit in different forms ranging from rowdiness through rudeness, symbolic and verbal violence to pitch invasions, brawls, riots and killings. The examples also reinforce the point that violence associated with displays of physical competition is not new. Nor can it be narrowly understood as a modern social phenomenon, whether produced by the worrying problem of social breakdown in troubled peri-urban areas and housing estates or indeed by the impact of poverty on a section of the population.

Three factors would seem to distinguish hooliganism from the forms of crowd violence observable at sports events since ancient times, namely the frequency of violent incidents, their specific association with the sport of soccer, and the fact that hooliganism was initially confined to one particular country – Great Britain. Questions inevitably arise as to how and why this sport and this country were affected sooner and to a greater extent than others.

Hooliganism and football today

The first reason is structural. When the English invented modern sport and developed it in its collective forms from the mid-nineteenth century onwards (Elias and Dunning, op. cit.), they established spaces in the middle of towns and cities where physical activity had to obey certain standards and rules. These centres for regulated spectacle and confrontation, quite different from the impermanent venues of physical competition in the past, were the sports stadiums. In parallel with the development of sport went that of stadiums – requiring that competitive physical exercise take place in a local venue measured out for the purpose, where specific regulations applied (Beaulieu and

Perelman, 1977) – which had the effect of bringing together ever greater numbers of spectators confronting their rivals in the context of a shared purpose (a passion for sport) and a specific aim (the increasingly partisan support of a particular team). In 1930 Duhamel wrote of crowds in America occupying stadiums like "conquered fortresses" and noted that the spectacle of sport, far from being limited to events on the pitch, was situated most particularly "on the terraces, among the crowd" (Duhamel, 1930).

Alongside the actual sporting events, the stadiums – and also their periphery and immediate environs – thus became places of competition for cultural and social visibility and therefore places of symbolic and actual confrontation, reinforcing the very essence of sport. For it must be borne in mind when discussing the ambivalent relationship between sport and violence that the principle which brings individuals together in sport is the will to pit oneself against one another (Jeu, 1972, p. 156). While this is expressed in the first instance through the sport, it is unimaginable that differences of culture and identity should not connect with this sporting opposition in such a way as to stimulate more violent forms of conflict. To ignore this would be to deny that sport is part of society, or at least to create the impression that everyone entering a sports ground leaves their day-to-day anxieties and problems (including problems of sociability) at the gate.

There are no clues, however, as to why the spread of soccer-related violence throughout Europe and beyond was slower than that of the game itself. Certain aspects of the British experience were probably more conducive to the development of a particularly stable and virulent form of hooliganism. Yet it is also likely that the early rise of the phenomenon in the United Kingdom and its intensity there had the effect of partially obscuring its spread in other countries, leading observers to overlook the hooliganism that was on the increase in Europe in both football and other sports, including at amateur level. Basketball matches in Greece and Turkey have been affected by violence, for example, as have cricket matches in India and the European Water Polo Championship match, when rival Croat and Serb supporters clashed. Incidents have also marred lower-division rugby matches in France, and groups of French students were involved in brawls at inter-university games in 1997 and 1999. Nonetheless, these manifestations of violence have been infrequent. Soccer is the only sport to have been affected by hooliganism both in Europe and throughout the rest of the world and at every level of competition – for violence is certainly not confined to the professional football matches that have become media spectacles.

This observation is interesting inasmuch as it invites a further question: why should football, more than other sports, be not only a backdrop but also a vector for this type of violence?

Word play

The 1960s saw the emergence in the United Kingdom of new forms of violence associated with soccer matches. There had been brawls and clashes at matches since the late nineteenth century but the types of violence now seen in and around football grounds appeared less spontaneous. They were not necessarily triggered by anything in the game itself, the match result or incidents on the pitch (refereeing decisions, fouls, players' behaviour on the bench or during play), nor even by the sporting rivalry provoked by the competition itself. On occasions, too, they were extremely violent and involved large numbers of people. The violence was no longer occasional or impulsive, related to results or specific events in a pattern of frustration and aggression; instead it was organised, premeditated and often collective. The emergence of hooliganism as a concept marked both a change of behaviour and a change of paradigm (Bodin, 1999). In order to describe the events taking place, and eager to coin a new term, a journalist dubbed the violent fans "hoolihans", from the name of an Irish family, the heads of which were arrested in Victorian England for highly anti-social behaviour and rioting. No one knows, however, at what point or why the word shifted from "hoolihan" to "hooligan". The explanation may lie in a printer's error, the letters "g" and "h" being adjacent on the qwerty keyboard. In any event the term came into being, marking the emergence of new types of behaviour, and began to be used throughout Europe. It should be noted, however, that the British themselves favour the word "thugs", which comes from the name of a murderous religious fraternity in India, worshippers of the goddess Kali. The choice of terms is thus significant in itself, given the pejorative connotations. By the words used to describe them, the hooligans are already stigmatised as abnormal individuals on the margins of society and classified in advance as offenders, whatever the origins of their violence or the reasons why they engage in hooliganism.

The United Kingdom as the birthplace of hooliganism

We can trace six stages in the emergence of hooliganism in Europe.

Changing patterns of violence

The first phase covers the period from the late 1950s to the early 1960s, when journalists and researchers – sociologists for the most part – saw an increase in organised violence not only outside but also inside football grounds. The types of violence being observed were, on the face of it, different from what had gone before: there was a shift from "ritualised dionysiac violence", associated with the logic of the game and the antagonisms it aroused, to "premeditated violence" (Bodin, op. cit., p. 19). The customary manifestations of violence had previously been more or less sporadic, reflecting and rooted in the ambiguous essence of sport itself – which, as we have pointed out, has the function of bringing people together all the better to divide them (Jeu, 1992). Between the early twentieth century and the 1960s, violent incidents arose from spectators' perceptions (always partisan to some extent) of the refereeing or the play, and also from general sporting rivalry. They tended to reflect chauvinism, irritation or spontaneous rowdyism, all part of the culture of the typical football match crowd, drawn mostly from the working classes. These forms of violence can still be found today in other sports such as rugby. The distinct emergent forms of conflict, however, also highlighted social and cultural divisions.

From this period onwards hooliganism came to be defined as violence that was deliberately perpetrated in an organised, structured and premeditated manner, not so different, in fact, from organised crime (Dufour-Gompers, 1992, p. 94). To approach the question of hooliganism in this way is to externalise its possible causes and to create a number of problems from the outset. First of all, in drawing the distinction between spontaneous and premeditated violence, researchers have excluded from the scope of their studies factors associated with the game, the results, or indeed, with excessive alcohol consumption. It is true that not all hooligans arrested are inebriated. Likewise, violent behaviour on the part of spectators does not necessarily occur after mistakes by the referee, controversies on the pitch or even defeats. So violent incidents cannot be regarded simply as the work of an intoxicated, fanatic crowd without a conscience (as depicted by Brohm (1993)), enslaved to a sport whose purpose and domestic political function is to be an "opium of the people" obscuring social conflict and problems. Yet if we choose not to explore what may be at stake in sporting terms and the uncertainties of match results, or to ignore studies of individual and collective frustration and its potential impact on passionately partisan fans, we are left with a definition of hooliganism that is confined to socioeconomic factors. Thom, on the other hand, uses catastrophe theory to explain that the paradigm of any indeterminate situation is conflict (1980, p. 308). Individuals who watch conflict – albeit the ritualised conflict of a match – tend to identify with one of the protagonists, and everyone's preference is to identify with the winner.

Drawing a parallel with the theatre, Thom goes on to argue that so long as there is a reversible situation inherent in the plot, we are in the realm of comedy. By contrast, as soon as outcomes appear irreversible, comedy shifts towards tragedy (op. cit., p. 310). That shift from reversible to irreversible and from comic to tragic may well explain in part why football supporters resort to violence. To opt for the limited definition of hooliganism is thus to take any study down a predetermined path. By confining research to the observation of physical violence, analysts effectively exclude other explanatory factors that have now been identified in relation to juvenile delinquency – banter, verbal jousting, goading, the history of antagonism in a given situation, the gap between expectation and reality – all of which may be present in the lead-up to fights, brawls or riots (Lepoutre, 1977; Duret, 1996, 1999; Wieviorka, 1999; and Roché, 2001).

Marsh (1978) was to criticise this conception of hooliganism as being too simplistic. In his view, it was not possible to focus only on physical violence to the exclusion of psychological and symbolic forms of violence, for to do so was to deny the existence of "aggro" – the ritualised enactment of violence designed to intimidate an adversary. Appearing strong and dangerous and attempting to strike fear into one's opponents was often more important than any physical action – the latter occurring only when the tacitly accepted rules of "aggro" were breached (by an attack on a girl, for example),[6] or when the police stepped in. Among hooligans, the ability to scare one's adversaries so effectively that they run away without even seeking confrontation is seen as a vital indicator of fighting spirit. Yet the dividing lines between physical, psychological and symbolic violence can be almost imperceptible. Violent acts simply represent moments or stages in social processes and they feed or exacerbate other forms of violence and may cause them to get out of hand (Wieviorka, op. cit., p. 17). Psychological and symbolic violence – "aggro" – is thus in many cases the base for a pattern of extremely violent clashes or antagonisms between groups of supporters that can persist for years.

A new type of football crowd

Nonetheless, in accepting that the nature of the violence among sports crowds has changed, we have still not explained why football more than other sports should be particularly affected by violence. The factor that offers an answer to this question – namely a change in the composition of football crowds – represents the second phase in the development of hooliganism. From the 1950s onwards, soccer in the United Kingdom underwent a number of transformations. In the first half of the twentieth century England had dominated the other European countries. England had invented the sport and it was in the United Kingdom that it first became properly organised, democratised and popularised. Wahl (1990) notes that schools played an important role in the spread of soccer throughout all sections of the population: in 1948, 8 000 schools were members of the English School Football Association. Yet by the 1950s soccer clubs were attracting fewer people. British society was changing and modernising, and individuals were gradually freeing themselves

---

6. This example is, in itself, revelatory of another aspect of the issue, namely the role of gender in physical and sporting activity.

from social constraints in a process that had its roots in the de-Christianisation of society from the 1930s onwards.

The period of reconstruction immediately after the war was one of prosperity. Leisure time was increasing and people were enjoying the newly carefree atmosphere by seeking out new and different recreational pursuits of many kinds. This was the beginning of the more individualistic and individualised consumer society. Sport became just one pleasure among others that included days or evenings out, trips to the cinema and holidays. It was no longer the only or the chief form of working-class recreation. Certain more individual sports, such as judo, appeared on the scene at this time, and other sports were democratised inasmuch as they became more affordable, so that the practice of sport became accessible to greater numbers of people, while others chose to switch to emerging forms of sport that were more playful or simply trendy.

Football was no longer the only form of entertainment that everyone could afford, and match attendances were falling. Broadcasting rights and sponsorship in its modern form were not yet factors in the situation. While some players were semi-professional and others were still amateur, they were all funded essentially from ticket sales, unless they were employees of particular industries. The British solution to the problem of disaffection was to make the game more spectacular and to professionalise it, to improve the level of comfort for spectators and to reconstruct the stadiums so that they could hold more people. Typically this involved building new stands – known as "ends" and corresponding to the "curves" of oval stadiums – on the short sides of the rectangular grounds, behind the goals. The democratisation of football and its growing popularity with all strata of society combined with the new facilities to attract different types of people; the crowds became more socially mixed and possibly less knowledgeable about the game. These changes revolutionised the social function of stadiums and upset the celebratory, convivial atmosphere that had previously prevailed in them. The development of football and its transformation into a spectacle altered the standards of an activity that had previously been regarded as class-based, being not only played but also watched mainly by the working class.[7]

That was not the only change, however. There were those such as Bromberger (1995) who used photographic records to show that crowds were getting younger.[8] There were a number of reasons for this. The first was

---

7. See the work of Bourdieu (1979, 1984) and Pociello (1981, 1995).
8. We must beware, however, of the idea that a radical change had taken place. There is no doubt that there were more younger fans but, at the same time, as people enjoyed better health care and were better fed and clothed they presented a contrast in photographs with their counterparts of previous generations, who may not have been as old as they looked.

sports-related, for with soccer being promoted in schools it was only natural that the new crop of young people who had played it would become keen amateurs or passionate fans. Then there were social factors, as this was a period of comprehensive change in society, especially with the trend towards greater autonomy among young people, who were gradually developing leisure pursuits distinct from those of their elders. The third reason for the change was an economic one: by offering cheap seats in the "ends", football clubs encouraged young people to gather in this "down-market" section of the ground. Finally there were cultural reasons as the United Kingdom saw the emergence from the 1960s onwards of various adolescent cultures and sub-cultures, most notably roughs, teddy boys, skinheads and punks. Football was thus no longer a "family pursuit" characterised by restraint and parental control. Families no longer went to the football ground together as they might have done to the theatre to share a common enthusiasm that cut across the generations. The "ends" became the territory of the young, who gradually began to group themselves not only according to the teams they supported but more particularly according to the areas they came from and the sub-cultures to which they belonged. They formed distinct communities, each with its own identity, rituals, emblems, symbols, loyalties, signs of recognition and dress codes: the elements used to form groups of fans. All they lacked by comparison with similar groups nowadays were names linking them to the clubs they supported. Xenophobic political ideologies were also imported into the stadiums at this stage (by the teddy boys and skinheads notably), and gangs (of skinheads and roughs) made their appearance there.

The celebratory ambiance previously associated with matches gave way to a climate of sporting rivalries combined with clashes of identity and cultural and social antagonism. The introduction of this new brand of more active, committed and unconditional support for soccer teams, along with the existence of distinct sub-cultures, was to lead to the emergence of hooliganism by creating a culture of opposition that was no longer purely sport-based. Pitch invasions and fighting between groups of supporters became more frequent. Hooliganism as an extreme expression of adolescent sub-cultures imported into football grounds is a common theme in a whole series of studies and commentaries (Elias and Dunning, 1986; Taylor, 1971, 1973 and 1982, in relation to the United Kingdom; Zimmerman, 1987, writing about Germany; Ehrenberg, 1991, on the United Kingdom; and Mignon, 1993 and 1995, who compared the British and French experiences).

As early as 1968 Lord Harrington noted in an official report on soccer hooliganism that hooligans who had been arrested were genuine fans, they were young (under 21) and well-informed, with a thorough knowledge of football, of the clubs they supported, the players and the technicalities of the game, and that many of them displayed the distinctive insignia of the groups to which they belonged. The Harrington Report ought to have settled a debate that, in fact, rumbles on today in both the United Kingdom and France: the fact is that hooliganism is committed by genuine football supporters and not by outsiders unconnected with football who choose to come and misbehave in stadiums. There are several reasons for the persistent misconception about where hooligans come from, and they are straightforward. The football world not only wants to maintain a "clean" image of sport (Ehrenberg, op. cit.), but also wants to shake off any moral responsibility for having attracted fans of a new type, and consciously or otherwise having allowed them to break the law. Ultimately, too, it wants to disengage from any financial responsibility for offences committed.

Rather than serving its aim of preventing violence, the policy of separating rival supporters by erecting fences inside stadiums actually exacerbated the problem. The effect of dividing up the "ends" and segregating the different groups was to "territorialise" the stands, to focus attention on them and to promote inter-group rivalry. Each group – driven by the desire to assert itself, confront its rivals and demonstrate its superiority, as well as the urge to be seen and recognised, avenge defeat or prolong victory – would seek to conquer the opponents' "end". Processes of "antagonistic acculturation" were gradually triggered, in which violence became one means among others of forging an identity. While the establishment of security cordons around stadiums, in conjunction with the policy of erecting fences, was to reduce levels of violence inside the grounds, it did not succeed in eliminating violence.

> "As a consequence of the official policy of separating rival fans – a policy introduced in the 1960s as a means of preventing football hooliganism, but which appears to have had greater success in enhancing the solidarity of 'football ends' and driving the phenomenon outside grounds – large scale fights on the terraces became relatively rare during the 1970s and early 1980s" (Elias and Dunning, op. cit., p. 247).

The active, organised fan scene that emerged in British soccer in the 1960s (Broussard, 1990) was quite different, however, from the "Ultra" culture that prevailed among supporters on the curves at French and Italian stadiums. Whereas the Ultras mounted *tifos* (motley, multicoloured displays and sequences of movement), using large plastic sheets or coloured-paper effigies identifying their club or their community, many British football fans displayed only scarves and badges, but sustained their support vocally throughout the matches, with an endless succession of chants and provocative slogans.

Social problems exacerbate hooligan behaviour

Many researchers (Taylor, op. cit.; Clarke, 1978; Elias and Dunning, op. cit.) see the third period in the development of hooliganism as corresponding to the sharp socioeconomic decline of the United Kingdom in the 1970s and

1980s. Successive Labour governments (under Harold Wilson from 1964 to 1970, then again from 1974 to 1976, and James Callaghan from 1976 to 1980) failed to curb inflation and rising unemployment. The country was on the verge of bankruptcy. In the early 1970s, the proportion of the United Kingdom population living below the poverty line was 14%, a figure never reached in France, where the poverty rate stabilised at around 10% in the 1990s. The United Kingdom rate of inflation hit 25% in the mid-1970s and the unemployment rate rose from 3.8% in 1972 to 11.5% in 1983. Three million jobs were lost in the British industrial sector alone between 1966 and 1986; France, by comparison, took until 1993 to shed the same number of jobs right across the economy. It was this economic collapse that heralded Margaret Thatcher's coming to power and the introduction of a policy of rigour and austerity, privatisation and the development of strict free-market economics. The political choices of the day were clear: economic recovery was the imperative, albeit at the expense of the working class and the socially disadvantaged. The single episode of the miners' strike succinctly evokes the British working-class experience in that era: the strike lasted a full year before it was forcibly broken by the Conservative government. It is one example among others of the economic de-structuring that took place and the social division that set in. Anti-working-class economic and social measures acted as a catalyst for the development of hooliganism.

> "The brutality of the Thatcherite plan to wipe it out culturally and politically is a potent factor explaining the growing autonomy of the football fan phenomenon and the strategies that hooligans used to achieve public prominence" (Mignon, op. cit. p. 22).

Hooliganism, however, was less a reflection of the class struggle than a mechanism for survival and social recognition. Soccer violence existed alongside, without being linked to, urban rioting. Hooligans were not overtly proclaiming their social loyalties or defending the working class. Nonetheless, as shown by Coser (1956), hooliganism is a danger signal to the community and in the United Kingdom it was an indicator of deep-seated social dysfunction. Like urban rioting it is a type of violence that testifies primarily to the fact that political and institutional responses to social demands have been exhausted (Wieviorka, op. cit., p. 30). Football became an instrument and channel of expression for the socioeconomic rootlessness of young people excluded from society.

On the basis of socioanthropological studies, Taylor (1973) and Clarke (1973) describe the formation of groups of supporters – complex entities within which social bonding took place. At a time when British society appeared to be disintegrating, supporters' groups offered their members reassurance, approval and solidarity. The groups came into being not only because their members were in the same situation of being socially excluded, but also as a defence against the alien, against "foreigners" who were stealing British jobs. Certain groups (predominantly skinheads and right-wing extremists) no longer made any attempt to conceal their ideology but openly chanted racist slogans. They attracted to their ranks growing numbers of disaffected young people who lacked a sense of direction or prospects and had given up on achieving any sort of social status.

The racism displayed by these supporters reflected not a rejection of the modern world but rather a fear of being excluded from it; of being excluded, too, from social progress and of being unable to find any position or status in society (Wieviorka, 1998, 1992). Racism was not some sort of "natural state": in this context it was a reaction to exclusion. The football supporters were "driven" by their social situation and the socioeconomic proximity of immigrant communities to seek a "scapegoat" (Girard, 1972, 2004). Hooliganism was for them a way of being, a manner of presenting themselves and standing out from the crowd, a way of cultivating what made them different (Broussard, op. cit., p. 308). Fan culture and violence offered an alternative to a miserable and sordid day-to-day existence. They represented an escape from a deadly-dull routine and provided a base and a sense of purpose for people who lacked any vision of a future. The extreme violence practised by such groups earned them social recognition and enabled them, as suggested by Van Limbergen et al. (1992), to forge an identity which might have been exceedingly ugly but was preferable to contempt and social denigration.

Certain groups organised themselves into so-called "fighting crews", among them ICF (the "Inter City Firm") at West Ham, the "Main Firm" at Cambridge, the "Service Crew" at Leeds and the "Headhunters" at Chelsea. Sporting rivalry became compounded by inter-group rivalry, and existence depended on being seen. Media coverage of the violence brought the groups greater social recognition. The typical image began to develop of the shaven-headed, tattooed football fan wearing Doc Marten boots and a bomber jacket, possibly adorned with neo-Nazi insignia – an idle fanatic with extreme right-wing views. The ICF was one of the most representative and most violent of these groups, going so far in 1982 as to stab an Arsenal supporter on the way out of a Tube station and leave a "calling card" on him, with the words "Congratulations. You have just met the ICF". It was, of course, commonplace to find manual workers and young unemployed people among the membership of supporters' clubs and, by extension, among the hooligans.

Football is part and parcel of working-class culture and exalts the values of that culture: effort, physical commitment, solidarity, virility, organisation, submission to collective discipline, and team spirit. It is one of the ordinary enthusiasms that are open to everyone and with which many people can identify, for football and football players embody the democratic ideal that anybody can become "somebody" (Ehrenberg, op. cit.). But in Thatcher's Britain the gulf was widening every day between the players, who were getting richer, and their supporters, many of them excluded from society and without prospects. Taylor, and later Clarke, were to identify the increasingly bourgeois nature of football and the growing distance between fans and players at this time as additional reasons for supporters' turning to violence. Some observers described what was taking place as a struggle for self-preservation. Wahl suggested it was part of a trend that had been perceptible for some time.

> "Signs of regression are appearing in Europe. The warmth originally associated with the game has gone. The closeness between players and supporters is merely a memory; fans no longer acknowledge a player as one of their own who has made good" (op. cit., p. 109).

For certain supporters, hooliganism had thus become a means – an objectionable and frightening means perhaps but nonetheless a means like any other – of making sense of their existence, of making themselves socially visible and, in that way, of transforming exclusion into recognition and failure into success.

> "They embody a working-class refusal to become bourgeois, a defence of principles based on roughness ... Through their skinhead style they proclaim a violent masculinity and a spirit of loyalty ... they are racist ... they set the style for the stands at the end of the stadium because their systematic toughness is an ideal that many share" (Mignon, op. cit., p. 24).

Through violence they acquired a status that replaced their actual status, giving them a recognised, enhanced identity that they lacked or were denied in everyday life.

Hooliganism as a "normal" form of violence for young, excluded working-class people

The fourth period was to be documented by Elias and Dunning (op. cit.) as they extended Elias's core work on the civilising process in western societies (Elias, 1969, 1985) into the realm of sport. Elias contended that societies are built, on the one hand, around the establishment of standards of civility (politeness, courtesy and the settlement of disputes by verbal means) and, on the other hand, around state control of violence (the "courtization"[9] of warriors and the monopolisation of violence). They are also built by individuals as they gradually internalise processes of self-control. Sport is one means among others of controlling violence in society, or violence practised by

---

9. As the warrior nobles, with their vassals, their own armies and their tax-raising powers, were transformed into a courtly nobility gathered in one place under the "protection" of a monarch, they gradually lost any interest in engaging in armed conflict among themselves.

society, because it offers a "social enclave where excitement can be enjoyed without its socially and personally dangerous implications", a place where players and spectators (in the generic sense) can give free rein to their emotions, but it is also a place where standards of sociability apply, encouraging obedience to rules and the control of emotions. Elias and Dunning thus approach the phenomenon of hooliganism by asking a simple question: given that modern sport was originally intended in part as a means of controlling violence, how has it spawned this type of violence in football?

Building on earlier work, Elias and Dunning noted that most hooligans were members of the rough working class, the lowest tier of the working class, and in fact belonged to the most disadvantaged sections of that social group:

> "at the bottom of the social scale ...., the gap between them and the dwindling lower working class ... has widened. Although their numbers may have started to grow again in the course of the current recession, it is these groups of 'rough' working-class people that tend to behave in ways that approximate most closely to the standards generated by what Suttles terms 'ordered segmentation'.[10] Such youths and young men ... constitute the majority inside the core groups who engage in the most serious forms of football hooliganism" (op. cit., p. 262).

The authors nonetheless found it impossible to generalise or to equate hooliganism automatically with a particular social class. In order to understand why the link existed, it was necessary to look beyond status and to examine what happened in practice. First of all, while it was true that most hooligans seemed to come from disadvantaged social strata, the converse did not apply: all the socially disadvantaged individuals who attended football matches did not necessarily become hooligans or delinquents. Secondly – and while this was not a question specifically pursued by Elias and Dunning it is one to which we shall return – not all those arrested as hooligans were, in fact, members of the rough working class.[11] In the authors' view, the significant factor was not membership of the working class but rather the way in which the working class functioned, its forms of socialisation and sociability. If violence was attributable to the rough working class, it was because the members of that class were less advanced in the civilising process.

In Elias's work a key aspect of the civilising process depends upon a change in the pattern of social bonding, comparable to what Durkheim (1893) calls the shift from mechanical to organic solidarity. Elias, in describing this aspect of the process, uses the terms "segmental bonding" and "functional

---

10. The system by which gangs were observed to operate in Chicago, characterised by a high level of segregation, importance attached to norms of masculinity and an elaborate system of alliances.
11. By extension the lowest section of the working class – in which violence is still a meaningful element of social functioning.

bonding". He argues that the social functioning of the rough working class is characterised by segmental bonding. In this pattern, violence is a traditional means of resolving conflict. For Elias and Dunning it is thus an inherent and irreducible part of the way in which these groups function socially. In behaving violently at football matches the hooligans were merely reproducing what was for them normal and familiar behaviour: "The fighting norms of such segmentally bonded groups are analogous to the vendetta systems still found in many Mediterranean countries ..." (op. cit., p. 235).

Elias and Dunning observed four aspects of hooliganism that confirmed this concept of its social function:
> "1. the fact that the groups involved appear to be as, and sometimes more, interested in fighting one another as they are in watching football;
>
> 2. the fact that the rival groups appear to be recruited principally from the same level of social stratification, that is from the so-called 'rough' sections of the working class. This means ... one has to explain the fact that their fighting involves intra as opposed to inter-class conflict;
>
> 3. the fact that the fighting of such groups takes a vendetta form in the sense that ... particular groups and individuals are set upon simply because they display the membership insignia of a rival group. The long-standing feuds which develop between rival groups of hooligan fans, and which persist despite the turnover of personnel that occurs within such groups ... are an indication of the very great degree of identification of particular hooligans with the groups to which they belong;
>
> 4. the remarkable degree of conformity and uniformity in action that is displayed in the songs and chants of football hooligans. A recurrent theme of these songs and chants is enhancement of the masculine image of the in-group, coupled with denigration and emasculation of the out-group" (op. cit., p. 242).

The gender composition of the groups, the generally accepted norms of aggressive masculinity, male dominance, the pattern of close-knit gang membership from childhood onwards, the complex system of alliances (which Elias and Dunning term the "Bedouin syndrome")[12] and the consumption of alcohol were all factors that made recourse to violence easier.
> "The intense feelings of in-group attachment and hostility towards out-groups of such segmentally bonded groups mean that rivalry is virtually inevitable when their members meet. And their norms of aggressive masculinity and comparative inability to exercise self-control mean that conflict between them easily leads to fighting" (op. cit., p. 243).

This approach requires some comment. The first problem it raises is that of defining what constitutes a norm and consequently what constitutes deviant behaviour. Is a deviant a person who circumvents norms established by a section of the population for the purpose of keeping the peace in a community

---

12. The friend of a friend is a friend; the enemy of an enemy is a friend; the friend of an enemy is an enemy.

and maintaining social cohesion? Or is this a judgment that certain people pass on behaviour they regard as abnormal because it is not that of the majority or the mainstream (Becker, 1963)?

As Elias saw it, modern societies were turning into pacified social territory. As we are confronted by violence less and less frequently, each of us now tends to be increasingly fearful of it. Conflicts today tend to be settled by consensus and we have a lower level of tolerance for violence. The very idea of violence now appears unacceptable. Brawls between football supporters are disturbing because in the early twenty-first century they are not considered "normal". People regard them as a danger and an indicator of rising insecurity. But is that really the case? The second problem raised is that of ascribing the responsibility for violence to people who are "less civilised", or less advanced in the civilising process. For example, in response to the assertion that "because it is difficult for males from the 'rough' sections of the lower working class to achieve meaning, status and gratification and to form satisfying identities in the fields of school and work, there is a greater tendency for them to rely for these purposes on forms of behaviour that include physical intimidation, fighting, heavy drinking and exploitative sexual relations" (Elias and Dunning, op. cit. p. 258), we can legitimately ask whether it reflects contempt for the working class or at least constitutes an exaggerated generalisation about its social and emotional functioning. There is also the possibility that it reflects, in the specific and admittedly restricted context of hooliganism, a theory that certain writers such as Taylor (op. cit.), Williams (1991) and Hargreaves (1992) have been quick to denounce as tainted with latent evolutionism. It may, however, be going too far to label the theory "evolutionist". The core contribution of Elias's figurational sociology – based as it is on the central theory of "civilising processes" and concern to balance the ideographic and nomothetic approaches – has been to describe the development, learning and refinement of those standards of socially acceptable behaviour that led to the formation of western societies between the Middle Ages and the twentieth century (Bodin, 2002).

Yet beyond the limited context of hooliganism, studies carried out in many different parts of Europe have shown that people do not necessarily behave more violently because they are manual workers as opposed to members of the intelligentsia or the upper classes. Work on the violence directed against children and women sadly confirms this (Jaspard et al., 2003; Marinova, 2004).

The media as a catalyst for hooligan violence

While research carried out in the United Kingdom has provided a number of interpretations both divergent and convergent, depending on the chosen terrain and the researchers' approach, it is clear that one effect of the Heysel tragedy was to promote the extension of hooliganism to Europe generally, while at the same time significantly shaping public perception of it.

In May 1985, Liverpool (victors in 1984) and Juventus of Turin (who were to win the match) met for the final of the UEFA Champions League at the Heysel stadium in Brussels. While Liverpool fans were not among the most dangerous in the United Kingdom, they did have a fiery reputation that had been fuelled by a number of recent incidents. For example, in March of the same year they had been involved in violent clashes with Austria Vienna supporters, and in June 1984, during an AS Roma v. Liverpool match, forty people had been hurt in fighting with Italian Ultras, and some fifty supporters had been arrested.

This was on top of a range of violent acts committed over previous months and years by supporters of other United Kingdom clubs and of the England team. There was a strong police presence at Heysel and the officers had been instructed to take a firm line. Supporters of the two teams had been allowed into the stadium early and were separated only by a fence. As they waited they exchanged provocations and insults, tried to intimidate their rivals, drank, and threw beer cans. Then panic set in as a few English supporters managed to infiltrate the Z block, reserved for Juventus fans, and charged forward. The police were caught out and failed to intervene. Panicking Italian fans in the back rows of the stand then began pressing down the terracing, crushing their fellows – who did not know what was happening above them – against the fence at the bottom. For several long minutes stewards awaited the order to unlock the fence gate at the base of the stand. Had they done so sooner the fans would not have been crushed. What occurred was not a direct clash of any severity but rather a failure of passive security in the stadium despite the presence of 2290 police officers. A response came on 19 August 1985 with the adoption of a European Convention on Spectator Violence and Misbehaviour at Sports Events and in particular at Football Matches.

It was a belated effort to stem a phenomenon that could have been foreseen, part of a recurring campaign (Becker, op. cit.) to introduce standards and control measures that would reassure the public. A committee of inquiry was also to show that tickets had been sold to anyone and everyone, in defiance of basic security rules. Whatever the time pressures on the journalists who reported the Heysel disaster, by continually repeating an interpretation of events that focused on British hooliganism they played a major part in shaping public perception of the phenomenon: hooligans were now definitively young, English, male, socially marginalised yobos who had had too much to drink. No one took time to explore the origin of the antagonisms between the two groups nor even to ask whether the Liverpool supporters were indeed responsible for triggering the tragedy. We are entitled to ask, as Kapuscinski (2002) did, whether the media were actually concerned with reflecting reality or whether – information having become a commodity – truth had taken second place to the imperative of selling it.

Hooliganism was definitely no longer an insular phenomenon, for by commenting on, reworking and incessantly reshowing the same images – in a classic journalistic tradition of relying on the weight of words and the shock of pictures – the media gave football fans and hooligans an unprecedented public profile. Up to that point, their prime purpose had been to support their teams, with hooliganism as the ultimate hard-line expression of fan culture, but from then on they were to enjoy increasing recognition as their activities were authenticated. The excessive media coverage of Heysel thus accelerated the spread of hooliganism at European level. But it was merely an acceleration, for the phenomenon had already existed in continental Europe for quite some time. Visits by English fans to other European countries had already encouraged mimicry of their behaviour, resulting in various violent incidents in the years 1975-80. It is surprising that neither the press nor national and international football bodies chose to comment on what was happening.

In France, hooliganism had been occurring at Paris Saint-Germain matches since 1979 (Rouibi, 1989) and at fixtures involving Marseilles, Strasbourg and Nantes since 1980. Belgian football had been experiencing similar problems since 1980 (Dupuis, 1993a/b), and in West Germany, Italy and the former Yugoslavia there had been numerous cases, since the early 1980s, of matches being disrupted by clashes between rival fans. Broussard (op. cit.), in his detailed research into European football Ultras, records similar incidents in virtually every country in Europe from around the same period. Contrary to the general perception, hooliganism was not therefore something exclusively British.

Why, however – apart from the fact that it experienced socioeconomic problems at an earlier stage than other countries – was the United Kingdom so particularly affected by and involved in this type of violence?

There are a number of quite straightforward reasons. The first is a feature that the United Kingdom shares with Belgium and the Netherlands, which also experienced very violent hooliganism, namely the physical proximity of the soccer clubs. In 1996 there were no fewer than eleven English Premiership or First Division clubs in greater London alone. The land area of England – the part of the United Kingdom worst affected by hooliganism – is just a quarter that of France or Spain and half that of Italy, while Germany is two and half times bigger (to take only the examples of those countries with the strongest tradition of professional football). Belgium and the Netherlands are each smaller than the French region of Aquitaine. Mobility is therefore significantly facilitated: supporters can travel to matches easily, frequently and in large numbers. Thus, while antagonistic behaviour (in the ethological sense) was quite commonly part and parcel of sporting rivalry, it was exacerbated by the physical proximity of the clubs, bringing to the fore local and territorial antagonisms that had their roots in the particular history of cities, countries, social classes and periods of recession (Bromberger, 1995, p. 242).

The second reason concerns the media. The role of the media in the spread of hooliganism was not confined to the excessive media coverage of Heysel. As a means of combating hooliganism, sections of the British press created what they dubbed the "thugs league". The aim was, in itself, an honourable one: to counter groups of hooligans by stigmatising them and holding them up to public condemnation and opprobrium. But the young supporters, hungry for public attention, took up the system of classification and put it to their own use. Topping the thugs league gradually came to be the primary aim of all the hooligan groups. The tactic had misfired (see Boudon, 1977), and was actually to sustain and fuel inter-group rivalry and violence. A similar process occurred in France, too, with the launch of *Sup'Mag* [Supporter Magazine], a publication originally founded to report on the activities of fans and to publicise and celebrate their *tifos*, but which gradually stoked animosity and rivalry by including an official league table of the "best" supporters. The content of the magazine became progressively more extremist, reflecting a harder-edged fan culture and including many articles about hooligans:

> "… football grounds began increasingly to be 'advertised' as places where fighting or 'aggro', and not just football, regularly took place. This drew in young males from the 'rough' sections of the working class …" (Elias and Dunning, op. cit., p. 264).

While the media were not the cause of hooliganism, they nonetheless helped to trigger, amplify and fuel it. They made a substantial contribution to its dissemination, promotion and validation, at least among those people who were to identify with it as a way of life and a means of attaining social recognition.

Hooliganism spreads throughout Europe

The public profile that young hooligans could now enjoy not only promoted an increase in levels of violence at football matches, but also contributed to the spread of the problem across Europe through a process based on imitation and rivalry. European fans sought to emulate their English counterparts, and to be recognised in the same way as impassioned hard-liners, capable of defending their team, their club and their own image as supporters – violently if need be. Rivalry was a factor too because the unofficial supporters' league table demanded that each group try to outdo the rest: travelling in greater numbers to away matches; loyally attending all home games however the team was performing and whatever level it was playing at; organising *tifos* or well co-ordinated manifestations of support; disrupting the efforts of rival supporters and provoking them. The "contagious" spread of fan groups who measured themselves against one another by competing for territory in the stadiums made violence an inherent feature of fan culture everywhere in Europe. Indeed, violence helped to forge group identities on the basis of a history of conflict and antagonism. By relating stories of violence, even from a totally subjective and distorted perspective, each member of a given group could achieve personal validation through belonging. And violence was also a factor that held groups together because it required their members to confront the dilemma of either uniting to oppose rivals or individually backing off, with the result that the group would cease to exist.

As hooliganism spread throughout Europe, more researchers began to explore the phenomenon in different countries, although a significant number of those working in the field taught at British universities. Two quite distinct approaches gradually emerged. On the one hand there was a body of work, done mainly in France, that was concerned solely with fan culture, regarding hooliganism as a marginal phenomenon (Charroin, 1994; Bromberger, 1995 and 1998; Roumestan, 1998; Nuytens, 2000) while, on the other hand, more specific research projects sought to understand and interpret hooliganism at national and local levels by exploring the internal workings of fan groups and seeing hooliganism as part and parcel of supporting one's team and the ultimate expression of the fan culture (Giulianotti, 1995, in relation to Scotland; Zani and Kirchler, 1991, in relation to hooligans in Naples and Bologna; Zimmerman, op. cit., in a German context; Van Limbergen et al., 1992 and 1989; Dupuis, op. cit., in relation to Belgium; and Bodin, 1998, 1999 and 1999a in France). Three authors stand apart from these approaches: Mignon, who made a comparative study of hooliganism in the United Kingdom and France (1993 and 1995), Tsoukala (1993 and 1996), who studied the development of penal policy in relation to hooliganism, and Comeron (1992 and 1993), who from 1992 onwards set about promoting "fan coaching" on the basis of work done at Standard Liège in Belgium.

British in origin, fan coaching involves, on the one hand, maintaining a dissuasive presence and monitoring supporters inside the stadiums with a view to preventing violence (essentially the role of stewards) and, on the other hand, preventive work in the run-up to matches, including a range of activities for young fans (sports fixtures, trips and sports activities not connected with football). This second aspect is similar to types of youth work done on the streets. Fan coaching is currently the theme of a European project, and organisations in different countries in Europe are doing similar work at national level.

These various projects challenge the processes whereby fans learn violence via mimicry and conformity to group norms, in the quest for status within a group or via inter-group rivalry, thus turning hooliganism into a sub-culture within fan culture. There was also a structural change in the nature of hooliganism in the wake of the Heysel disaster. Control measures (ranging from the adoption of European conventions and national legislation to the erection of security fences around football grounds and the introduction of frisking and video surveillance) led to the emergence of a new brand of hooligan. These were the "casuals" (Redhead, 1987),[13] violent fans who no longer dressed in a way that marked them out as members of a particular group. Instead they wore clothes designed to inspire confidence and to make them anonymous. Police officers and stewards carrying out security checks at stadium gates had to engage in the sort of physiognomy more familiar to night-club bouncers, relying on visible characteristics to assess those seeking to enter, and stopping people because they didn't like the look of them. Young fans decked out in group or club insignia tended to be more frequently singled out for frisking, but by dressing in a neutral or smart way the casuals inspired confidence and found it easy to gain entry. The hooligans became if not invisible at least hard to spot.

Van Limbergen et al. meanwhile pursued their work on social exclusion among Belgian hooligans and introduced the concept of societal vulnerability. Police files on hard-core fans who frequented the Belgian "sides" (the equivalent of the "ends" in Britain) showed a pattern of family and social problems: 40% of those concerned had cut short their education; only 16% of those of school age were attending school regularly; many were socially and financially deprived and tended to reject traditional bourgeois values (of politeness, discipline and respect for the law); and 75% had a police record dating back to childhood.

Whatever their approaches, the different authors were united in highlighting two points. Firstly, hooliganism was, without doubt, attributable to fans and not to outside individuals unconnected with football. All the hooligans belonged to organised groups. Echoing a type of assertion more familiar in the context of drug addiction, we can thus say that while not all football fans would become hooligans, all hooligans were indeed football fans. As Ehrenberg suggested, hooliganism was the ultimate excess of fan culture.

> "Specifically, what distinguishes hooliganism from traditional forms of supporter behaviour is the movement of the hooligans towards the terraces: while the match is in progress on the pitch, two rival teams of supporters will enter into a parallel physical contest .... The hooligans' behaviour thus has its roots in cultural and

---

13. The name was derived from their casual style of dress. The most hard-line fans wore "normal" clothes in order to merge into the crowd.

sporting traditions which they take to extremes and transform. The aim of their violence is to make the terraces the focus of attention rather than the pitch" (Ehrenberg, op. cit., p. 58).

Secondly, hooliganism was, in consequence, the work of a limited number of supporters: the hard core of a given group, comprising its leaders and certain individuals who attended all the matches in a season, both home and away. The numbers involved varied between a dozen and as many as 300. While the term "hard core" in this context cannot be defined in the same way as it is in relation to juvenile delinquency, the pattern was identical. As Roché (2001) and Debarbieux (2002) have demonstrated, 50% of hooligan acts could be attributed to a "hyperactive core" of 5%.[14]

It is, in fact, hard to dissociate the question of hooliganism from the research that has been done into urban violence, youth crime and violence in schools because, at least in the main, the persons involved are the same. Hooligans and other types of young offenders often share the same sociodemographic profile.

Hooligans as ordinary young people

Nonetheless, the above observations on the origins of hooliganism pose a number of problems for they have the effect of "naturalising" and "sociologising" fan violence, inviting an overly narrow, if not caricatural, interpretation of it, in a sort of social determinism that rules out other possible causes such as factors to do with the game, with frustration or with the rationality of those involved.

How can the development of hooliganism in Europe be assessed?

Initially the only criterion used for defining and explaining hooliganism was the structured nature of the violence, which from the 1950s onwards appeared to be increasingly the work of organised gangs of young people. But as football crowds were changing and tending to organise themselves, to a degree at least, into groups, it seemed only logical that the violence should be carried out by groups. Yet this was not the nub of the issue. The interesting question was whether violence was becoming more or less frequent in and around football grounds. Apart from the work of Tranter (1995) analysing the Cappielow riot of 1895, Lewis (1996) studying British local newspapers between 1880 and 1914, and Roversi (1991) on the increase in hooliganism in Italy between 1970 and 1980, no research had been done on this question despite its prime importance in terms of assessing whether the situation was getting worse or whether, in fact, researchers, the media and the public were simply giving way to what we would now call a sense of insecurity.

---

14. For discussion of the limitations of this concept see Debarbieux (2002), pp. 105-112.

The problem of failure to define hooliganism

A further problem is that of how individuals, or indeed groups of individuals, are categorised as "hooligans". Apart from misdeeds committed and damage caused – in other words the purpose of hooliganism – we have no real defining criteria for it. Should we classify as hooligans only those who have recourse to violence on a regular basis? Or should we extend the definition to include those who engage in it occasionally, or simply as a reaction to perceived dangers? The fact is that there are various types of hooligan, ranging from those who have only occasional recourse to violence to "chronic" hooligans – those individuals who take pleasure in hooliganism and make it a way of life. Yet does this mean there is no element of pleasure in occasional hooliganism? Are occasional acts of hooliganism accidental or a reaction to provocation or danger? Are they part of a defence mechanism? Or are they actually the prelude to a long career of deviant behaviour (Becker, op. cit.)? Is the "chronic" hooligan also a "chronic" delinquent in everyday life? The answers to these questions would enable us to refute, confirm or qualify the assertion that hooligans are ordinary delinquents. However, the "hooligans" listed as such by the various European police forces rarely are hooligans. On the one hand, there is sometimes a tendency to lump different phenomena together but there are also gaps in the available information. Individuals under the influence of alcohol may well be arrested and listed as hooligans. Acts of violence that take place at some distance from football grounds are often overlooked and go undocumented. It is also the case that acts of violence are treated differently by the police and courts depending on the social background or history of the individuals accused. Official statistics are inevitably inaccurate and incomplete (Bodin, 2003).

The vision of hooliganism depicted above also fails to take account of the fact that regulations governing sports events are changing. As new directives, laws and rules are introduced, certain social groups are, in effect, creating deviancy by setting standards the breach of which constitutes deviancy (Becker, op. cit., p. 32). The simplest example is that of the smoke canisters and flares that supporters use to "brighten up" the stands. Setting off these devices is in keeping with the festive atmosphere and celebrates support for the team, yet it is sufficient in France to get an individual listed as a hooligan or at least as a "violent fan or fan responsible for violence" under the official classification system of the French Central Directorate for Public Security.

Just ordinary young people

Alongside the grim image of individuals of low status, poorly integrated into society or belonging to the most deprived social classes, anthropological and sociological research (by Armstrong et al., 1991; Bodin, 1998, 1999a/b and

2001; Dupuis, 1993a/b; Giulianotti, 1995; Williams, 1991; and Zimmerman, 1987, among others), based on *in situ* observation and information on hooliganism supplied by those actually involved, depicts a more subtle social reality and throws up a number of similarities in the different countries studied.

The first observation is that three quarters of those who admit to having committed acts of hooliganism belong to the hard core of supporter groups. Two characteristics are common to the majority of them: 88.2% are male and 74.9% are aged under 27. While female hooligans do exist, they are less involved than their male counterparts in the most violent acts, although this is not to say that they bear no responsibility for violence or that they do not play specific roles in it (Bodin et al., 2004a/b). The findings on hooliganism tie in here with those on ordinary delinquency: exclusion is not in itself a sufficient explanation for delinquency and deviant behaviour. It is merely one risk factor among others. It is only when different indicators of social disadvantage accumulate – low family income, poor housing in a run-down area, large families – that we find a significant statistical correlation between poverty and delinquency (Fillieule, 2001, p. 66). While hooliganism may be explained in part as socially determined, it is important not to mistake a factor for a correlation. Not all hooligans are socially disinherited individuals ill at ease with their lives and lacking prospects. An unduly specific reading of hooliganism excludes other analyses that could shed light on the phenomenon.

The findings of the researchers mentioned above differ significantly from those of the British studies which, it must be remembered, were based on police data as opposed to information supplied by those actually involved in violence. Thus far the description of hooliganism reflects the sociodemographic factors commonly put forward to explain ordinary delinquency: it is the work of young males in groups. Yet is this not merely a tautology? Of all sports, football draws the youngest audience and it is an audience attracted by the ambiance of the crowd and the affinities and sense of fun among the groups of fans. Because it is fans who are involved in hooliganism, it is a form of violence present in football to a greater extent than in other sports. Youths aged under 17 – the age by which individuals normally become committed to fan culture – will gradually adopt antagonistic forms of behaviour through imitation. Such behaviour is a means of gaining recognition and acceptance from their elders and of integrating with them. By behaving aggressively and violently the young individual can also achieve higher status and a more important role within the core group. A further explanation for these young people's violent behaviour, however, lies in the fact that they do not relate to social norms in the same way as adults do. While age is a discriminating factor, it is unrealistic to talk of a dangerous age band (Dubet, 1987). The simple fact is that violent outbursts of this type are a feature of what is a transitional period in people's lives when individual identities are being forged; a period of "psychosocial latency" (Dubet, op. cit.) during which young soccer fans, like young people generally, have not yet assumed an adult role and are, as Galland suggests, less sensitive to the norms and rules; as they grow older they gradually adopt adult roles and adult status (1998, p. 28). Most criminological studies show, in fact, that young people are more tolerant of physical violence and do not tend to condemn it, or at least do so to a lesser extent than adults, provided that it does not involve the use of weapons (Roché, 2001).

Hooliganism and social disorganisation

There are, at the same time, certain factors that have had a considerable effect in promoting the emergence of new forms of hooliganism in European football.

Social anomie

Sociological studies of deviance[15] have shown for some time that a situation of anomie, in which a sense of social norms is lacking or crumbles, can trigger violent or delinquent behaviour. The concept of anomie, encompassing the vague notion of social deregulation (Boudon and Bourricaud, 1982), is actually a catch-all term for various concepts, as evident from the different ways in which Durkheim uses it in his works *The Division of Labour* (1893) and *Suicide* (1897). Merton (1965), introducing the notion of social disorganisation, sees deviance as marking the point at which certain individuals break with the normal rules of social exchange. Pushed aside by other members of society, despite the fact of sharing the same goals, certain individuals come to develop deviant and conflictual behaviour patterns. Anomie thus becomes a reinforcing process that makes it harder for them to become involved in activities legitimately and has the effect of driving some to rebel or challenge authority.

The first point to be made in this context is that there is little real relationship between those in charge of football clubs and the supporters' organisations.

Absence of relationships and a laissez-faire attitude leave room for hooliganism

There are several possible explanations for this situation. Firstly, the age of the fans (referred to above) influences the desire for independence on the part of their groups, most of which are formed without any assistance from

---
15. In this context, evasion of the norms and rules generally accepted as regulating life in society.

the football clubs. This is compounded by young people's desire to act independently and make their own decisions as they make the transition from adolescence to adulthood. A number of researchers have also commented on the ever-growing gulf between players and supporters that was observed by Wahl (1990). A similar distancing process is apparent in the absence of relationships between football club management and the supporters' clubs. Broussard comments that:

> "the growing gulf between the fans and the rest of a club inevitably accentuates the feeling of isolation experienced by the extremists. As a result, ignored or treated with contempt by the managers of their own club, they become more entrenched than ever in their conviction and end up persuading themselves that only they truly love the team and are prepared to defend it through adversity" (1990, pp. 210-211).

Each group has an independent existence centring on a shared object of interest and a particular place and insists upon the justification for and relevance and importance of what it does.

Experience with fan coaching or "fan embassies" (Comeron, 2002) has shown, however, that where contractual-type relations can be established (in both spirit and letter) between groups of supporters or between supporters and club management this seems to have a moderating effect on fans' behaviour. Age, once again, is a key factor here: as Broussard (op. cit., p. 210) comments, many club chairs do not regard these young people as acceptable partners in dialogue. Relationships in most clubs would appear to be conducted largely on an ad hoc basis, the aim being to guard against various types of incident, without any concerted policy of regarding fans as genuine interlocutors with a stake in the development of the club. Those in charge of the sport seem to be primarily interested, as Ehrenberg has put it, in asserting that "these yobos have nothing to do with football". Ehrenberg comments that this attitude is understandable: it is a way of maintaining the "purity" of the sport and dissociating supporters who are clearly nothing but a burden (1991, p. 47). Football as a phenomenon is changing: in effect, it is no longer simply a sport or even a sporting spectacle in which spectators can genuinely participate and which they can help to influence. Nowadays it is something else:

> "... because attention has been focused on advertising revenue and television broadcasting rights, because the prime interest of the clubs has been self-promotion ... after all, football also belongs to the wretched paying public" (Broussard, op. cit., p. 211).

It is thus reasonable to ask whether hooliganism might not stem, at least in part, from social disorganisation and a social void, of which the supporters take advantage.

As fan culture spread and became more organised more or less throughout Europe in the late 1970s and early 1980s, most young people saw it as a means of escape and an outlet in the face of economic and social uncertainties. Football, a universal sport, was the preferred object of their passion. A simple popular sport that they could all understand and most of them played, it celebrated social success and meritocracy. Young people identified with the players, their clubs, their successes and failures. It was at this time that football underwent a profound change. It had not yet come to monopolise the media and it needed to attract a larger audience in order to boost its revenue, confirm its credibility and become still more professional. By appealing to more people, offering cheaper seats and providing a higher-quality spectacle, football managed to attract larger and more enthusiastic crowds. As fans organised themselves into groups, the managers of the clubs had neither the expertise (for such was not their job) nor the desire (for it was not a factor in their ambitions) to control passions that they themselves had created and encouraged – or at best they applied themselves to the task too late. While they may not necessarily, or not directly, have provoked this type of fan culture, they nonetheless permitted a social void to develop within which that culture and its most extreme manifestation, namely hooliganism, evolved and became organised of itself, without co-operation, assistance or communication, and equally without points of reference or boundaries.

Such a situation created problems because the young fans, who were more permissive than their elders with regard to social norms, were less likely to condemn deviant or rude behaviour (Galland, 1998, p. 27); instead they socialised separately from adults, among their peers and beyond the pale of standards and rules. Group membership led some of them to adopt violent forms of behaviour as a means of defiance, an expression of opposition, or an aid to identity-building, in pursuit of vendettas or in a quest for status and a recognised role (Linton, 1936; and Goffman, 1961). Some police reports, notably in France, take this idea a stage further, commenting on the total laxity of club managers in relation to the emergence of an extremely violent fan culture within their clubs. Deputy Chief Constable Rouibi, for example, states that: "Those in charge at PSG appear overwhelmed and alarmed by a trend that their own laxity and commercialism can reasonably be said to have encouraged in the past" (Rouibi, 1989, p. 4).

Hooliganism and the line between laissez-faire and collusion

Some supporters go further again, asserting that there is real connivance between the management of certain clubs and groups that are known to engage in violence more frequently than others. Deputy Chief Constable Rouibi's report echoes this suggestion, noting that:

> "... those responsible for security at the clubs commonly find themselves torn between conflicting aims. While they are aware of the risk of violence posed by

the presence of hooligan elements, they will readily assert that all football teams need fans of this type to 'pressurise the players'" (op. cit., p. 39).

Are such views simply fanciful – or do they reflect an attempt to denigrate the supporters of rival clubs? The question remains unresolved. Yet a few examples will suffice to demonstrate that relationships between the management of football clubs and their supporters can be highly ambivalent.

One club, for instance, hired a chief steward[16] who was a former supporter of neo-Nazism and whose photograph (showing him dressed in military style and giving a Nazi salute) circulated among supporters' clubs throughout France not so long ago. While it is understandable that the club in question may have wished to achieve greater insight into violent political extremism by engaging an "expert", it has to be asked whether such an individual could have any sort of credibility among his former comrades.

The second example concerns an incident reported in *L'Equipe* on 18 April 1996: the managing director of PSG had been indicted for complicity in the introduction of smoke canisters into a sports ground during a match between PSG and Metz on 30 March 1996. He was acquitted.

The third example is that of the request by a security official at a French first division club to the police superintendent responsible for the Jacques Chaban-Delmas stadium in Bordeaux that he should drop proceedings against two supporters arrested for violence in the stands. The official suggested it would be better to "settle the matter internally".

The fourth and final example concerns the same stadium, where a supporter physically restrained by the Bordeaux stewards after attacking another fan announced that he was the son of a former minister. Despite the existence of procedures to be followed in such cases, no action was taken against him.

These are just a few of the possible examples from French football alone and many more could be cited from all over Europe.

Be that as it may, the absence of any relationship, or the ambiguous nature of the relationship, between club management and fans could not but have the effect of reinforcing social anomie and provoking extreme behaviour such as hooliganism. In some cases, rules have been broken as the result of a convergence of interests. For has not football benefited, or at least derived a quid pro quo, from the deviant behaviour of fans inasmuch as they inject atmosphere and animation into the stands and enhance the sense of partisanship? Becker (1963, p. 150) made the observation that rules were broken with impunity

---

16. In France, stewards have been employed to prevent incidents at stadiums since the passing of the "Pasqua Law" requiring the organisers of sporting or cultural events to put in place their own security at the venues.

because two groups derived mutual advantage from turning a blind eye to what was happening. How otherwise could one explain that it was so easy to bring quantities of flares and smoke canisters into stadiums despite rules in most European countries prohibiting them and requiring that fans be searched? Yet failure to apply the law can reasonably be regarded as a vector of violence (Bodin, 1999a) – a point made by the head of security at Girondins de Bordeaux FC: "When the law was introduced, calm was restored in the stands and the area around the stadium, but when it gradually became apparent that nothing had changed, that they could carry on as before and the law would not be enforced, well, they went at it more than ever".

This forceful, lucid and logical observation stands in contrast to the examples cited above and demonstrates, if demonstration were necessary, that rule-breaking and violence are social constructs and part of a process of complex interactions.

Without subscribing to the school of thought that prioritises security above all other considerations – and well aware that our argument reflects a utilitarian approach to penal policy under which the threat of punishment is often seen as sufficient to prevent the offence – there can be no doubt of the need to punish manifestations of violence. The sanctions taken must, however, be fair and appropriate in order to avoid inflaming feelings of opposition that can lead to an endless spiral of transgression/punishment/aggression (Debarbieux, 1992, p. 23). Socialisation has to entail an aspect of repression, otherwise the individual desire for self-control – a shared human condition – will disappear. While social deregulation is certainly not the only explanatory factor, it is evident that violence more readily takes root where those in charge of football clubs leave a social void between themselves and the fans. That void – that careless, laissez-faire ethos, "complicity" or indulgence – has echoes in the work and writings of Debarbieux (1996) on the separate field of violence in schools. Such violence tends to occur most readily in those secondary schools where there are conflicts among the staff and the school has no clear sense of direction and purpose.

Could this then be a factor behind the violence associated with football: the absence of any agreement or shared strategy for making the sport, in real sense, a "total social phenomenon" mindful of everyone involved in sporting society? For surely inclusion, co-operation and the recognition of individual contributions offer other means of establishing rights and duties, opportunities and prohibitions.

The consequences of applying or failing to apply social rules

While the police may be aware of, and even have files on, disruptive and dangerous individuals, they rarely call them in for questioning. In some cases the individuals concerned may not have been caught in the act, but the point has also been made that the law is applied selectively (Becker, op. cit., p. 36).

Laws and regulations[17] for the prevention of "hooliganism" were enacted belatedly in the aftermath of violent events heavily covered by the media. The 1985 European Convention on Spectator Violence and Misbehaviour at Sports Events and in particular at Football Matches was adopted a few weeks after the Heysel stadium tragedy. In the United Kingdom it was not until 1984, with the passing of the Police and Criminal Evidence Act, that the police were empowered to search and control hooligan fans; these powers were reinforced by the Sporting Events Act 1985 and a year later by the Public Order Act 1986. In Italy, because the authorities had not considered hooliganism a sufficiently serious problem (Tsoukala, 1996, p. 113), no measures were taken until 1985. In France it was not until 1993 that the Alliot-Marie Act on safety at sports events reached the statute book. The act had been in preparation for some time but it was the events of 28 August 1993 in Parc des Princes, when television viewers saw a riot police captain being beaten up during live coverage of a PSG v. Caen match, that gave impetus to the process, highlighting the urgent need for legislation to address such behaviour. Yet there had been a sufficient number of similar incidents, not only in the countries mentioned but right throughout Europe,[18] to warrant legislation at a much earlier stage. It is true that new rules are not always introduced solely in order to provide a legal framework for tackling hooligan behaviour or to institute measures to prevent it; they may also be part of a campaign to reassure the public and prevent the spread of a feeling of insecurity potentially damaging to society in general or at least to football as an institution (Bodin and Trouilhet, 2001).

Following the Heysel tragedy the Council of Europe addressed the problem of controlling and preventing spectator violence, adopting two major texts on football and a further one which extended their provisions to indoor sports, as well as a number of recommendations. The most important of these are listed below.[19]

– The European Convention on Spectator Violence and Misbehaviour at Sports Events and in particular at Football Matches, signed in Strasbourg on 19 August 1985, under which the states parties undertake to try to

---

17. We do not intend to discuss the civil liability and criminal responsibility of those who perpetrate violence at sports events, a question that has been studied by Lassalle (2000).
18. See Chaker (1999) for more detail on developments in the law.
19. Only the most important conventions and recommendations are cited here. For more exhaustive coverage see the summary of Council of Europe recommendations in *The prevention of violence in sport*, Council of Europe (2003).

prevent violence at sports events by taking measures to ensure security, policing, checks and screening, separation of rival supporters, exchanges of information between the signatory states, the identification of trouble-makers, etc. A Standing Committee, comprising representatives of the signatory states, was also set up with the task of monitoring and preventing violence on the part of athletes or spectators and taking all the measures necessary to facilitate its control. The convention is not designed to take responsibility away from the signatory states; indeed Article 3(4) provides that they should make every effort to put their own legislation in place.

– Recommendation 93/1 on measures to be taken by the organisers of football matches and public authorities, adopted by the Standing Committee of the convention (T-RV) at its meeting in Strasbourg on 3 and 4 June 1993. The purpose of this recommendation was to introduce a "standard checklist of measures to be taken by the organisers of football matches and public authorities". The checklist includes more than sixty points in relation to checks, preventive measures and organisation, to be observed in the preparation of sports events, responsibility being divided between the different parties involved, including stadium owners, event organisers, sports federations, UEFA (the Union of European Football Associations) and public authorities. The aim is to ensure that no measures are overlooked and to identify the function, duties and areas of responsibility of all those concerned.

– Recommendation 94/1 of the Standing Committee of the convention (T-RV) on measures to be taken concerning high-risk indoor sports events, which provides for measures similar to those required in stadiums in relation to protection and the prevention of violence, and contains recommendations on ticket sales and improved security at indoor sports events.

– In 1999 the Council of Europe produced a number of recommendations with a view to the European Football Championships in 2000, including one on football hooliganism.

– In July 2001 the Committee of Ministers adopted Recommendation Rec(2001)6 on the prevention of racism, xenophobia and racial intolerance in sport, which came into force a month later, calling on governments to adopt measures and institute a policy for combating racist and xenophobic behaviour in stadiums and in connection with sports events.

– In January 2003 the Standing Committee of the convention approved, in the context of the Council of Europe's Integrated Project on Responses to Violence in Everyday Life in a Democratic Society, Recommendation 2003/1 on the role of social and educational measures in the prevention of violence in sport.

The Council of Europe's efforts to tackle the problem of spectator violence have not been confined to recommendations and conventions. It has also set up a system of monitoring signatory states' observance of their undertakings, which entails on-site visits to assess implementation of the various texts. In the run-up to major tournaments (such as the World Cup and European Championships) the Council also organises co-ordination meetings between representatives of the host state and participating states. The European Union, for its part, has addressed the recurrent problem of hooliganism by focusing on the implementation of specific measures to prevent violence, notably through improved co-operation between the police forces of member states, including the setting up of an information network. These measures aim, *inter alia*, to:
- identify hooligans;
- prevent their leaving their own countries during major international competitions;
- prohibit their entry to, or facilitate their expulsion from, host countries;
- promote international exchanges of information.

UEFA, meanwhile, has issued a number of guidelines on safety in stadiums at competitions held under its auspices. The latest of these, dated June 1993, provide "binding instructions to the organisers of, and the associations and clubs participating in, matches played in any of the UEFA competitions, regarding precautionary measures to be taken to ensure safety and security in the stadium, and to prevent crowd disturbances". At each relevant event a UEFA delegate is charged with monitoring implementation of the measures in question.

The difficulty of introducing an effective crowd control policy

The main effect of the conventions, recommendations and national and international laws and regulations has been to introduce a twin-track policy for controlling crowds at sports events: preventive on the one hand, involving fan coaching and "fan embassies", and dissuasive on the other hand, with screening and control measures. There are many problems with the implementation of such a policy, however, given the evident clash between the recommended measures and the principle of freedom of movement within Europe.

Limitations on preventive policies

Although well intentioned and necessary, these preventive policies[20] pose a problem inasmuch as they are not unified or standardised and thus depend

---

20. For further information on the preventive policies advocated by the Council of Europe see *The prevention of violence in sport*, Council of Europe (2003).

for their effectiveness on the commitment of those in charge of sport. Their implementation at club level is contingent on a favourable or co-operative attitude on the part of sports bodies. For club bosses they pose the further problem of requiring them to acknowledge that violent or potentially violent fans are nonetheless "their" fans and furthermore that hooliganism is a "side effect" or unforeseen by-product of professional soccer. Making such an acknowledgement implies assuming responsibility for the violent acts that their supporters may commit – and they have no wish to do that. There is a strong temptation not to introduce genuine prevention policies at club level because, by working to prevent violence and getting involved in preventive and co-operative activities with their fans, the clubs could find themselves morally and financially required to assume the burden of criminal responsibility for those fans. As a means of "preventing" or guarding against heckling, jeering and violence some club bosses attempt to curry favour with fans by turning a blind eye when smoke canisters are brought into stadiums, or by sponsoring supporters' groups and the displays they put on. Others interpret prevention as entailing nothing more than the deployment of stewards inside sports venues.

Such an attitude is in the clubs' interest in several respects. Firstly, violent fans are regarded as outsiders, unconnected with football, who come to stadiums in order to misbehave. The introduction of violence prevention policies not only involves clubs in a long-term moral and financial commitment, but also requires them to acknowledge their connection with the violent fans, something they are reluctant to do. Secondly, financial interest is a factor, for if violence is committed at a distance from the football stadium it is no longer a problem for sport but rather a problem of law and order, for which civil society is financially liable. The third type of interest at stake has to do with the nature of professional football, which nowadays – given its revenues from advertising and the media – has no need of the impassioned supporters on whose ticket money it once relied for the resources to build a professional sport.

The concern to prevent violence is thus in conflict with the new commercialism in professional football, which can probably be regarded nowadays not so much as a sport, or even a sporting spectacle, but rather as a kind of board game geared towards promoting particular companies and achieving social recognition for the individuals who run them. The soccer world today is thus less concerned with preventing violence than with making it invisible so that law and order can be maintained inside football grounds (Roché, 1996) and the sport itself can retain a healthy, honourable image. This, surely, is the attitude reflected in the policy of keeping the "ends" seated and thus pacifying those who occupy them, and in the selective impact of higher ticket prices. Making them pay up, shut up and sit down (Bromberger, 1995) would seem to be the strategy of choice for curbing fan behaviour, a strategy already in place at British football grounds, where supporters can find themselves barred for life simply for standing up.[21]

Repressive measures

Repressive measures can be classed for the most part under four headings: legislation and regulation (and anti-hooliganism laws have been passed in most European countries); security measures (separation of rival fans, a police presence for the arrival of away-team supporters, establishment of a security ring around football grounds, use of frisking and body searching, and checking procedures at stadium gates); surveillance measures (installation of video surveillance in stadiums, and a police presence among groups of fans and in the stands); and information gathering (exchanges of information between police forces and between sports clubs on the numbers of fans expected at matches and how they are travelling).

Yet these repressive measures are problematic. In certain countries, including France, body searching is governed by the same rules as apply to police searches under warrant. It cannot therefore be carried out by stewards inside security cordons or at the gates to football grounds. Only public law-enforcement officers are empowered to search people in this way as part of their official policing function of maintaining or restoring order. Stewards can do no more than frisk people seeking to enter a stadium – i.e. carry out a brief surface check. While this sort of check may reveal sizeable objects it does not pick up darts or batteries, which are sometimes hidden in sandwiches, or coins with sharpened edges that are concealed in shoes. The Paris Bar Institute of Human Rights Training (IFDHBP) has pointed out in this context that the powers of stadium security personnel are the same as those of private security companies and that the courts have drawn attention on numerous occasions to the fact that body-searching procedures are unlawful (1995, p. 15). Clubs can get round this restriction to some extent, however, through arrangements whereby notice is given on tickets and at points of access to the stadium that persons entering will be searched. Giving notice of the search procedure in this way may enable clubs to refuse entry to persons who do not comply but it does not allow them to insist on searching any individual, or the personal effects of any individual, who objects to such a search despite having received prior notice of it (op. cit., p. 15).

Screening and frisking procedures are also hampered in many cases by the sheer influx of spectators at a match. Arrivals tend to peak shortly before

---

21. In April 1995 Manchester United supporter Steve Briscoe was barred from the team's ground for life for having remained on his feet in the stands shouting encouragement to the players, despite repeated warnings from security personnel.

kick-off, making it impossible for those in charge of security to check each spectator without holding up the crowd and provoking unrest. In such circumstances the police and stewards carry out spot checks, using their instinct to select individual spectators or fans for searching on the basis of their apparel or potentially aberrant conduct – hence the emergence of the "casuals". Frisking arrangements are further complicated by the fact that a shortage of female police officers and stewards can make it impossible to search women entering the ground. This being so, women are often used to bring in prohibited items (Bodin et al., 2004a/b).

In order to make their security measures work, clubs need to adopt very specific internal rules which must be clearly displayed at points of entry and ticket sales points. Legal experts argue that this formal requirement must evolve into a contractual obligation linking spectators and organisers. The IFDHBP has proposed that the following should be printed on the back of tickets:

> "The ticket holder acknowledges that he or she has noted the rules of the stadium (or club), constituting general conditions of sale, as displayed at the entrance to and around the stadium and made available at the point of purchase or reservation of the ticket. The ticket holder accepts that, having purchased a ticket, his or her access to the stadium depends upon acceptance of the club's security measures, including passage through security arches, searching of personal effects and body searching, and video surveillance under the conditions specified in the rules and subject to the safeguards provided. In return for the spectator's acceptance of such measures, the organisers will accept liability under a supplementary collective insurance policy for any bodily injuries sustained during the event, subject to the conditions and limits set out in the agreement made available to the spectator" (op. cit., p. 39).

Installing video surveillance systems in and around stadiums is also highly problematic. While such systems are clearly intended to prevent incidents and identify troublemakers, it is nonetheless true that – like video surveillance in town centres – they raise the problems of interference with the individual's right of personal portrayal, on the one hand, and of ensuring that the only areas surveyed and filmed are the stadium itself and access ways to it. The fact is that most stadiums are sited in built-up areas and the video cameras sweeping the exterior must be positioned so as not to impinge upon the privacy of the ordinary people of the area. In the countries with the most detailed legislation in this regard there is a further issue concerning the length of time for which images are stored. In any event, spectators may not be filmed unless it is clearly stated at the entrance to the stadium and on the tickets that they will be.

The task of security and prevention (in the broadest sense) at sports events is thus a difficult one that often runs into conflict with human rights. It is not at all uncommon for policing and stewarding arrangements to be focused on management of the general interest – a focus located somewhere between strict application of the laws and regulations, respect for the celebratory atmosphere that normally exists at any sporting fixture, and the need to take account of the stadium's urban location. Clearly those in charge must do their best to accommodate three conflicting perspectives. People who live near sports stadiums experience various types of constraint and nuisance as well as heavy traffic and problems when the crowd leaves the stadium. The task of keeping order and providing security in inner cities involves meeting a number of requirements quite apart from those connected with any given sports event – ensuring safety on the streets, securing and protecting public buildings, ensuring the safety of residents – but at the same time it can involve controlling a crowd of anything from 30 000 to 60 000 people (equivalent to the population of a small town) and getting them in and out of a venue. In many cases therefore it is a deliberate choice to prioritise the public interest and to allow offenders in and keep them under observation, rather than turning them away in strict compliance with the law, the aim being to prevent incidents elsewhere. In their concern to manage problems and incidents as effectively as possible, the police in different countries may turn a blind eye to certain activities that are in breach of the law. This means, in many cases, failing to apply the law in order to manage a football crowd as efficiently as possible with police resources that are not infinitely elastic.

> "Those whose job it is to ensure that the letter and spirit of the law are respected often make compromises, allowing certain acts to go unremarked and unpunished because taking further action would be too difficult, or because their resources are limited and they cannot prosecute everyone …" (Becker, op. cit., p. 208).

The task of the police and the courts is complicated because while failure to apply the law is bound to lead to excesses and violence, its rigid enforcement inevitably shifts the problem to other locations. The clashes that nowadays take place at some distance from stadiums are the clearest proof of this. The physical displacement of violence results much less from any intention on the part of supporters than from the efficiency of the crowd control arrangements that are in place.

Although the relevant laws and regulations are quite obviously geared exclusively to surveillance and punishment (Foucault, 1975), it would seem that in the case of football matches there is less emphasis on prevention – in the sense of recognising, interpreting and understanding deviance and violence on the part of fans in order to stop it happening – than on the suppression of all potentially criminal acts. It is simply a matter of maintaining law and order. That said, we do not take issue with the need to punish certain types of reprehensible behaviour; we would simply point out that there is currently an imbalance between the arsenal of repressive measures that is brought to bear (however deficiently they may be applied) and preventive or educational measures. We cannot but echo the following observation by M. Martins.

> "It is understandable that, in the past, when the logic of urgency prevailed, priority was given to adopting technical and safety measures to prevent the most dramatic events in the short term. However, action directed more at the root of the problem is now absolutely vital" (2003, p.5).

But does the football world really want to adopt such an approach? If incidents are not taking place close to the stadiums, club bosses can currently argue with righteous indignation that "their" fans are not responsible because the acts of violence do not occur at or during matches and the individuals involved do not even wear club colours. The violence is thus portrayed as the work of ordinary delinquents who, by fighting some distance away from the football grounds, confirm what the soccer world has always proclaimed: that the violence can be put down to social disorder. The world of sport thus merrily shrugs off any responsibility: it is up to society in the different European countries to respond to what are inherent failings in the social fabric.

With regard to structural decline of society, it is impossible to ignore the way in which political claims began to be voiced in European football grounds in the 1970s, and currently seem to be resurfacing with new vigour in some countries, notably in the former eastern bloc.

Political ideologies in the football stadium

In the beginning: the British skinhead movement

In addition to the phenomena habitually advanced as typical of hooliganism (physical violence among fans or between fans and police, and damage to property and infrastructure inside and outside sports grounds), one factor is the open display of conflicting political ideologies in many stadiums in Europe.

Discussion of the political ideologies publicly displayed at soccer matches often tends, however, to focus solely on extreme right-wing movements. Hooligans are equated with neo-Nazis and skinheads. As Broussard has suggested (op. cit., p. 305), it is a classic, almost clichéd image. Since Heysel it has been taken for granted that the neo-Nazis who attend football matches are British. When Gendarme Daniel Nivel was brutally attacked in France, it was the work of German skinheads and was thus automatically classified as part of a long tradition in that country, currently reflected in neo-Nazi movements. And an upsurge in xenophobia in Parma and Rome, which attracted universal shock and condemnation, was deemed to symbolise a resurgence of Italian fascism. Yet no one ever stops to ask whether skinheads and hooligans are, in fact, one and the same, or whether other ideologies might be present in the stands. Also, are the political ideologies that are flaunted and proclaimed really genuine? And what significance should be attached to such political and xenophobic displays?

We need to explore the notion of ideology not so much as a word or concept but as a whole system of meaning and presupposition that was almost certainly evident under other names long before Destutt de Tracy coined the term "ideology" in the late eighteenth century. It is understood in so many different ways that its very polysemy at best dilutes its force. Is ideology an ideal or set of ideas, precepts, beliefs and value judgements that tends to be imposed by societies on their members or on others? Or is it, rather, an ideal or set of ideas, precepts, beliefs and value judgments that individuals more or less collectively attempt to spread or impose in a society as a means of upsetting the established order? However we define it, ideology has to be seen as the active ingredient and basis of fanaticism and totalitarianism in many different guises (Arendt, 1972).

Fan culture and political ideologies

The link between fan culture and ideology goes back many years. Skinheads made their appearance in the United Kingdom in the late 1960s. Originally the movement, which was relatively small, was not racist. It reflected a reaction both to hippie culture and to the disintegration of the British economy. Essentially it was a counter-culture: hippies had long hair and went on peace marches, so skinheads shaved their hair and used violence as a means of proclaiming masculinity and virility. The skinheads, most of whom came at the time from working-class homes, shared many values with immigrants, who, like them, were kept on the margins of a crumbling society. They favoured ska and reggae music. In football, which at the time was an integral element of British popular culture, the skinheads found an affirmative means of expression and a place in which to express themselves. This brief outline of the genesis of the skinhead movement is far removed from the archetypical composite image of fans, hooligans, skinheads and right-wing ideology.

It was in the late 1970s that the skinhead movement really veered towards violence. The slogan of the day, "No future", was a succinct expression of the social disarray of which the movement was part. It became more radical and began to react against the growing poverty in British society and against a socioeconomic policy that marginalised working-class young people. The skinheads adopted as their rallying cry a shout – "Oi" – which gave its name to "Oi music", with songs challenging the Establishment, Thatcher's economic and social policy and the exclusion of the white working class (Johnson, 1982). The music moved into football grounds as certain groups wrote songs in support of particular clubs but also because the tunes could easily be fitted to chants for any team. Some of the fans identified with particular groups.

Skinhead groups gradually became more structured and more radical in reaction to the situation of exclusion in which they were (or perceived themselves to be) placed. Their violence was thus one of the ways in which social dysfunction (Coser, 1956) expressed itself. The emergence of the West Ham ICF (Inter City Firm, named after the train service) in 1975 was part of this process. Yet at this stage by no means did all skinheads flaunt a political affiliation. It was not until the early 1980s that the movement became significantly more radical. Most skinheads began to join one of two extreme right-wing parties, the British Movement and the National Front. The immediate consequences of this were not only to aggravate the violence but also to accelerate the spread of right-wing ideologies among young fans who were disillusioned by the traditional political parties and anxious about their future. In racism and xenophobia they found an outlet for their anger by focusing on a scapegoat for the problems (Girard, 1972).

A combination of social unrest and a process of mimicry led to the formation, more or less throughout Europe, of similar groups with names designed to be disturbing (the "Nutty Turnout" at Millwall, the "Headhunters" at Chelsea or the "Service Crew" at Leeds), to evoke the Third Reich (the "Army Korp" at PSG or the "Naoned Korp" at Nantes FC) or, by association with extreme right-wing organisations, to display a political affiliation (e.g. "Ordre Nouveau" ["New Order"] at PSG). In Spain, young admirers of Franco tended to support Español de Barcelona, while in East and West Germany the youth that identified with the Third Reich favoured the football clubs of Berlin, Dortmund and Leipzig.

The nature of ideology in the stadiums

Are these various ideologies equally dangerous? Although, as Bromberger (1995) points out, most of the displays described could be put down to fairly mundane and sporadic expressions of group opposition, or to efforts by individuals to mark themselves out, some did actually reflect the work of political parties. In these cases the fan groups concerned served as a form of shop window or a means through which the parties could infiltrate the stands in order to attract young recruits. Two groups of French fans which offer useful examples here are those of the Boulogne Kop at PSG and the south curve at Marseilles.

Ideology as a means of asserting an identity

In the period between 1980 and 1995 a rash of Celtic crosses and swastikas appeared on the Boulogne stand at Parc des Princes [home ground of PSG].

In this context the National Front periodical *Le Choc du mois* became an apologist for the Boulogne Kop, which it depicted as confronting a left-wing police force (Mignon, 1995). As in Italy, black players on opposition teams found themselves booed. Meanwhile at the Vélodrome stadium in Marseilles, the south curve – home of the "South Winners" group – began to be decorated with "A" (for "anarchy") symbols and images of Che Guevara.

While it is important not to read too much into these political affirmations and demonstrations, one must nonetheless be wary of them. They triggered clashes both between groups from rival clubs (Marseilles and PSG for example) and between groups from the same club (such as South Winners and Commando Ultra at Marseilles), and sowed the seeds for networks of inter-club alliances and enmities (supporters of Châteauroux, PSG and Strasbourg, for example, united against Marseilles fans). In such cases violence is fuelled by a political dimension that lends it a new *raison d'être* unrelated to sport. The purposes of the various ideologies are, however, quite distinct, as can be seen from the example of the two fan groups mentioned above.

Right-wing extremism in the stands: the case of Paris Saint-Germain

At Paris Saint-Germain the political affiliation was very clear, and PSG remains today the French club most heavily infiltrated by political activists. The Boulogne Kop came into being in 1987 at the initiative of a skinhead to whom we shall refer as S. A.,[22] a member of Jeunesses Nationalistes Révolutionnaires (JNR) [Young Nationalist Revolutionaries], a group attached to the Troisième Voie [Third Way] organisation. This was a period during which various French organisations including Troisième Voie, L'œuvre Française and the French and European Nationalist Party (PNFE) were trying to organise, recruit and structure skinhead groups. JNR actually had its headquarters at Parc des Princes. This tiny grouping was to structure and influence the Boulogne Kop. On 9 December 1989 S.A. founded the so-called "Pitbull Kop", a group that was to initiate numerous incidents of conflict and violence and was known for its xenophobic and pro-Nazi slogans. The PSG v. Strasbourg match on Saturday 16 January 1993 marked a turning point for the Kop, which from then on became 100% hooligan:

> "... consistent and homogenous in its politics and outlook. A combat area peopled by highly motivated activists who have nothing in common with ordinary football fans: there are no streamers, no animation. The only emblems on display are [political] flags. The stand is now solidly grey and black. Certain individuals play an active role as political party stewards" (Rouibi, op. cit., p. 4).

Here there was a genuine effort by the extreme right to infiltrate the stands, part of a strategy to maintain a high political profile through incitement to

---
22. His initials.

racial discrimination, hatred and violence. Posters for fan groups in the Boulogne Kop in 1993 make this quite clear.

Figure 1: Apologia for racial hatred on a Boulogne Kop poster from 1993

This shift into extremism had social implications. It reflected a dual desire to dominate and segregate (Wieviorka, 1998), rather than any reaction to growing poverty in certain sections of society. In fact it has been pointed out that the founders of the Boulogne Kop, particularly the skinheads, came from comfortably off families where the heads of households were lawyers or members of other middle-class professions (Mignon, op. cit., p. 31). Affiliation to the extreme right can thus come about for various reasons, reflecting individuals' different life experiences (Duret, 2004). The structured image of the Boulogne stand served as a recruiting device and a political platform. The most politically committed fans also acted as stewards for the parties of the extreme right. Although the flags bearing Celtic crosses and swastikas no longer fly on the stand, it is reasonable to ask why those in charge at PSG allowed the extremists to organise in the way they did. And what is one to make of the club's decision to recruit a former hooligan from the extreme right as a senior steward?

The Marseilles experience: being different in order to exist, with left-wing extremism as a pretext

While the political affiliation and ideology on display at PSG were genuine, that was not the case at Olympique de Marseille (OM), despite the images of Che Guevara adorning South Winners' banners. Posters advertising forays by the Winners to away matches depicted recommended weapons for each destination (e.g. baseball bats and truncheons) alongside slogans such as "KAOS" or "A" for anarchy.

Figure 2: South Winners poster for an away match in Lyon in 1998

In the unofficial league table of French fan groups the Winners long enjoyed the reputation of being the most violent and the distinction of being unbeaten. Yet their apparent political affiliation was merely a pretext that enabled them to assert their difference from other groups, and most importantly from the Parisians. Not only is there hereditary sporting rivalry between Marseilles and Paris but there is also historical enmity dating back to the days when the capital dispatched troops to quell insurrection in what was for many years one of the wealthiest cities in France. But the roots of the Winners' "ideology" lie elsewhere. The proximity of Italy and the experience of European Cup matches triggered a boundless enthusiasm for football among the young people of Marseilles in the 1980s. Imitating the practice of Italian fans, young supporters gathered in the south curve in a group initially known as "CU84". The group was a reflection of Marseilles itself: multicoloured and culturally diverse. But tensions quickly grew among its leaders until, towards the end of the 1980s, it split into three distinct factions, the Fanatics, the Ultras and the Winners, which nonetheless sustained a degree of unity for a time under the umbrella name of FUW. The break-up occurred primarily for reasons of ethnicity (Poutignat and Streiff-Fenart, 1995): the Ultras and Fanatics were essentially white although many, including the leaders, were of non-French origin, while the Winners were of mixed race. Cultural and social reasons also played a part, however. The Ultras and Fanatics came from more comfortably off backgrounds whereas most of the Winners lived in the northern districts of Marseilles or the Panier area, which in some years (1998 for example) had unemployment rates of up to 40%. Struggles for power and leadership were a further factor in the split, and age also played a not insignificant role. The founding members of the Winners were still at school, whereas the other groups tended to attract slightly older young people, most of whom had jobs or were in higher education.

The groups functioned in a familiar manner. For a group to sustain itself it has to assert that it is different, notably from other groups closest to it.

Identity is forged through opposition, and conflict plays a part in creating social distance. The Ultras were quick to become organised and some proclaimed what were essentially far-right views. The group dressed in navy blue bomber jackets and some hard-core members also wore Doc Marten boots with white laces – typical skinhead "uniform". In reaction, the Winners flaunted images of Che Guevara and anarchist flags in the south curve. Their hard-core members also wore bomber jackets but reversed them, wearing the orange lining on the outside, and some sported Doc Martens, this time with red laces in imitation of the "Redskins" (a far-left skinhead group). The leaders of the group acknowledge that all this happened in a more or less unplanned way, the intention being to provoke and to mark themselves out from the "fascists" in the opposing group, who labelled the Winners "Rebe".[23] The group's leftist stance was more feigned than real. In many cases the spirit that informed the emergence of extreme fan groups – combining a desire for independence from adults with militancy and an assertion of autonomy in the face of family constraints and parental authority – tended to place the young supporters in a libertarian tradition. Among the Winners, the most significant manifestation of a political dimension was in the day-to-day application of community values: solidarity, a rejection of large-scale profit-making, and the provision of financial and other forms of support to members. Quite simply, the libertarian spirit came into play here in a context of social hardship in which the young people had a sense of resourcefulness and realised they needed to share in order to get by. This *esprit de corps* was apparent even in the solidarity shown during physical clashes, although the leaders of the Winners regarded such violent incidents as quite specifically targeted and unrelated to the violence that young members of the group might face on the streets on a daily basis.

At OM, political infiltration was not an issue. The ideology proclaimed was quite clearly a pretext for staking out an identity. None of the Marseilles fan groups from the far left or right ever forged links with counterparts at other football clubs. On the contrary, the different Marseilles factions would put up a common front against PSG or Lyon fans, whom they labelled as fascists. Unlike the Paris fans, none was involved in a stewarding role for any political party. That said, it is not our intention to stigmatise one set of fans while depicting another as angels. We are simply reporting the experience on the ground, as confirmed in studies carried out by the Central Directorate for Public Security.

---

23. The word means "Arab" in the French street slang known as "verlan", which reverses the syllable order of words.

Emerging shades of extremism

Clearly, therefore, the various ideologies on display in football grounds were not all equally significant. Social reasons similar to those described above have been a factor behind the emergence of certain ideological currents among soccer fans in eastern Europe: the collapse of an economic system has provoked extremism among certain sections of the youth in reaction to poverty. One example was an incident when far-right Budapest fans descended on to the pitch to beat up their own team for not trying hard enough. While such behaviour has to be condemned, surely political leaders as well as those in charge of sport, have to acknowledge that soccer can take on the function of a "social testing-ground". If a country's economy undergoes upheaval so severe as to leave a section of the population by the wayside, surely a visible reaction to what is happening (in the form of violence and political extremism) ought to constitute a clear political signal to those in government. In our increasingly pacified and prevention-conscious societies the football stadium really is one of the last "social enclave[s] where excitement can be enjoyed without its socially and personally dangerous implications" (Elias and Dunning, 1986). Where else can ordinary individuals so exuberantly express their passion, joy, grief, uncertainties and discontent? If people were to gesticulate and vociferate in the street as they do at football matches they would soon find themselves escorted to the nearest police station. We need to accept the idea that while sport is a social outlet, it also provides an ideal context in which both to control impulses and to give way to them. This is by no means to say that we must permit racist, xenophobic and violent ideologies to take root in our football grounds. We may simply have to accept, however, that it is better for society if such ideologies are expressed in an enclosed, regulated and structured place such as a stadium, rather than in the street, and also that it is preferable to be able to observe social breakdown in the stadium context before it spreads irreversibly or more damagingly to society as a whole.

What is harder to accept is the failure on the part of sports bosses to react to the upsurge in racism and xenophobia among football crowds. In 2000, for example, Unesco's Courier newsletter carried an article that accused FIFA of "ducking the issue" after the football federation had condemned public demonstrations of racism. "Such statements", the article read, "do not disguise the lack of action against football administrators such as the President of the Turkish team Trabzonspoor, Mehmet Ali Yilmaz, who called the black English striker Kevin Campbell a 'cannibal' and 'discoloured', forcing him to go on strike before he was transferred to the English team Everton."[24] The

---

24. The article can be consulted on the Unesco website at:
http://www.unesco.org/courier/2000_11/uk/ethique.htm

incident referred to is not an isolated one: in 2004, Ron Atkinson, sports consultant to the British television channel ITV and former manager of Aston Villa, believing that he was off air, referred to French international Marcel Desailly as a "fucking lazy, thick nigger".[25] In an effort to combat racism in football, UEFA and FARE (Football Against Racism in Europe), at a joint meeting in London in March 2003, adopted a ten-point anti-racism charter. This represented an important step in the fight against racism, FARE having recorded 120 serious racist incidents over the previous decade. Nonetheless it is fair to note that it took some considerable time to produce the charter – necessary as it was in terms of condemning and preventing racism at matches – given that major manifestations of xenophobia in soccer were first apparent in the late 1970s.

Recent conflicts in the Russian Federation between extreme right-wing Moscow fans and supporters of St Petersburg need to be seen from a social perspective and not simply as a sporting expression of historical rivalry between, on the one hand, the capital of the Soviet empire and, on the other, the ancient seat of the Tsars and cradle of the Russian Revolution.

The fact is that other forms of ideology are emerging in sport today, the origins of which do not lie solely in the economic and social exclusion of a section of the population. These are proving, in the ways they are expressed, to be particularly dangerous and radical. The individuals involved are not demanding a place in society or even proclaiming social malaise. Their xenophobic violence is rooted in ethnic, cultural and religious conflicts such as those which surfaced in the last Balkan war. Violence of this type is harder to curb because it stems not only from prior assumptions, prejudices and value judgments but also from past atrocities that cannot easily be erased from individual and collective memory. Rather than being a substitute for war, sport thus becomes an extension of it, an arena in which each side seeks to avenge affronts or atrocities or to seal victories. Inter-ethnic conflict was already apparent in football within the eastern bloc several years before the fall of the Berlin Wall, providing a foretaste of more radical rivalry and conflict. It occurred, for example, at matches between Spartak Moscow and Dynamo Tbilisi, at the Dynamo Zagreb v. Red Star Belgrade match of 13 May 1990 when sixty-one people were injured, and in the recurring clashes between Slovakian supporters of Slovan Bratislava and Czech fans of Sparta Prague.[26] The fighting between supporters of Croatia and those of Serbia and Montenegro at the finals of the European Water Polo Championship on

---

25. Atkinson's words earned him a "red card" from *L'Equipe Magazine* (30 April 2004, 104, p. 19).
26. See the article on this subject by Ignacio Ramonet (1996).

15 June 2003 demonstrated how the phenomenon was spreading. The trouble started when Croat fans began to shout anti-Serb insults, triggering the sort of violence rarely associated with sports other than soccer: bottles were thrown, iron bars were wielded and supporters attacked their rivals with implements including rocket flares. Inter-ethnic conflict can thus use sport – an ideal context for forging and reinforcing national identities – as a vehicle for sustaining and extending war (Grubisa, 2003). Sport also mirrors existing political tensions, which are embodied, interpreted and expressed through an exaggerated, chauvinistic fan culture that promotes or accompanies nationalism. The example of the former Yugoslavia is not unique. Football was one means of asserting identity in Franco's Spain in the years 1936-75, and it has had the same function in other places more or less throughout the world (Colovic, 1998; Colomé, 1998; and Kapuscinski, 1986).

Ought sport to be any better than the rest of society?

Whether feigned or genuine, the types of political affirmation we have described – including those that are mere apocryphal constructs – have the effect of intensifying cultural rivalries and promoting antagonism. Sporting rivalry is thus reinforced by political affirmations and demands, leading fans (like juvenile delinquents) into an endless spiral of opposition and conflict. Already singled out and stigmatised for their exuberant passions and their youth, the fans are rendered all the more menacing by the ideologies they flaunt. Yet extremists in sport are no more numerous or more dangerous than they are in the rest of society. They simply have a higher profile. In some cases they receive media coverage as a result of their demonstrations of violence. But a football stadium can never be a sterile space: the crowd it holds may be equivalent in size to the population of a town, so it is inevitable that a whole spectrum of political ideologies will find themselves thrown together and on display there. Without approaching sport from a radically critical perspective, we must acknowledge that it cannot be depicted solely as a vehicle for education, integration, socialisation and health promotion. Sport – or physical and corporal exercise if we feel that the term "sport" does not adequately describe ancient games – has always involved exclusion and propaganda. The Greek games are just one example of this. Bodin and Debarbieux (2001, p. 14) have made the point that ancient Greece no more created sport as a pacificatory activity than it created the rationale for bringing rules and harmony to the ancient games and athletic contests. The fallacy of such notions was demonstrated long ago by Gernet (1917) and more recently by Vernant and Vidal-Naquet (1986), among others. The Greek ideal of sport was aristocratic and even during periods of democracy it reinforced discrimination and slavery. Sport was, after all, the preserve of nobles and free men. It had no place for the low-born, outsiders, slaves, or indeed women (and all these principles found an echo in the Olympic Games as resurrected by Pierre de Coubertin and also in Hitler's Germany). Certain victorious athletes in ancient times were hailed by the title "Gene",[27] thus doing their bit for Greek expansionism.

Yet if sport is a vehicle for ideologies, it is perhaps no more than a reflection of our societies. Elias and Dunning suggested that "knowledge about sport was knowledge about society" (1986, p.19). While sport can sometimes help to create social cohesion, it also has various domestic and foreign policy functions (Brohm, 1992) in which political ideologies can find a foothold. Bernard Jeu (1993) went so far as to call sport a merciless combat in a peaceful setting, resulting in the downfall or elevation of particular systems.

Disasters – another form of violence

Disasters (fires or incidents of crushing in stadiums) are another form of violence associated with large-scale sports events. They can happen before, during or after the event itself. Through carelessness or lack of analysis they are often equated with hooliganism and they mark the collective imagination because they tend to result in large numbers of people being killed or injured. Essentially, a disaster can be caused in one of four ways: through organisational failure on the part of the police or those in charge of stadium security, through ill luck, through the mercenary attitude of club bosses or because facilities are dilapidated.

Organisational failure or a poor response by police and security staff: Sheffield and Heysel

Although there had been some skirmishing in the Heysel stadium at the May 1985 UEFA Champions League final between Liverpool and Juventus of Turin, it was not so much these clashes that were responsible for the deaths of thirty-one spectators and injuries to 600 more, as shortcomings in the way in which the fans and spectators from the two rival camps were managed. No other interpretation can be put on the decision to allow the two sets of supporters onto the same curve two hours before kick-off, with only a fence to separate them, and with a long wait. The outcome was never in doubt: in this highly charged atmosphere of sporting rivalry, the wait, the boredom and the physical proximity of the two camps was bound to lead to provocative behaviour, insults and intimidation. The first organisational mistake was made at this stage in that the two groups of supporters were not better separated. In the context of crowd control in an urban area it is understandable that they were allowed into the stadium very early: it was preferable to keep them

---
27. A military leader.

together and channel them into the ground rather than run the risk of clashes occurring on the streets of Brussels. But the first mistake was compounded by a second one: when the Italian fans in the back rows began to panic and descend the terracing they crushed numbers of their comrades – who did not realise what was going on higher up – against the fence at the bottom. It took several long minutes for the stadium security staff to unlock the fence gates at the base of the stand. There is no doubt that had a decision been taken more quickly, in immediate response to what was happening and to the danger, the fans would not have been crushed to death. The police and security staff hesitated, however, probably fearing a pitch invasion and a clash between the two sets of fans. It is quite clear that Heysel happened because the stadium security was flawed.

In 1989 the Hillsborough stadium in Sheffield (England) was the scene of a different type of disaster, which also called into question organisational arrangements. The occasion was an FA Cup semi-final match between Liverpool and Nottingham Forest, and several hundred Liverpool fans who had no tickets were attempting to get into the ground. It was a familiar phenomenon. The last-minute rush at the gates is always the most difficult time in terms of crowd control. The police remained determined to prevent any unauthorised entry. Once again, the fans at the back were to crush those in front of them. The toll of death and injury was worse than at Heysel: ninety-five people were killed and 200 hurt, showing clearly that those in charge had not learned the importance of immediate response in crowd-control situations. The incident also exemplifies how hard it is, when controlling crowds of fans, to strike a balance between the strict maintenance of law and order and an approach based on "doing one's best" in the public interest. The Sheffield and Heysel tragedies are not isolated cases: similar disasters have taken place around the world and at different periods of history. Thuillier (1996) reminds us that deaths were caused by crowd movements in the Colosseum in Rome 2 000 years ago. In Cali (Colombia) in 1982, twenty-two people were crushed to death by a crowd, and, as recently as 2001, forty-three people died in similar circumstances in Ellis Park, Johannesburg. It would seem there is a general failure to learn from history. At the same time, however, one must acknowledge that, given the number of sports events held every year all over the world and the huge numbers of people who attend them, dreadful incidents such as those described are rare.

Ill luck

It goes without saying that sports fans will behave in an impassioned manner. While their passion can sometimes make them unreasonable and lead to reprehensible actions, its primary focus remains the sport itself and the celebration associated with it. In this respect, football matches are unlike any other sporting fixtures. With their *tifos*, songs and chants, shouts of encouragement and vociferation, the fans turn a match into a highly colourful spectacle. The flares that light up the curves contribute to the emotional intensity of the encounter. But the fact of turning the stands into a spectacle has caused many accidents. In 1991 in France, for example, a group of Toulouse fans known as the "Purples" were travelling by bus to an away match with Saint-Etienne and stopped along the way to buy ingredients for making flares: sugar, potassium chlorate etc. Back in the bus they began preparing the mixture. When someone inadvertently dropped a cigarette butt into it, the bus caught fire, killing one fan and seriously injuring many others. It was a case of bad luck turning what should have been a celebratory occasion into a tragedy, but it also highlights two security issues. The first concerns the consequences of the negative reputation of certain fan groups. In the case of the Toulouse fans, the bus driver had taken what he regarded as a precautionary step by removing the hammers used to break the windows of the vehicle in an emergency; it is possible that had he not done so everyone would have been able to escape. The second problem is that of smoke canisters and flares brought to football matches. Such devices are nowadays banned in European stadiums but fans continue to bring them in, taking advantage of what is often an indulgent attitude on the part of those in charge. At Paris Saint-Germain, for example, a head of security was charged with "complicity in allowing smoke canisters to be brought into a sports stadium" after fans questioned about an incident at a PSG v. Metz match on 30 March 1996 told police that they had the security chief's tacit agreement. The court subsequently found him not guilty.

Mercenary motives on the part of those in charge

Among other factors involved in many of the tragedies that have occurred is a mercenary attitude on the part of club bosses – in different sports and at different levels of competition – who have sometimes been prepared to sell excess numbers of tickets under dubious conditions, in an all too transparent attempt to boost gate receipts or indeed to create "slush funds".

The "best" example is probably that of the tragedy at Furiani stadium in Bastia (Corsica) on 5 May 1992. Just ten minutes before kick-off at a French cup final match between Bastia and OM a temporary stand gave way. The outcome was tragic: eighteen people dead and 2 332 injured. A committee of inquiry set up by the Prime Minister of the day, Pierre Bérégovoy, found that more tickets had been sold than there were places available and that terraces had been hastily constructed without any building plans or proper calculations, using what resources were to hand. Had Bastia simply agreed to the match being staged at a neutral ground capable of containing the large crowd anticipated for what was a major southern French "derby", the tragedy could probably have been avoided. One consequence of this disaster was the introduction in France of tougher safety standards and a ban on temporary stands (Pujol, Freydière, Bayeux, 2004). But again, this was not an isolated incident, nor one attributable solely to the fact that modern sport has become a commercial concern. For example:

> "In the year AD 27 an event promoter had built an amphitheatre without due attention to the foundations, and 50 000 people were maimed or crushed. In AD 52 there was a disaster at a mock naval battle, for which Narcissus, who had directed the preparations, and Agrippina blamed each other" (Jeu, 1987, p. 110).

Similar cases include the collapse of a stand in Glasgow (Scotland) in 1902 and walls giving way in Bolton (England) in 1946 and in Tolima (Peru) in 1981, to name but a few.

Dilapidated infrastructure

Run-down infrastructure is often cited as a cause of disasters and while it has been a factor in many cases, the problem is frequently compounded by poor organisation and the mercenary attitude of those in charge. The tragedy that occurred in Bradford (England) in 1985 illustrates this. During an ordinary match a stand caught fire. Fifty-three bodies were recovered, 200 people were hurt and eighteen were unaccounted for. The dilapidated state of the wooden stand was clearly a causal factor. At the time, stands of this type, which are now prohibited and have disappeared, were not uncommon in the United Kingdom. What aggravated the toll of death and injury, however, was the fact that all the emergency exits had been locked during the match in order to prevent fans using them to gain entrance. Spectators trying to escape the blaze rushed towards them believing they offered a way out, only to find themselves trapped.

Many tragedies could have been avoided, however, if the standards laid down in the European Convention on Spectator Violence and Misbehaviour at Sports Events and in particular at Football Matches (ETS No.120, 1985), and the recommendations following on from it, had been scrupulously observed. Too often in the event of a disaster, those in charge have to cope with the consequences of inadequate organisational arrangements (put together in haste), dishonest dealings, or simply the problem of recognising how an inherently impulsive, mobile and irritable crowd will react and being able to deal with it (Le Bon, 1895) – a problem significantly compounded by the impassioned context of the sporting event and its location in an urban stadium.

Sport, politics and the violence they have in common

No one today can be in any doubt about the close relationship between sport and politics, for it is a relationship that has been present in many guises throughout the history of modern sport. As long ago as 1912, Georges Rozet, analysing French failures at the Olympic Games, was to write that: "a nation's sporting worth, alongside other forms of prestige, is a contributory factor and by no means a negligible one in what may be properly called its social worth" (Thibault, 1991, p. 149).

In the years after the First World War, major international sports events became occasions of symbolic confrontation between nations, and indeed empires (Arnaud, 1999). In the inter-war period sport grew in status and drew international audiences, while at the same time contributing to the rise of totalitarian regimes, whose ideologies it reflected or purveyed.

Alongside this process, sport became an affair of state, a political consideration of sufficient importance to be a lever in attempts to influence the fate of nations. In this regard, the practice of boycotting – as used at the Montreal, Moscow and Los Angeles Olympic Games – was highly symbolic of political interplay.

At the same time, certain champions have carried the torch of national, cultural, religious or political identity far beyond the goal of sporting victory. Sport also became a means of promoting the demands of cultural minorities and downtrodden or dissident groups – the prime example being the moment in 1968 when Tommie Smith and John Carlos raised their gloved fists on the Olympic podium in support of the Black Panther movement and its struggle against the discrimination still endured by the black minority in the United States at the time. On occasions, sport has also been a crucible for terrorism.

Since the 1980s, as the economy of sport has opened up to the free market, the sports institutions that dominate international competition (the IOC and FIFA, for example), have set themselves up as alternative power bases capable of exercising a certain influence on political decision-making and indeed of promoting by political means a "sporting establishment" which – like such organisations as the UN, Unesco, WTO or IMF in their respective fields – has the capacity to bring about at least partial changes in the fate of nations and the international status quo.

In fact, sport's influence on politics is probably greater today than at any time in history, reflecting on the one hand its economic clout and on the other its increasing universality. The image of sport – a political image conveyed by international media networks – is now part of the development of sporting cultures, and the shared enjoyment of those cultures (deliberately engineered or not) is becoming a global reality.

This dimension of sport is most clearly evident in the general enthusiasm for activities like soccer that have spread across the world, soccer indeed having been termed "the most universal phenomenon, much more universal than democracy or the market economy, which are said to know no borders, but cannot rival the spread of football" (Boniface, 1998, p. 10).

As Arnaud and Broyer pointed out in 1985, sport in this respect has actually functioned like a colonial power, having sought out and all but exterminated traditional local and regional forms of physical exercise throughout the world (Arnaud and Broyer, 1985), albeit not without meeting resistance, as outlined in the many studies about how traditional local practices have fought back (Epron and Robène, 2004). The first point to be made here, with regard to political and cultural forms of violence, must be to condemn the universal process of westernisation via the hegemony of sports culture, a process similar to that described by Lévi-Strauss in the 1950s whereby arrogant western civilisation perverted the cultures and ecosystems of traditional worlds (Lévi-Strauss, 2001). The widespread phenomenon of sporting acculturation was on occasions used, both in the west and in imperial colonies, as a political tool for bringing national and colonial cultures into conformity during a period when Europe's nation states were taking shape. It is no mere coincidence, for example, that in India and Pakistan, both formerly part of the British empire, English cricket (rather than traditional Indian games) should today enjoy such political and cultural prestige that the Indian cricket team's arrival in Lahore on 10 March 2004 was "seen by the man in the street as the first sign of a thaw in relations between India and Pakistan" (*Le Monde*, 12 March 2004, p. 3).

It is true that the spread of sport around the globe and the popularity of certain activities owe much to an appreciation of sport itself, with its capacity for motivating people and the high degree of partisanship it can provoke, as well as the concept of victory at stake yet never quite attainable – in other words, all the ingredients of drama that are inherent in the unpredictability of sporting encounters, reflecting as they do the uncertainty of human destiny in the modern world (Bromberger, 1996).

Nonetheless it is impossible to analyse sport's place in contemporary society and the popularity it enjoys without reference to contexts that periodically help to reformulate its horizons. Economic forces are an important part of this process, and politics (which cannot of course be entirely separated from economic considerations) is also instrumental in shaping people's awareness of sport, mobilising its potential and making it successful.

Although sport ought to be capable of shaking off any lasting domination by political or religious ideologies, it is not impervious to various types of manipulation or to being used as a tool, and from time to time the sporting world thus finds itself split into highly sensitive zones of influence. As a showcase for propaganda, a political mirror to various forms of domination, an arena in which group identities are negated, preserved, exchanged or asserted, a means of retaliation, a tool of affirmation and a window on national consciousness as well as chauvinism, sport certainly offers unparalleled opportunities for activities involving different types of violence and counter-violence that are, in essence, political.

How sport is used as a political tool, and the political functions of violence in sport

Sport as a stage for political violence and counter-violence

Because sport can be used as a tool – a means of amplifying political passions and a backdrop for displays of political ideology – there is inevitably a problem of violence associated with this process. Sport's external and domestic political functions, the former helping to shape relationships between nations, and the latter reinforcing the structures and power bases of particular regimes, have been instrumental in generating different types of political violence (Brohm, 1992).

Efforts by the Greek Government to reinstate the Olympic Games in 1859 and again in 1870 (among the first such attempts in Europe) were, for example, a reflection of political considerations, notably the desire to mount a display of ideological propaganda reinforcing the Greek sense of identity with a sporting celebration to mark the end of Turkish occupation (Arnaud, 1993). A century and a half later, when the United States and Coca-Cola captured the privilege of organising the Games' centenary (1896-1996) – depriving Greece, whose bid had been supported by the Council of Europe (Druon, 1999), of a historically European sporting celebration – it was not just an indicator of the event's enormous economic implications and their practical consequences for sport, but also the result of a political decision. The effect of that decision was to confirm the hegemony of an America certain of its own prerogatives and rarely needing to rethink them but finding it, nonetheless, expedient to counter the aspirations of the emerging European counter-power.

In the battle for the prize of staging the Olympic Games, or any major sporting event, political affiliations have been and remain fundamentally significant. The political convulsions that took place in Europe in the inter-war period, in which sport and great sporting occasions were used as tools by various factions, offer a clear example of this.

In fascist Italy and in Franco's Spain the victories of national teams were seized on for propaganda purposes by the totalitarian regimes (Bromberger, 1996, p. 37).

Hitler's Germany drew kudos from the sheer scale and impact of the Berlin Olympics (in 1936), using them as a propaganda tool for Nazi ideology (Augustin,1999). Popular opposition to this political disfigurement of the Olympic ideal hardened into resistance in the form of plans to stage counter-Olympics in Barcelona, although the outbreak of the Spanish Civil War prevented their taking place (Arnaud, 1999).

The USSR, equally violently, sought to impose a state policy on sport, the aim of which was to promote the political regime and its totalitarian ideology. It wanted to cement its empire and to eradicate any demands for secession on the part of the Soviet republics by forcing them into the socialist sporting mould (Brohm, 1992).

In the 1950s, for example, Emil Zatopek, the "Czech locomotive", came to embody the "new socialist man". Breaking every world record from the 5 000 metres to the marathon, he flew the flag high for a dominating, unscrupulous regime. Not only that, but when British student athletes like Roger Bannister began to emerge in the west, the Czech became the champion of a political system, investing socialist muscle with a soul. It was thanks to this remarkable athlete from a satellite country that the USSR was able to make a successful entrance on to the Olympic scene in 1952.

Ultimately, however, the glittering story of the human locomotive was cut short by political violence when, some fifteen years later, Zatopek was publicly humiliated, renounced, deposed and stripped of his official functions in response to his fervent support for the Prague Spring (Rosé, 1997).

There have also been bloodier manifestations of politics as an external force expressing itself in sport, as international competitions have been held hostage to outside interests. Tragedy struck the Munich Olympic Games in 1972 in the form of terrorism, transferring a murderous conflict from the political arena to the world of sport: nine Israeli athletes were killed by an eight-strong Palestinian hit squad.

Violence found expression in another form a few years later when, after a series of boycotts,[28] the Olympic Games were again marked politically by events that had an international impact: several nations,[29] including the United States, refused to take part in the Moscow Olympics (in 1980) and in retaliation the USSR stayed away from the Los Angeles Olympics (in 1984).

From this almost caricatural depiction of political, and particularly cold war, enmities being perpetuated in sport and amplified by the huge charge of symbolism that sport carries, we can see at the very least how surely politics seeps into sport, and in turn draws from the symbolic rivalry of the sports field the means to renew itself, producing at the same time new forms of violence.

Observing how popular sport is in Europe today and how it has come to be dominated by economic constraints over the last twenty-five years, it is easy to overlook the fact that as an aspect of human culture it constitutes more than simply regulated physical competition subject to the laws of the marketplace. In effect it is a sounding board for the various types of violence associated with political, nationalist, cultural, ethnic and racial tensions: they permeate it and find a way to express themselves through it, sometimes with horrendous consequences.

It is particularly revealing to look at how various forms of nationalism express themselves in sport. As the multinational empires of eastern Europe imploded into separate states after the fall of the Berlin Wall, the immediate effect was to increase the number of national teams competing in Europe. The emerging European nations were quick to seize on sport as a way of affirming their new political status. Soviet, Yugoslavian and Czechoslovakian teams had ceased to exist and, for better or worse, were replaced by respectively fifteen, five and two separate national squads – for worse inasmuch as sport (and not just football), highly charged as it is with symbols and identities, was soon to become a backdrop for violent clashes, the water polo rivalry in the former Yugoslavia providing just one example.

The issues in the former Yugoslavia are complex because they concern the affirmation of cultural and political identities and are influenced by the resentment that recent and well-remembered wars and massacres have injected into this geopolitical region – with the possibility of integration into the European Union as an additional background factor. The intense rivalry apparent at sports events and the highly sensitive nature of some of them

---

28. Most African countries, for example, boycotted the 1976 Games in Montreal in protest at the decision not to bar New Zealand for having hosted a visit by the South African Springboks a short time after the Soweto massacre.
29. The United States, Canada, Japan, the Federal Republic of Germany and China.

indicate how human investment in sport retains a very real political dimension alongside its economic aspects.

It was in this context that in 2003, at a Serbia and Montenegro v. Croatia water polo match in Kranj, Slovenia, not only fans but also politicians and journalists behaved in a manner that was disturbing, to say the least. On the one hand, the language and body language of the Croat fans was unusually violent as they shouted racial insults and death threats. On the other hand, Serbian Foreign Affairs Minister Goran Svilanovic, far from trying to calm things down, had the bright idea of jumping into the water to celebrate his team's victory, thus compounding the general confusion (Grubisa, 2003). More seriously, in the wake of the incident the Croatian Minister of Foreign Affairs cancelled a visit to Montenegro. It was a political decision taken after a "counter-attack" from Belgrade and vandalism against the Croatian embassy there in protest at the behaviour of the Croat fans. Meanwhile, a Croatian journalist who had condemned the actions of his own team's supporters over the air, and had subsequently been attacked in the commentary box by fans who could not take the criticism, was asked by his bosses to keep the matter quiet. As Damir Grubisa notes, this general attitude tarnished the image of a country queuing up to join the European Union. The Croatian journalist also pointed out that a large share of blame for the fans' behaviour lay with politicians who were unable or unwilling to curb the inequalities and violence rife in civil society in Croatia. Serbian commentators were no less critical of the political authorities in both countries. The Serbian newspaper *Politika* editorialised as follows:

> "One is entitled to wonder whether a sporting encounter between our two countries can actually take place under normal conditions ... After the vandalism of the Croatian fans in Slovenia and the Serbian riposte, questions have to be asked about a generation of young people who grew up under the regimes of Franjo Trudjman and Slobodan Milosevic" (Grubisa, 2003).

This case clearly illustrates that, just as political violence spills over into sport, sporting violence contaminates the political climate in a situation where those concerned attach ever increasing importance to sport, and the fact of winning or losing takes on a hugely symbolic charge, severely aggravated by the bitter legacy of past conflicts.

While such violence is a product of political identities brutalised by a chaotic geopolitical context, the convulsions of war and oppression in many forms, history shows too that sport can help give expression (including violent expression) to truth by juxtaposing two aspects of what is a single phenomenon: submission to a dominant regime and the expression of resistance to authority.

One example of this is the history of the magnificent Hungarian soccer team of the 1950s – the team of Puskas, Czibor, Hidegkuti and Boscik – which gradually came to symbolise a people who refused to toe the line and contested Soviet political domination. Having been regarded for many years by the regime as a political propaganda tool, this team, which won the admiration of the entire world for the quality of its game, showed how it could rise above the vicissitudes of political history, from the bloody Rakosi years to the Budapest insurrection, incarnating a Hungarian identity that refused to limit itself to that of a people's democracy. Another example is the creation of the famous FLN football team at the time of Algerian independence. By permitting the expression of nationalism through sport, football suddenly became a tool of political counter-violence in opposition to colonisation, war and all its attendant suffering, and an affirmation of national identity that was as much political as it was athletic. It was giving voice to the aspirations of a former French colony for freedom and independence.

It has to be said that French-Algerian relations as expressed in and through sport regularly take on an ambiguous quality, probably because – if one reads between the lines of the game – each competitive event dramatises and highlights a political struggle, with the protagonists symbolically re-enacting the war of independence. The painful history of these two countries has almost certainly left resonances which, warped by the impact of current social problems and the sufferings they generate, by the realities of immigration and integration, periodically find expression in sport, often to mixed effect.

It was the Algerian national game of football which – for the space of a match at least, a "friendly" against France on 6 October 2001 – became a vehicle of unrest when a section of the crowd booed the French national anthem in a gesture perceived by some as the expression of social and political problems, and by others as disrespect and a form of violence. The incident effectively marked the end of a dream of political and social integration through sport, a dream that had quietly crept into being with the victory of the French *"black-blanc-beur"* [black, white and North African] team in the 1998 World Cup.

This sad incident had a sequel a few months later at the French cup final between Lorient and Bastia, when a large section of the Bastia supporters booed during the playing of the *Marseillaise* (*Sud-Ouest,* 12 May 2002). The political struggle between the state and one of its regions – represented on that occasion by the Corsican supporters in the stadium – thus spilled over into sport, and senior soccer officials felt themselves obliged to make amends for this overt use of a football match for political ends.

On the other hand, those who practise sport have, on occasions, used it as a platform for expressing views on national political issues, as for example when French athletes mobilised against Jean-Marie Le Pen in April 2002 (*Le Monde*, 3 May 2002, p. 28). Likewise, sport has helped to promote the message of tolerance, as when Lilian Thuram spoke out in Italy against racism at soccer matches. It can serve, too, to prick the conscience of former European colonial powers and bring home certain political truths, as it did when New-Caledonian-born footballer Christian Karembeu refused to sing the *Marseillaise* as a mark of respect for his grandfather, one of the "natives" displayed at the French Colonial Exhibition of 1931 (Bancel and Blanchard, 2003).

Sport as a means of retaliation or sanction

In the course of the twentieth century sport was often used as a means of political retaliation or reprisal, not always in the best advised or most balanced way, and with varying degrees of sincerity.

During the conflict with the Federal Republic of Yugoslavia, for example, the EU foreign affairs ministers called on European sports federations to exclude Yugoslavian athletes and teams from their competitions as a form of sanction. The gesture had powerful symbolic value because the Federal Republic of Yugoslavia was at the forefront in a number of sports, including basketball and football. The sports federations concerned, as well as some national Olympic committees, signalled a reluctance to follow the Council of the European Union's recommendation. This show of independence on the part of the sports bodies was subsequently criticised by the sports directors of the EU member states (meeting in October 1999).

Similarly, the former South African National Sports Council decided in May 1998 to act on the threat of isolating South African rugby because of the deliberate failure by Louis Luyt, President of the national Rugby Football Union, to observe the principle of avoiding racial discrimination, which had been applicable since the end of apartheid. Europe was asked to lend its support when the National Sports Council requested that Ireland and Wales cancel planned tours by their teams in South Africa (*Le Monde*, 9-10 May 1998).

When used in the interests of tolerance and by international consensus, the threat of exclusion may be justifiable and, in turn, may justify recourse to pressure through sport. Yet there is often no international consensus and this can lead to sporting activities and contacts being interpreted in a way that runs counter to sport's basic principles. This has happened where nations have themselves acted in such a way as to demolish the politically utopian dream of apolitical sport (Thibault, 1991). By using sport unilaterally as a political tool and a means of blackmail for purely national purposes, these countries have done much to turn it into something it was never intended to be. As long ago as 1980 the Council of Europe felt it necessary to condemn this type of national posturing, at odds with the fundamental principles of sporting competition. The member states passed a resolution:

> "Noting with regret that the Olympic Games are moving further and further away from the ancient ideal which it was sought to revive at the close of the last century [and] deploring the fact that they have become a political and commercial competition between major states and large cities [and] that, instead of contributing towards peace, the Games are a source of discord in international relations ..." (Resolution 738 (1980) of the Parliamentary Assembly of the Council of Europe, on the Olympic Games and the outlook for their future).

The resolution did not refer explicitly to any particular national position and the boycott of the Moscow Olympics was merely hinted at, yet the text clearly staked out boundaries for an apolitical approach to sport in the modern world. It served to highlight a gradual accumulation of abuses that had slowly turned the Olympics into a political platform.

The question of sport's independence from politics arose at a very early stage. In the immediate aftermath of the Great War, the Inter-Allied Games of July 1919 were organised in a way that made them the first example in modern history of sport used for the purposes of political reprisal. The Games offered the United States a unique opportunity to make propaganda in France and – approaching the situation in black and white terms, an attitude that has become more familiar in very recent times – to present a contrast between the pacifism and civilisation of the victors and the barbarism of the vanquished (Arnaud, 1999). History records how the Allies sustained this form of pressure by keeping the defeated nations beyond the pale in international sport for a large part of the inter-war period. Examples include their exclusion from the Antwerp Olympics of 1920 and from almost 100 international competitions (in football, rugby and athletics) that involved the three Allies, France, the United Kingdom and Belgium between 1920 and 1924.

During this period the Olympic committee, and indeed sports bodies generally, were completely submissive to political authority. In France, national sports policy was made by the Ministry of Foreign Affairs in co-operation with Gaston Vidal of the Service des Sports [Sports Office], which was set up in 1920. This was logical inasmuch as athletes were gradually becoming ambassadors for their countries in a political sense. With more than half a century of hindsight, we in Europe need to ask ourselves whether the exclusion of former enemies, which lasted for twelve years after the Armistice, was not in fact a form of political violence. It was not until 1931 that Germany and France – both footballing nations – were to play each other again. Similar isolation measures were applied to the sports teams of the Axis powers after the Second World War, re-emphasising how sport could be a political tool of reprisal.

"In 1948 Germany and Italy did not take part in the London [Olympic] Games and they did not compete in the Football World Cup in 1950. Permitted to compete in the 1954 World Cup in Berne, however, Germany made it to the final and won" (Thomas, 1999, p. 12-13).

The use of sport as a tool of politics did not stop with the Allies' exclusion of Germany and the nations that supported it in the two world wars. Areas of incompatibility also emerged between western Europe and the Bolshevik Revolution and the differences were quickly transferred into the world of sport. The French Government, for example, banned the Internationale Sportive Rouge [Red Sports International] from holding workers' sports competitions in Paris in June 1924, refusing to issue visas to the invited athletes.

The other side of the coin was the Soviet refusal to send teams to the "bourgeois" Olympics, a stance maintained until 1952.

Thirty years later the United States and USSR monopolised both sport and politics, dwarfing the rest of the world to an extent that destabilised the Olympic Games and undermined the very meaning of the Olympic ideal.

This was a form of political violence that the United States seemed, at the time of writing, prepared to repeat, at least according to former Olympic swimming champion Mark Spitz. He spread the impression that the very real political threat posed to the Athens Olympic Games by international terrorism might well cause the nation which had promoted the 1919 Inter-Allied Games to keep its athletes at home in 2004. Were it to do so, the gesture would signal the forceful return of politics to the Olympic arena – the only alternative interpretation being that other (doping-related) problems were prompting the Americans to make a prudent withdrawal, and again this would clearly be laden with political overtones.

Sport as a seedbed for violence in politics

Sport is also capable of nurturing political fundamentalism and, through its own processes, can generate a type of violence consubstantial with competition, which has the potential to cross over into politics. Apart from the Croat and Serb violence at the water polo final described in an earlier chapter – demonstrating how sport, as well as being an alternative means of prolonging war, to paraphrase Clausewitz, can, on occasions, actually turn into war – there are other examples of more discreet but no less significant types of behaviour that have left their mark on the sporting world.

Straightforward refusal is one: refusing to compete with someone of a different religion or with an athlete because of a political, cultural, religious or other controversy. There is, however, a wider problem, in connection with gender in sport. It is true that the question of whether or not women participate in cultural activities – which is both a political issue and an aspect of exclusion – is confined neither to sport nor to the modern era. The Olympic ethos as reinvented by Baron Pierre de Coubertin, for example, drew strongly on ancient times for its discriminatory attitude, borne out by his pithily conservative and discriminatory declaration that there could be "no female Olympiads". In the context of present-day sport, however, the perpetuation of segregation constitutes a form of violence at two levels: it contravenes the basic principles of sport as a cohesive, fair and dignified activity, and it admits the existence around sport of a grey area in which there remains some doubt about the applicability of national and international civil law. The ambivalence inherent in sport's theoretical separation from politics, and in the equally utopian idea that it can be independent from political considerations, is also to blame in this regard.

At the Barcelona Olympic Games in 1992, thirty-five countries had no women athletes in their teams and one of those teams refused to walk behind a Spanish woman athlete at the opening ceremony (Council of Europe, Vol. 1, p. 194).

Nonetheless, the Parliamentary Assembly of the Council of Europe has taken a very clear stance in support of its humanistic vision of sport:

> "Wherever fundamental human rights are infringed, the Assembly considers it has a duty to intervene in the internal affairs of any state, irrespective of whether it is a member of the Council of Europe. Even if there are cultural differences and traditions, this should be no argument for accepting any policy of discrimination against women in sport" (Resolution 1092 (1996), Council of Europe, Vol. 1, p. 194).

Looked at from another angle – in connection with the political violence practised by governments – sport has regularly produced its own share of disparities, where the sporting elitism inherent in competition has contributed to state-sponsored inegalitarianism. This linkage between politics and selection in sport was developed particularly in the countries of central and eastern Europe.

The first country to be affected was the German Democratic Republic (GDR). Sports champions there had traditionally emerged from the masses but a policy gradually developed of identifying them at an increasingly early age, picking them out and placing them in special training facilities quite separate from the traditional sports clubs circuit. Building on its own logic of excellence, sport thus came to create within itself a permanent divide that was sustained, managed and fostered by the political authorities: on the one side was an elite, the showcase of the nation; on the other, the ordinary mass of sportspeople. Inevitably this exaggerated push to promote the top level led to a decline in overall participation in sport.

> "The raising of records in those sports, such as athletics and swimming, where results are measured in time and distance, led to a fall-off in the practice of sport as a mass activity" (Thomas, 1999, p. 14).

In the case of the Soviet Union, this policy of elitism based on a political reading of the competitive impulse in sport actually had a perverse effect by inflicting a dire lack of sports resources on the rest of the nation.

> "Outside official pronouncements of the basic Soviet doctrine, mass sport was sacrificed, particularly from the 1950s onwards, in order to promote an elite" (Bourg and Gouguet, 2001, p. 85).

In 1992, 60% of the pupils at Russian primary schools still played no form of sport – a fair reflection of the virtual abandonment in which the population was living: 75% of Russian schools at the time had no gymnasium, 80% had no playing fields, and there was one swimming pool for every 125 000 head of population (Bourg and Gouguet, op. cit.).

Sport and reasons of state

Physical and ideological conditioning

Among the types of violence that give political regimes power over the bodies of athletes, the forcible physical conditioning of athletes for reasons of state stands out as a factor in the sporting success of many European countries. In seeking to understand this phenomenon we need to identify and consider the different levels at which this form of violence operates, as well as the extent of the constraints it imposes and the damage it does.

Three examples, at three different levels, will help to give us a working picture of how these types of political violence operate.

At the first level, violence is inflicted through actual physical and psychological conditioning, making the athlete subservient to the regime he or she is destined to represent. Before the collapse of communism, eastern and to some extent central European countries, which epitomised central planning, were those that practised such systems most intensively.

According to researchers who have sifted through the available archive material (including the mass of East German archives), this athletic and political conditioning was based on a combination of procedures: methods for selecting athletes at an early age; widespread doping under medical supervision; and close political and administrative monitoring.

While it may not be credible, as Hurtebise has suggested, to continue demonising east European sports training systems such as that of the German Democratic Republic, at a time when abuses are gradually being uncovered throughout the world of sport (the Festina case in the 1998 Tour de France springs to mind here), it is nonetheless true that those in charge of East Germany's state "doping policy" were "unique in having made such substances [chiefly anabolic steroids] available in a systematically organised and officially monitored manner" (Hurtebise, 1999, p. 39).

The author goes on to point out that those responsible also opened the way to unauthorised excesses on the part of irresponsible coaches and doctors (ibid.). We can clearly conclude, at the very least, that the strictest controls were not applied with equal zeal in every area or every sport.

In certain disciplines (including weight lifting and body building), those in charge have acknowledged that they lost control as the system developed a momentum of its own and the uncontrolled use of doping products became possible through unofficial channels. Official East German sports bodies such as the German Gymnastics and Sports Confederation (Deutscher Turn- und Sportbund or DTSB), under the presidency of Manfred Ewald, are reported to have tried unsuccessfully to stem such developments. They had all the more reason to do so after the relevant substances were proved to be harmful to young people, especially girls. Probably the most serious aspect of the whole affair was the fact that, under the official system, athletes were not told the nature of the substances they were given (Hurtebise, op. cit., p. 40).

At the second level we shall consider here, the conditioning of athletes by means including doping is revealed as neither an East German speciality nor a thing of the past. Once again there is apparent state implication although, in terms of political affiliation, state centralisation and the concept of the "state athlete", there is no direct comparison with the East German experience. Nonetheless, the key issue is the same: state control over dubious means of preparing athletes for competition.

The example concerns a case in Italy where an inquiry led to charges being preferred against a university researcher in December 2002. The Ferrara centre, where the scientist worked, had the task of combating doping and had received financial support from the Italian Olympic Committee (CONI) ever since it had opened in the 1980s. Eventually, however, it proved to be at the centre of a system of organised doping (Sobry, 2003).

CONI admitted that the funding had been used not only to conduct blood tests but also to carry out research on erythropoietin (EPO) – research that provided a cover for the drug to be used in preparing athletes for competition.

Ultimately the affair amounted to a form of state-sponsored doping, and the violence exercised by the state against the athletes concerned was no less serious than that practised by the East German doctors.

A third level of conditioning is at work when states place their mark on the bodies of a sporting elite through a policy, in certain sports, of special training under the auspices of a sports institution.

In the case of gymnastics in France the link to the world of politics functions through the official recognition of excellence coupled with the right to represent the country: "French athletes receive their identity, status and social position from their federation by virtue of authority delegated from the state" (Papin, 2001, p. 89).

The first point to be made here is that, far from gymnastics being a conscious and fully-controlled vocation, accession to the highest level is much more the product of the individual's response to a highly ordered system of selection, over which the state retains control. The process of inculcating a will to excel in the sport – something commonly assumed to stem from the individual and his or her capacity to stick to an apparently freely chosen plan – is also well structured and reflects, as a rule, preparatory work done by the staff of the gymnastics federation at all the levels of its own system (Papin, op. cit., p. 91).

The second point is that, within the system, the approach to the body is determined by and geared to performance; it involves athletes learning to live with pain, continual effort and injury, so that they can carry on training. This policy is accepted by athletes generally, including those – like the Russian athlete Dimitri Karbanenko, a French national since 1996 – who had to adapt to the rigours of the French system at a relatively late stage. Karbanenko was quoted in a national newspaper as boasting that the strength of a gymnast lay in the ability to perform faultlessly even when injured (*Le Monde*, 28 April 1998).

The accepted notion that athletes have to suffer, coupled with the idea that injuries are a normal condition, and the forms of asceticism that the federation imposes on gymnasts, have gradually come to dominate the approach to performance (which is the sporting expression of the system's power). In a much clearer way than those who are part of the system will normally admit, this conditioning represents a form of political violence inflicted on the bodies of the athletes by the sports personnel whose task it is to produce a gymnastic elite destined to represent the state and obtain impressive results in international competition.

The state, and forms of political violence in sport

Among the different types of state violence that have exploited people's relationships to their bodies and sport, there are some that have left a particular mark on European history. Prime examples are the way in which young people were dragooned into sport under the banners of fascism in Italy, Nazism in Germany, and Pétainism in France (Augustin, 1999; Arnaud, 1999; and Robène, 2002).

In a separate process, the war itself – while extending the brutality and ideological ignominy of Nazi authority – also spawned symbolic forms of violence similar to those generated in politics. The occupying forces' confiscation of sports fields, as in Bordeaux between 1940 and 1944 (Robène, ongoing research, Bordeaux municipal archives, Series 1828 R2, 1828 R3, 1828 R4), illustrated how the German powers at local level sought to do more than simply impose their control. They deprived the Bordelais of the pleasures of sport in order to favour their own troops. Access to the football stadium and swimming pools was gradually restricted to a small number of soldiers while the local people were excluded, and ground newly designated for recreational use was also ruled out of the equation as it was taken over for billeting the troops (Robène, 2002).

Fifty years later we find an example of a group initially mobilised around sport going on to become a reliable recruitment ground for those choosing to exploit it politically in acts of barbarism.

During the conflict in the former Yugoslavia, the Serb warlord known as Arkan (real name Zeljko Raznatovic) transformed a group of diehard fans of the soccer club Obilic Belgrade (of which he was a fervent supporter) into a commando unit. These hooligans joined the Serb volunteer forces as the "Tigers", with Arkan as their self-styled commandant.

The Tigers operated under cover of the Serbian army to wipe out entire villages using grenades and Kalashnikov rifle fire. The supporters' chants were turned into hate-filled war cries as their violence spilled beyond the football ground and found expression in the vilest acts of "ethnic cleansing" (Coadic, 1995; and Colovic, 1998).

The violence inherent in sport and in the antagonisms associated with cultural identity had apparently found a barbaric echo in ideology, which in turn had channelled it into political violence. This sick relationship goes to the heart of the matter. For beyond the trail of suffering generated by these violent acts in the context of war, an issue arises with regard to sport's impact and responsibility – as an organised force shaping alliances and enmities – in the emergence of such behaviour. Actions that are utterly opprobrious would probably not have taken place with such ease had the protagonists not already felt themselves united in one and the same cause and part of the same structured Serb hooliganism.

We thus have to ask whether sport is merely an object of politics and always likely to be marked by political excesses, or whether in some cases its own nature and structures can cause it to generate violent behaviour which then becomes part of, and indeed goes beyond, political violence, so that war becomes an extension of sport by other means.

Whatever the answer, the link between politics and sport is a complex and not always obvious one. At the same time, real or perceived violence (however much deplored) continues to be generated when sport is compromised by politics.

To take a less tragic example, it is interesting to analyse the violence regularly perceived by Spanish football lovers at matches involving Real Madrid. An incident arising from a disputed decision by the referee at a match between FC Valencia and Real Madrid on 15 February 2004 highlighted how politics can find its way into sport in the form of violence experienced or perceived by the spectators. The award of a penalty – interpreted as a political decision – was enough to plunge the entire nation into seemingly endless debate. "It was a political penalty!" declared Valencia defender Amedeo Carboni, convinced that his club had been the victim of an injustice rooted in collusion between the Madrid-based side and the government (*Le Monde*, 21 February 2004). The incident underscored how Real Madrid is identified with authority and the arbitrary hand of politics. Rightly or wrongly, Real (the name means "royal" in Spanish) has become, in the collective imagination of Spanish football lovers, the team of the regime or the government. It is regularly accused of receiving special treatment from both referees and politicians – effectively of "winning to order" (*Le Monde*, op. cit.).

Naturally, the allegations can be explained in part in terms simply of rivalry between teams from the capital city and those from the provinces – something familiar in virtually every country in Europe. In France, the opposition that has grown up between OM and PSG is rooted in similar folklore: the image of football in Marseilles is one of a popular sport followed with unbridled enthusiasm, while the relatively formal VIP stands in Paris often function as a showcase for those in power. Observers of the Spanish football scene monitor the preferences of their politicians, one journalist noting with surprise, for example, that former Prime Minister José Maria Aznar only attended Real Madrid home games (*Le Monde*, op. cit.). The attachment of current Prime Minister José Luis Rodriguez Zapatero to FC Barcelona runs counter to the established trend (*Le Monde*, 27 April 2004).

At another level, however, it is clear from the political history of the Madrid club that the criticisms directed at it for any form of compromise have their roots in the 1950s and in certain actual events. There were the club's links to the Franco regime, for example, and the arbitrary decision by General José Moscardo, as President of the Spanish National Sports Council, to assign Argentinian player Di Stéfano exclusively to Real Madrid following a transfer dispute between the Madrid club and FC Barcelona: the player was to have returned to Barcelona but never did so.

More recently, in 2001, Real Madrid managed to wipe out €80 million in debt by obtaining planning permission for club-owned land in the city, thanks to its good relationship with the City Hall and the regional council – both controlled by the ruling Popular Party. Real club President Florentino Perez pulled off a highly lucrative real-estate deal, with the official justification that the city needed land in connection with its bid to host the Olympics. At the time of writing the Olympic construction programme has been considerably scaled down.

There can be no doubt that this set of circumstances contributed to the emergence of a very particular form of political violence, based on the general impression that the Madrid club is officially favoured and enjoys special attention and privileges.

It should be re-emphasised here that it is not uncommon in a dominant sport for a capital-city-based club to serve as a showcase for those in power, but it is nonetheless true that in certain situations in Europe sport has been turned into a political tool in a way that amounts to manipulation and is perceived as a form of violence.

In Romania, for example, under the Ceaucescu regime, the team supported by the president's eldest son was regularly assisted by referees who were acting under orders, and its opponents were sometimes "prepared" for matches by the infamous Securitate (Bureau, 2002).

Violence in sport from an economic perspective

Sport underwent a radical transformation in the last quarter of the twentieth century as a world sport market emerged, characterised in Europe by an upsurge in demand for – and the supply of – major events. High-level sport became part of a trade system dominated by the media and event promoters and, in turn, attracted sponsors as the corporate world invested in a sector promising high returns (Andreff, 1988b; Andreff and Nys, 2001; Bourg and Gouguet 2001; and Sobry, 2003).

As growing volumes of capital were pumped into sport from increasingly international sources, Europe also experienced application of the free-market principles of freedom of movement for persons, goods and services. All this had the effect of undermining the traditional pyramid-shaped European model of sport, already under pressure from the secessionist ambitions of the wealthiest clubs and from plans for closed leagues along American lines. There is no doubt that one effect of the overall process was to increase and shed light on the flows of capital in sport. These had hitherto been carefully contained, in pursuance of cultural principles rooted in once-dominant conceptions of sport that originated in Britain and with Baron Pierre de Coubertin and centred on social elitism, amateur status and voluntary effort.

Two factors combined at an early stage to spur the changes (Miège, 2000). On the one hand, the decision taken by the IOC in the early 1980s to open the Olympics to professionals triggered commercialisation of the Olympic movement on a vast scale, ushering in an era of entrepreneurship in sport and enabling clubs and athletes to assess their prospects in straightforward commercial terms. At the same time, European television channels – recently freed from public-service constraints, their numbers swelled by newly formed companies joining the market, and riding high on the tide of new information technologies – threw themselves en masse into the business of sports coverage. In the race to boost ratings and win market share, they helped to create the conditions for what was in effect a speculative bubble (Economic and Social Council, 2002, pp. 1-3). Apart from these two engines of change, a further factor affecting sport was the social and economic transformation wrought by the phenomenon of increased leisure time in post-industrial societies. It was the fact of having more free time that made Europeans available for sport, and it was because television understood the new demand that sport became an integral part of the mass entertainment business, attracting very substantial investment.

Generally speaking, the massive influx of capital into European sport in recent years visibly reflects both the dynamism of a rapidly expanding sector and its excesses. The new order has imposed a commercial rationale, around which sport has had to reconfigure itself (Bourg, 1999, p. 52).

Sport today, as both activity and spectacle, needs to be financed and managed. As a productive activity it generates markets estimated to represent on average 1% of GDP in all the developed countries (Nys, 2003), with a concentration of capital in professional and high-level sport and high-profile events (Andreff and Nys, 2001). More generally, around 3% of world trade is sport-related (European Commission, DGX, 1998).

Sport's conversion to the market economy does, however, pose problems, particularly as it has led to certain abuses that cannot be reconciled with the sporting ethic or the set of values on which, by common consent, sport is based: equality of opportunity, respect for the rules and one's adversary, fair play, self-control, integrity etc. Problems are also posed by the shift away from a type of social and political economy in which ownership of sport, as an aspect of culture and heritage, a practice and a spectacle, rested with the people, who supported and nurtured it. Addressing this problem means, at the very least, taking account not only of the worrying divide between elite and mass sport but also of the attack on freedom implied by television companies' monopolistic control of sports coverage. Further problems arise from the fact that this commercial vision of sport is largely at odds with the cultural, social, educational, health and civic concerns which inform the approach of bodies like the Council of Europe, which are attempting to consolidate a European model of sport based less on increasing profits and profitability than on building genuine co-operation between peoples and exploring sport's potential in terms of humanism, fairness, sound ethics, tolerance and solidarity (European Commission, DGX, op. cit.).

There is no doubt that investment and financial support have been instrumental in the growth of sport. In the Europe that is taking shape today, injections of public and private money are essential in order to channel the growing enthusiasm for sport and to improve sports provision substantially: catering for as many people as possible, developing sports infrastructure and enabling growing numbers of Europeans to participate – voluntarily involving themselves in a cultural phenomenon with a momentum of its own and the capacity to create a shared culture. At the same time, while "the growth and variety of sources of funding for sport are helpful to its development" (Council of Europe, 14th informal meeting of European Ministers responsible for Sport, CDDS (98) 90 Vol. I, p. 177), we also have to see sport's recent subjection to the logic and laws of the market economy in the light of the collateral damage it can cause: disparities and inequalities, exclusion, corruption, law-breaking and mafia-type activity, exploitation and the treatment of human beings as commodities.

In the words of journalist Jennie James, writing in *Time* magazine about the economic transformation of European sport: "Money may not be the root of all evil, but its ability to taint is becoming acutely apparent" (James, 2000, p. 51). Money exercises authority in sport today at two levels: as the engine of the sports system, which it helps to develop in an uneven way, and as the corruptor of values traditionally equated in Europe with sport's basic principles.

With all this in mind – and before any consideration of the prospects for improving or consolidating the way in which sport is organised in Europe – the following chapter sets out to survey certain major fault lines apparently caused by a narrowly financial and free-market conception of what sport is. At the same time we will consider the relevance of projects being overseen by the Council of Europe in an attempt to curb the spread of economic violence in sport and promote a vision firmly focused on the development of a sports ethos that is humanistic.

Money and sport in Europe: strengths and fault lines

Economic portrait of sporting Europe shows considerable disparities

The first observation has to be that there are glaring disparities throughout Europe with regard to economic resources for sport. While the issue is a highly complex one and funding sources are still relatively patchy (Andreff et al., 1995; Le Roux and Camy, 1995; Miège, 1996, and 2000; and European Commission, DGX, 1999), the fact is that the disparities and imbalances in sports budgets (whether based on public or private money), the different ways in which capital is channelled into sport, and the practical barriers (recession, wars etc.) that still divide the main sporting nations of Europe from the "satellite states" all amount to discrimination. There is discrimination firstly in the provision of services, which is a precondition for access by Europeans, without distinction, to all the types of sporting activity available in Europe. Secondly, discrimination affects the competitive balance between athletes at international level (in terms of resources, preparation for major competitions, training and equipment). This is particularly so within the federation system, which is crucial to the European pyramid model of sport, intended to ensure solidarity and fairness.

Given the current state of research, it is hard to paint a comprehensive picture of the imbalances that exist in Europe in terms of sport's economic impact and the sources of finance for it. Nonetheless it is worth suggesting certain avenues of study which offer an insight into the most glaring disparities.

In general terms, it is estimated that in the year 2000 the national sports federations of the European Union's fifteen countries included some 700000 clubs and associations, with a total of around 100 million members (Miège, 2000; and *Organization of sport in Europe,* Society of European Sport Studies, 2004). From a broader perspective, embracing both organised and non-organised sport, the European Commission estimated in 1996 that 125 million people practised sport (European Commission, DGX, 1996).[30]

Studies designed to assess the economic impact of sport in Europe and to identify its sources of funding (Andreff et al., 1995; Miège, 1996 and 2000; and European Commission, DGX, 1999) have highlighted areas of convergence. For example, generally speaking, finance for sport from private sources – chiefly household spending and, to a lesser extent, corporate sponsorship – outweighs public funding from governments and local and regional authorities. The public/private variable is a significant one because it is reasonable to assume that countries with a strong growth rate and a high standard of living will consume more sports products, thus boosting national sources of finance for sport.

Studies have also highlighted certain differences that arise from the existence of two distinct models for state involvement in the management of sports-related matters – what might be termed a "liberal" model in northern Europe and a more interventionist model in southern Europe (Miège, 1996).

Generally speaking, throughout Europe, household spending (on sports goods, club membership fees etc.) tops the list of sources of finance for sport; local and regional authorities are the second most important source of funds, with the state in third place (Andreff et al., 1995). In the case of both public and private financing, however, there are considerable differences in the proportion of overall budgets devoted to sport.

In relation to private financing – the biggest source of funds for sport in Europe – the disparities are very clear, with figures ranging from 0.32% of GDP in Hungary and 0.34% in Denmark to 1.45% in Spain and 3.27% in Switzerland.

The differences are less marked in the realm of public financing, where the figures range from 0.18% of GDP spent on sport in Switzerland to 0.42% in France and 0.61% in Portugal (Miège, 1996 and 2000).

---

30. The reliability of the figure is subject to the recurring difficulty of defining what constitutes sport.

A closer look at the statistics on public financing (Le Roux and Camy, 1995) allows us to take account of the degree of decentralisation in different countries as a determining factor in the provision of public funding and economic resources for sport. From this perspective the countries fall into several groups. On the one hand are those where public money represents a high proportion of financing for sport (including Denmark, where the figure is 39%, France, with 38%, Portugal, with 35%, and French-speaking Belgium, with 33%). This group sub-divides into countries where public responsibilities are heavily decentralised (in Denmark, for example, local authorities disburse 84% of total public financing, and in France the corresponding figure is 76%), and those such as French-speaking Belgium and Portugal where there is little decentralisation (and the breakdown of financing between state and local government is more balanced). On the other hand we see a group of countries with a high proportion of private financing (Spain, 86%; United Kingdom, 84%; Italy, 81%; Germany, 73%; and Flemish-speaking Belgium, 70%). Again the group sub-divides into those countries where public spending is strongly decentralised (including the United Kingdom, where local government provides 95% of public resources for sport, Germany, where the figure is 98%, and Spain, with 76.2%) and those with less decentralisation (including Flemish-speaking Belgium and Italy, where the public/private split is more even).

At the other end of the chain, additional information is also available about the way in which sport is practised in Europe. A survey conducted in 2003 (Eurobarometer, 2003) by two directorates general of the European Commission (Education and Culture and Press and Communication) shows great differences in the extent to which Europeans are involved in sport and other forms of physical exercise.

The first significant finding is that only 15% of EU citizens claim to practise a sport or take regular physical exercise. This figure is much lower than the corresponding one in Commission statistics from the 1990s (European Commission, DGX, 1996). By contrast, 88% of Europeans report that they watch television at least three times a week, and 19% are regular users of the Internet.

The first finding is a surprising one. It raises doubts as to whether sport really is a regularly practised mass activity in Europe or, at the very least, questions about how the different states apportion sports budgets between high-level events and development policies designed to make sport universally accessible. Bourg and Gouguet's concept of creating a link between revenue from sports events and spending on the mass practice of sport is an interesting one (Bourg and Gouguet, 2001). In order to work fairly, such a principle would probably have to be introduced at European level, where it could have a balancing effect in terms of rates of participation, although factors other than financing (cultural, social and political considerations, for example) obviously also need to be taken into account in any effort to get more people involved in sport.

Recorded levels of participation currently show great disparities. Although the overall rate is 15%, northern Europeans tend to practise sport and engage in physical exercise to a greater extent than people in the south.

The national figures for the proportion of the population practising sport at least once a week are 70% in Finland and Sweden, 53% in Denmark, 47% in Ireland and 43% in the Netherlands. They are just 19% in Greece, 22% in Portugal, 31% in Italy and 32% in France and Spain.

It is also important to note the high proportion of people in Greece and Portugal who practise no form of sport or physical exercise (70% and 75% respectively).

Another interesting variable is the context in which people practise sport. A majority (47%) say they are involved in sport in settings other than sports clubs. Only 23% of those who practise sport do so in a club context. On the other hand, 20% say they go to a gym. Non-organised sport is most popular in countries such as Finland, Sweden and Austria, where 73%, 67% and 58% respectively say they practise sport in non-club contexts. In Greece and Spain the proportion of people practising sport in gyms is higher. In the Netherlands, clubs are the most popular context (43%) while in Italy the highest figure (30%) is recorded for sports centres.

It is, of course, very difficult to draw detailed conclusions from all these data, and attempting to make any direct correlation between the statistics on methods and levels of funding for sport and those on rates of participation throughout Europe is even more problematic. All we can hope to do is to show the wide range of national situations and to appreciate the extent of the disparities even within the EU. Looking towards central and eastern Europe, at the accession countries, we find that generally less favourable economic conditions, problems with decentralisation, and, especially, tragic circumstances such as wars or their aftermath, produce more obvious types of discrimination.

A Council of Europe report produced after a seminar in Sarajevo in October 2001 – involving twenty-five representatives from Albania, Bosnia and Herzegovina, Bulgaria, Croatia, Romania, Slovenia, "the former Yugoslav Republic of Macedonia" and the Federal Republic of Yugoslavia – highlights for example how the conflict in the former Yugoslavia was followed by a "period of setbacks". The report noted that sport in this part of Europe was "heavily dependent on state funding" because "there [was] no wide membership base; the volunteer movement was in its infancy in most countries [and] the commercial sector [was] still in a stage of early development" (*The Council of Europe and Sport,* 2001, p. 30).

Generally speaking, the east-west divide observed by Andreff and Nys (2001) seems much more alarming than the subtler distinctions between southern and northern Europe. Among the socialist economies in transition, countries including Russia and the former German Democratic Republic – that once had a thriving sports scene based on the official conception of sport as a showcase for the nation and the ruling regime – have seen sources of funding for sport dry up since the fall of communism. Financing sport is no longer a budgetary priority, foreign sponsors hesitate to get involved, and athletes from eastern Europe find they can earn more from their talents in the west. These factors have combined to create a highly problematic situation: in former East Germany, for example, sports club membership is reported to have fallen off by 48% (Andreff and Nys, 2001, p. 120). The former GDR *Länder* have found themselves unable to finance the development of sport. The same applies in the Russian Federation, which has had difficulty finding the necessary resources to implement a new sports law passed in 1993. The tricky transition from a planned and centralised economy to a market economy has seen a sharp decline in sport as a mass activity. Some forty Second and Third Division soccer clubs went bankrupt in 1998 and a total of almost 1 500 athletes and sports professionals emigrated to western Europe or North America (Bourg and Gouguet, 2001). In Hungary, involvement in sport has been halved since 1989, and spending on sport has fallen steadily, dropping in the mid-1990s from 0.28% to 0.13% of the national budget (Andreff, 1996).

This is a generally worrying situation inasmuch as it confirms the emergence in Europe of a slow lane, if not a very slow lane, for sports development. According to a report compiled by the Council of Europe in 1997, the level of public participation in club-based sport in central and eastern Europe is very low: around 0.5% in Lithuania, 1.1% in Ukraine, 1.2% in Bulgaria, 3.6% in Estonia and 4.7% in Latvia. By comparison, the rates of participation in sports clubs and associations in western European countries seem remarkably high: 22% in France, 29% in Germany and 36% in Denmark.

The most obvious conclusion must be that greater Europe – coping with a range of political and economic situations – does not currently offer the conditions for balanced levels of involvement in sport, whether in terms of access to all the generally available sports or in terms of financing, or indeed in terms of national representatives' preparation for major competitions (although in the case of countries like the Russian Federation, whose athletes have very recently become competitive again, the situation in high-level sport is more complex).

The inequalities become even clearer when we consider the following figures: in Ukraine there is one sports club per 34 000 head of population; in Bulgaria the figure is one per 5 700 and in Latvia it is one per 4 900. In the reunified Germany there is one club per 965 inhabitants (Bourg and Gouguet, 2001).

There are two lessons to be drawn from these observations. The first is that, through its focus on profit and profitable investment, the liberal economic model being adopted throughout Europe contributes, albeit indirectly, to the pressures of economic disadvantage and to discrimination when it comes to "sport for all" because it produces or re-instates inequalities among European citizens with regard to sport.

The second lesson is that this type of discrimination constitutes a form of violence more insidious than others inasmuch as its effect on international competition – if only through the inequality in terms of available resources – is to break the tacit agreement whereby sport is supposed to offer all competitors an equal chance from the outset (with regard to preparation, equipment, training and support). Money is a means of discrimination that can suit those practising sport at a high level – a notion hinted at by Swedish athlete Ulf Karlsson when he commented that only the richer countries could afford jumping pits (a situation that suited him very well) whereas athletes from all the continents of the world could line up on the running track (*Le Monde*, 27 August 2003, p. 21).

In the 1990s, in response to this situation, the Council of Europe initiated a policy of co-operation with disadvantaged countries in eastern and central Europe, in line with the principles of the European Sports Charter, one aim of which is to make sport universally accessible. The Council admitted some twelve east European countries as members and tasked the Committee for the Development of Sport (CDDS) with implementing the co-operation policy. In 1991 a programme entitled SPRINT (Sports Reform Innovation and Training) was set up to develop the provision of expertise and exchanges. Financed from the Sports Fund, the programme aims to promote the democratisation of sport and to prevent abuses such as violence and doping. It covers exchanges and training placements as well as seminars on sports law, the financing of sport, sports management training and the development of voluntary involvement in sport.

Unequal provision of sports infrastructure and equipment

An aggravating factor in the inequality among nations with regard to sport is the unequal provision of equipment and infrastructure. It is a fact that lack of sports infrastructure is nowadays seen as a straightforward reflection of under-development and symbolises the exclusion of the nations concerned from the ranks of those that really count. Juan Antonio Samaranch, President of the IOC, once remarked that the Third World could not organise the Olympic Games for the simple reason that it could not organise anything (Ramonet and De Brie, 1996, p. 9). Sadly, such apparently unacceptable cynicism is founded on an economic reality that cannot be occluded by occasional sports co-operation plans or gestures of goodwill such as the holding of the football World Cup outside the rich countries (De Brie, 1996).

A majority of nations are excluded from the sporting order, including the (still too long) list of developing countries (Andreff, 1988a). Within Europe, the eastern and central regions of the continent lag significantly behind the others.

As well as suffering from the negative image that a lack of sports infrastructure conveys in our societies – where the emergence of a sports culture is generally seen as an expression of modernity – those countries prevented by an initial lack of resources from holding major international or world events (such as the Olympic Games or World Cup) are denied the material and economic advantages generated through return on investment. It should be borne in mind, for example, that in the recent history of the Olympics, the Soviet Union is the only east European country to have staged the summer Games (held in Moscow in 1980).

As noted in 1994 by the Conference of European Ministers responsible for Sport: "the increasing cost of major international sports competitions ... tends to exclude the less well-off countries, thus contravening the ideals of the universality of sport and of equal opportunities" (Council of Europe, 14th informal meeting of European Ministers responsible for Sport, op. cit., p. 177).

Those countries that have managed to join the EU seem to have resolved the problem to some extent. The examples of Euro 2004 – with the construction of seven soccer stadiums in Portugal – and of the 2004 summer Olympics in Athens, for which Greece had to pull out all the stops, demonstrate that once the initial threshold of recognising a country's ability to stage an event has been crossed, sport can sometimes be a driving economic force, revitalising entire regions.

At the same time, it is clear from domestic political debate that the choices of Portugal and Greece also represented an economic risk. It is hardly surprising that Portugal's successful bid to stage Euro 2004 came as a shock in some quarters, given the extent of the construction work required (*Le Monde*, 2 December 2003). The Portuguese Government, which put almost €170 million into the tournament, covered 25% of the cost of each site. It was confident of obtaining a rapid return on its investment through increased tourism, with visitor numbers projected to rise by 3-6% from 2005 onwards. The opposition, notably the extreme left, disputed the projections and dismissed the choice as a "historic mistake" in a country with a steadily rising unemployment rate. For its part, Greece, which drew criticism even from the upper echelons of the Olympic movement (*Libération*, 1 March 2004), had major problems with a series of delays in transport development and construction work. The main delays were in completing the roofs of the Olympic stadium and pool and in the installation of equipment for broadcasting coverage of the competitions (*Le Monde*, 7 and 8 March 2004). Media participation in the form of payment for broadcasting rights accounted for 37.5% of the total cost of staging the Games and was thus crucial to their success (*L'Equipe*, 21 April 2004).

It is true that there is another aspect to investment risk in such cases. Countries whose economies are still developing have been prepared to mortgage their resources and run up huge debts in order to assert or reassert their presence in the community of nations by organising sports events of world importance. When Moscow hosted the Davis Cup in 1995 it made a huge hole in the Russian Federation's budget because the commercial television networks associated with the event were not sufficiently well equipped to cover the competition properly and thus to generate income from broadcasting rights. The problem surfaced despite a high level of public response to the tournament and the fact that tickets were reasonably priced, at US$5-10.

An attitude of ostracism – which has proved hard to break and contributes, in the name of economics, to maintaining a gulf between those European nations deemed worthy of hosting international sports competitions and the under-equipped "satellite states" – is compounded by the genuine cultural and material disadvantages confronting potential athletes in a nation with few or unevenly scattered sports facilities.

In eastern and central Europe, economic problems have followed on the heels of political changes. As the Russian Federation made the transition to a market economy there was a decline in the practice of "sport for all" and this was largely aggravated by a lack of facilities. In 1982 the country had only 1 154 indoor swimming pools and in 1996 there were just 2 100 tennis courts, of which 96 were indoors. Not only were existing facilities and equipment in the region obsolete but they were unevenly spread, being concentrated in Russia, to the detriment of the former Soviet republics, and in urban rather than rural areas. It was reported that in 1990 rural sports facilities included only forty indoor swimming pools and one ice rink (Bourg and Gouguet, 2001, p. 85). The shortage of facilities in schools was no less marked: 75% of schools had no gym and 80% lacked sports fields (ibid.).

In addition, the low level of national sports goods production was not enough to meet the needs of the sporting public. In the winter sports market alone, ski production could hardly meet 50% of the demand. In tennis, domestic manufacturers could meet just 10% of the demand for rackets, while there was an overall shortage of kit (especially tennis shoes). Moreover, as the general cash squeeze saw the end of public subsidies for maintaining community sports facilities (such as gyms and pools), the cost of hiring and using them inevitably rose, to the detriment of the less well-off – a phenomenon which resulted in "new types of rationing" (Bourg and Gouguet, op. cit.).

The low level of physical provision for sport dictated by difficult economic circumstances (as countries made the transition from a planned, state-run economy to the free market) entailed a double handicap for the states concerned. On the one hand, at grassroots level, it hampered the development of sport as a popular activity because not all those who might wish to play sport had regular access to facilities. On the other hand, it excluded these same countries from the circuit of spectator sport by setting them apart from the group that hosted major international events – even though such events might have helped to offset their financial deficit. These aspects of economic discrimination were sadly compounded by the impact of political upheavals (abrupt changes of regime, the collapse of political systems, wars, destruction and the rise of organised crime).

Images likely to haunt anyone who followed the course of the conflicts in the former Yugoslavia include those of the Olympic facilities in Sarajevo utterly destroyed by war, and of an ice skater who movingly described how he patiently tried to keep himself fit for competition – despite battles, bombings and the lack of an ice rink – by "skating" around the wooden floor of his bedroom on cloth pads.

Among the relevant texts adopted by the Parliamentary Assembly of the Council of Europe, Recommendation 1190 (1992) on European sports co-operation states:

> "The Assembly has taken account of the implications for sport caused by the political changes in central and eastern Europe. It considers that action is urgently needed on the parliamentary level to assure sports provision."

The recommendation acknowledged that sports provision in central and eastern Europe (and related legislation) were matters of concern (Council of Europe, CDDS (98) 90 Vol. I, p. 193).

Money in sport, and the imbalances between different types of sport

Within organised sport and in federal, national and international budgets for sport, as well as private sources of funding, not only is money unequally distributed in general, but there are also obvious discrepancies between different types of sport and thus between sportspeople, and these too contribute to exclusion.

The Council of Europe has been aware of these factors for a number of years. The informal meeting of European Ministers responsible for Sport in 1994 clearly identified "the financial inequalities with regard to the needs of top-level sport and those of Sport for All, between popular sports and less popular sports, between the few televisual sports (whether at national or international level) and other sports" and acknowledged that these growing disparities "[divided] sport and [undermined] its solidarity" (Council of Europe, Vol. 1, CDDS (98) 90 Vol. 1, p. 177).

In some cases, imbalances are the result of deliberate choices as certain countries prioritise particular sectors at the expense of others that are considered less in keeping with the national sports tradition, or give preference to the sports in which they reckon they have the best chance of winning medals at international level.

In Sweden, strategic choices were made to support certain branches of athletics. The development of athletics, with high-quality facilities including forty covered stadiums, has focused on the jumping events, which have received the lion's share of the federal sports budget (€3.7 million) (*Le Monde*, 27 August 2003). In the Russian Federation, ice sports are still alive and well and receiving enough funding to nurture the hope that "Russian will remain the leading language of the rinks" (*Le Monde*, 6 February 2004). In Turkey, sports such as weightlifting receive financial preference to the extent that athletes are sometimes attracted from other countries (*Libération*, 15 and 16 November 2003).

Other more typical forms of inequality are based on the idea that certain sports are better investments than others. This conception of sports, which is concerned with their spectator and media value, has contributed in Europe to the creation of a rigid budgetary hierarchy. The result has been more discrimination between athletes of different kinds, the implicit discrediting of those sports with a lower profile and the undermining of solidarity in sport.

In France, the disparities are evident when we compare the budgets of different types of sports clubs in the 2002-03 season. From a budgetary point of view, leading clubs can be classed in descending order of importance as follows: soccer (far ahead of the rest); rugby; basketball; handball and volleyball (Source: Sporeco, 2004).

The financial situation of volleyball, to take this sport as an example, is far removed from that of soccer. The average budget of a football club in the First Division is around €34 million, compared with an average of €900 000 for a comparable volleyball club. The total budget of the fourteen French Pro A volleyball clubs – €12.59 million – is scarcely greater than that of Corsican soccer club Ajaccio (which, with €12 million, has the smallest budget in the French First Division). It is particularly striking that the difference between the volleyball club with the biggest budget (Paris, €1.5 million) and that with the smallest (Avignon, €0.5 million) pales by comparison with the gap between the richest soccer club (Lyon, with €100 million) and poor relation Ajaccio with its €12 million. Lyon has 8.33 times more money than Ajaccio, whereas the difference between the volleyball clubs' budgets is a factor of three.

Only in rugby is the corresponding figure smaller (a factor of 2.6), although in terms of overall financing rugby has recently moved into second position, behind soccer, the average budget of a rugby club in the "top sixteen" being €5.69 million.

The average budget of a basketball club is €3.4 million and the differential factor between the richest club and the poorest is 4.4. Handball clubs have an average budget of just €1.07 million, but the differential factor is relatively high at 5.37 (Source: Sporeco, 2004).

With few exceptions, the budgetary rankings correspond to the amount of television airtime devoted to the different sports. Of the ten most televised sports, soccer tops the table, with rugby in second place; basketball occupies only seventh place, while handball and volleyball are not in the top ten (Nys, 2003).

Among the inequalities created by the uneven spread of money in sport, a more remarkable type of discrimination is that generated not between different disciplines but between men's and women's sport (considering both at the highest levels of competition). Financial "rewards" and "penalties" are thus applied according to gender. In the 1998-99 season, for example, the average budget of a First Division soccer club was seven times that of a male basketball club competing at a comparable level – and thirty-four times that of a female basketball club at the same level. The ratio of an average (male) First Division soccer club budget (to take a dominant club in a dominant sport) to that of a female Pro A basketball club (an underdog club in an underdog sport) was approximately 87:1 (Bourg and Gouguet, 2001).

At the same time, these disparities in a European country with relatively few economic problems do at least reflect a certain vitality, even if the diversity of sports and sports organisations is accompanied by excessive budgetary inequalities, which both contribute to and reflect discrimination.

Further east, the problems associated with the collapse of communism and the old system of state-run sport have actually threatened the existence of some sports federations and clubs, and have highlighted the relationship between capital investment and discrimination. The transition to a market economy has particularly accentuated disparities in countries like the Russian

Federation, where only high-level sport has managed to adapt, under certain conditions, to the pressures of the market (only elite clubs that take part in international competitions have been able to attract private capital).

In soccer, most Russian First Division clubs have successfully constituted themselves as limited companies. By contrast, some forty Second and Third Division teams have simply ceased to exist, among them Spartak Chukotka after wealthy regional governor Roman Abramovich declined to invest in the "local" side, preferring to spend £140 million on a majority shareholding in the English club Chelsea (*Courrier international*, 664, 24-30 July 2004, p. 26).

On the other hand, foreign sponsors and investors have been hesitant about moving into the Russian market. In practice the input of private capital from different sources – including sponsorship, the use of brand names and the sale of television rights – has acted like a filter system, accentuating the hierarchies among sports, clubs, teams and players.

While Europe as a whole is affected by the phenomenon of disparity introduced by private investment, the effect has been much more marked in the central and east European countries.

In the Russian Federation, inequalities related to the input of private capital are compounded by the problem of seeking sources of foreign currency to offset an absence, or low level, of public funding. Specifically, sports bosses face an ongoing dilemma: by transferring their best players to the west in order to rescue their finances they simultaneously render their clubs less attractive to potential investors.

Generally speaking, it is clubs in the dominant sports that have successfully converted to the market economy. Those concerned include, in football, such elite clubs as Torpedo, CSKA Moscow and Dynamo Kiev; in ice hockey, CSKA, which was rescued by American investment; in basketball, Moscow Dynamo and CSKA; as well as a few cycling, athletics and tennis clubs. These are the sports which, since 1989, have managed to attract a number of European sponsors.

The most obvious conclusion to be drawn is that, structurally speaking, sport in Europe is still strongly hierarchical, with money determining the ranking of the different disciplines. The sports economy works through competition and segregation, defining promising investment areas and relegation zones, particularly so in those countries still undergoing economic conversion. The uneven nature of the cash flows helps to keep certain sports and those who practise them out of the public eye. At the lowest level, women and other categories of athletes (including those with disabilities) who are excluded from the lucrative markets struggle to keep their sports going and to remain competitive.

Budgetary inequalities among European clubs: the example of football

In European football the budgetary disparities among clubs have reached alarming proportions. They are reflected in practical terms in the uneven spread of talent and technical and human potential, and they pose a fundamental problem for sport with regard to fair competition. The key question is: does the richest club deserve to win?

The inequalities help to generate growing economic segregation by inexorably widening the gulf between those clubs with the lowest revenue (some of which simply give up) and an elite including Spain's Real Madrid and numerous other European soccer clubs, notably in Italy and the United Kingdom, which function as stables for the star players.

Journalist Jennie James, commenting in *Time* magazine on what amounts to a social divide in high-level sport, noted that the influx of capital coupled with free-market thinking in sport had a kinetic effect: "The rich get richer because they can afford the high-priced players that attract the fans and investors" (James, 2000, p. 51).

Disparities between clubs in terms of sporting performance thus stem in part from the relatively simple phenomenon of rising returns: those clubs that perform best attract most spectators, win sponsorship contracts, are more attractive to television operators and can draw in fresh sporting talent, which in turn helps to make the team more profitable. This kinetic effect can also work in the other direction, however: if a team's results are mediocre, its following will melt away and it will lose the support of its financial partners. In fact, various indicators, including average performance at championship level over the previous ten seasons, stable presence in the First Division or its equivalent and frequency of competition in the European Cup, confirm the persistent nature of the differences in clubs' performance (Bourg and Gouguet, 1998, p. 169). In other words, generally speaking and over a relatively long timespan, we find the same clubs dominating championships and the same clubs being dominated – a reflection of a fairly stable order dictated by levels of financial input. Countering the trend is still a very difficult undertaking, as demonstrated by the worthy efforts of French club Saint-Etienne, which is currently attempting to attract investment in the hope of recreating its "glory days" (*Le Monde*, 3 May 2003).

There is an ambiguity in today's highly unequal situation. According to the logic of sport, it should be possible to sustain maximum uncertainty about the outcome of championships and tournaments by balancing the capabilities of the different European teams, which would mean ensuring that the best players were not permanently concentrated in the teams with the lion's share of funding. To an extent, this is the principle suggested by the sport system in the United States and it is one that could conceivably work in Europe through a process of regulation involving equalisation of revenue and capping of the sum total of salaries in each club. By contrast, the free market in European football is currently polarising cash flows and sporting potential in a way that is anything but egalitarian.

The European soccer hierarchy is based essentially on invested cash, which ensures the mass recruitment of star players. Certain big-budget teams – and they are always the same ones – hold their position in the leagues, are the most attractive to watch, corner a major share of the profits and can thus recruit talented new players who will ensure that they sustain their hegemony.

The richest European clubs (Manchester United, FC Barcelona, Juventus Turin, Bayern Munich, Real Madrid, AC Milan, etc.), which constitute a hard core in competitive terms, are also those that conclude the most transfer deals and thus have the power (i.e. the financial resources) to retain players or to move them on. The same economic logic is reflected in the fact that the big football clubs are based in Europe's major industrial and financial conurbations (Ravenel, 1997).

In fact, these top European clubs possess the economic resources to plan over the long term and seek to improve or stabilise their sporting performance at a very high level through two complementary strategies, namely transfers, which enable them to fine-tune their competitive potential, and a policy of paying very high salaries, which allows them to hold on to talented players. To give some examples, in the late 1990s the sum total of salaries as a proportion of the overall club budget was 69% at AC Milan, 68% at Newcastle, 50% at Juventus Turin, 43% at Dortmund and 42% at FC Barcelona.

As most economic analysts of the situation have noted, this process, involving various market operators, with their respective strategies, has the effect of creating a core group of teams with large and stable budgets and a high level of profitability (Bourg and Gouguet, 1998, p. 176).

Economic analysis apart, in addition to the forms of violence inherent in an activity perpetually dominated by capital and its "pulling power", there are underlying types of violence deriving from the very form of negotiation imposed by the free market in sport.

The disparities we have described among the European clubs automatically affect the recruitment of players and help to create disproportionate differences between them in terms of conditions of employment, salaries and position. Christian de Brie has commented, for example, that the law of the marketplace means more inequality and insecurity, and less justice and solidarity (De Brie, 1994, p. 22).

The power of money also opens the way to other possibilities such as the dissimulation of profits, further widening the divide between those in sport who simply work hard for a living and their fellows who are paid astronomical salaries:

> "Already corrupted by salaries, bonuses and fees out of all proportion to their talent (although that talent is undeniable), the affluent in soccer also shamelessly engage in forms of tax fraud simply unavailable to more modest taxpayers, which are systematically organised in complicity with their employers" (De Brie, 1994, p. 22).

The scheming inherent in the dynamics of "free-market" competition is also carefully concealed behind the front of football as "one big family". The suggestion of open-hearted camaraderie conveyed in this much-vaunted image of the sport is dismissed by certain former club presidents who have experienced the bitter realities.

In France, Laurent Perpère, former president of PSG, is one of those to take issue with the idealised illusion of high-level professional sport as a force for solidarity: "The big football family is a façade behind which everyone does their own little deals" (Le Monde, 6 June 2003). His observations are supported by Pierrat and Riveslange, who comment on the excesses of no-holds-barred trading on the transfer market, where such "minor matters" as verbal or even written agreements seem to count for nothing (Pierrat and Riveslange, 2002, p. 140).

Such wheeler-dealing is part and parcel of a certain conception of what football is. While soccer teams – unlike manufacturing companies, for example – cannot do without competitors, for in the absence of credible rivals they would no longer have any reason to exist, they nonetheless function within a preferential system in which invested capital counts for more than sporting and competitive performance. In other words, by organising themselves and operating as they do, they deny the very essence of sport, which is the will to rise above oneself through one's own efforts.

It is worth quoting here the utterance of former Girondins de Bordeaux President Claude Bez in 1984, which so accurately foreshadowed the mounting reality of economic violence in sport, in relation to professional football: "I don't like to see little clubs doing well. If money wins, that's fine" (Pierrat and Riveslange, 2002, pp. 64-65).

Obviously this dismal economic reality did not come from nowhere: the current way of running professional soccer, with all the inherent disparities, has its roots in a period when the sport was hijacked by those who imagined they could give it a new image by pumping in vast amounts of money.

Certain European soccer club bosses thus bear a heavy responsibility for the wage inflation and inequalities now besetting European sport. An example is that of Jean-Luc Lagardère and the Matra Group. At a time when free-market economics seemed to be sweeping all before it, and riding high on the successes of the French international side (World Cup semi-finalists in 1982 and again in 1986 and winners of the 1984 European Nations Cup), they invested massively in a club to which they gave the corporate brand name "Matra Racing". In an interview with *L'Equipe,* Lagardère quite unabashedly explained that the aim was to achieve "with human flesh and blood" what the group had already achieved with their other products. With a budget of 100 million French francs, he believed the new club could cut through any opposition. On the one hand, the fact that the venture was relatively unsuccessful and that the club was simply abandoned in 1989 demonstrated the limits of a vision of soccer dominated by a balance sheet. On the other hand, the introduction into the sport market of extravagant salaries was significant in signalling the start of a race that subsequently exhausted many European clubs and left them with heavy debts.

The relentless inroads made by free-market philosophy set in train a disturbing inflationary trend affecting both salaries and transfer fees. Cut-throat competition between clubs became the norm and this was reflected in alarming losses and levels of debt. With a few exceptions, European clubs recorded heavy losses. In the 2000-01 season alone, French clubs accumulated losses of €120 million and reported a total debt of €290 million; Italy's Series A clubs had combined losses of around €400 million; the total deficit of Spanish clubs was €700 million, and 80% of British clubs were loss-making (Sobry, 2003).

When contrasted with the budgets of certain hard-up sports, or the overall sports budgets of countries excluded from world economic growth, such figures seem senseless.

Does the economic domination of sport in Europe inevitably generate inequality?

The logic of business is currently taking over European sport, posing various threats to the pyramid model which has made it what it is and which, to some extent, gives it a framework of solidarity.

This economic domination finds different forms of expression in Europe, from investment, sponsorship and patronage to shareholding and stock-exchange floatation, and including the acquisition of holdings and the development of companies that are, in turn, part of huge business empires in which sport is just another investment area. As a result, sports clubs are coming to think and behave like straightforward businesses.

At Real Madrid, Florentino Perez, who took over as President in June 2000, soon had the reputation of seeking to generate for the soccer club the sort of revenues that had made him, in the space of a few years, one of Spain's highest-profile businessmen. Real Madrid was no longer to be just a football club, but rather a "sports business", diversifying its activities (notably through merchandising), marketing its brand abroad (a strategy worth €58 million in 2002-03 and a projected €80 million in 2003-04) and branching out into areas far removed from soccer, with hugely profitable property deals (*Le Monde*, 26 November 2003, p. 18). Some supporters of the club criticised this style of management, however, sensing in a confused way that it represented the beginning of something that could prejudice the interests of the game itself. Paradoxically, Real's defeats were often interpreted as the negative outcome of a balance-sheet-based approach to sport. One ardent fan, dismayed that this style of managing the team had failed to "produce results", neatly summed up the criticisms: "It's all down to the President, Florentino Perez. He is a good businessman but he knows nothing about football" (*Le Monde*, 27 April 2004, p. 24).

In Italy, Antonio Giraudo, managing director of Juventus Turin, declared that the club's aim was to be "a business like any other" (*Le Monde*, 30 September 2001). Controlled by the holding company IFL – part of the empire of the Agnelli (Fiat) family – Juventus floated 35% of its capital on the stock market in early 2002 (Sobry, 2003). The floatation was part of a very particular approach which entailed sublimating the sporting aspect of the business, the better to extrapolate from it, for Juventus was planning not only to purchase its stadium on a co-ownership basis with Turin's number two club Torino, at a cost of €120 million, but also to open a €130 million theme park entitled Mondo Juve. The latter venture inevitably invites comparison with "Manchesterland", the Manchester United Soccer School for 7-14-year-olds, a joint venture by Britain's Manchester United, the world's richest club, and the Disneyland Paris Group (*Sud-Ouest*, 27 April 2004). This new trend towards diversification of the "sporting product" – already begun with initiatives by other European clubs, including Real Madrid, hailed as the "symbol of football business" (*Le Monde*, 26 November 2003) – poses two basic problems. On the one hand, the purpose of the activity is called into question when sport is used to market a giant fairground, and on the other the endless spiral of money-making in the inevitably circumscribed context of the game presupposes the accentuation of inequalities in terms of performance and competitive potential.

In fact, this mutation of high-level sport (the clearest example of which is seen in Europe in football) involves turning it into a commodity in a way that gives serious cause for concern on more than one count. Under the transfer system it encourages a trade in human beings, the most sought-after and most vulnerable of whom are often young. It reduces what was a cultural activity to its economic expression, a shift that will sooner or later threaten the very existence of voluntary club-based sport, and it also creates an ever-widening gulf between professional spectator sport and the more intimate events that characterise sport as a mass activity.

Sport is thus being organised and reorganised in ways that fundamentally change the spirit behind its development. In 1998 the editorial director of *France Football* warned that, if vigilance was not exercised, soccer would soon represent not a form of contact between countries and cultures, societies and individuals, but a form of trade between multinational companies and stock markets (Ernault, 1998, p. 15).

One of the first indicators of the changes – which proceed quite logically as a series of adjustments to achieve commercial viability and maximise profits – was the announcement of plans to develop private leagues in sports such as football and basketball that attracted large television audiences.

In football, in 1998 – at the initiative of Media Partners, an Italian group backed by United States bank Morgan Stanley and communications groups based in Germany (Kirch), the United Kingdom (Murdoch) and Italy (Berlusconi) – a plan was devised for a closed-circuit competition independent of the European federal set-up. This sprawling commercial venture promised participating clubs a total of €1.91 billion, compared with the "mere" €128.06 million distributed by UEFA. The system was to operate as a closed league, with no risk of relegation and therefore little risk of loss of investment for those who promoted, sponsored and funded the competition (chief among them private television companies and cartels): "Investors are attracted by the prospect of eliminating the uncertainty that goes with sport because it is becoming harder for them to reconcile their speculative interests with the risk of teams failing to make it in the Champions' League" (Bourg, 1999, p. 57).

In basketball, in May 2000, seventeen European clubs federated in the Union of European Basketball Leagues (ULEB)[31] – in turn sponsored by Spanish company Telefonica – laid the foundations for a European competition independent of the International Basketball Federation (FIBA). Two parallel championships were thus instituted: the "Suproligue" (under the auspices of FIBA) with twenty clubs, and the Euroleague (ULEB) with twenty-four clubs, each of which had paid a million-dollar deposit to play in the first three seasons. The fact that these projects currently seem to have failed in no way diminishes the threat they pose in principle. Like European professional soccer, which also sought to group its major clubs in a closed competition system comparable to that operated in the United States, the Euroleague made

---
31. There is no European Basketball Federation.

dangerous distinctions on the basis of money. The system is a good example of the current misguided trend in European sport, with efforts to side-step the federation set-up and the principles of promotion and relegation (which, although they impose constraints, also ensure a degree of sporting solidarity) in order to lock clubs into an arena where they are guaranteed a constantly high profile and their shareholders and sponsors are thus ensured long-term return on the investment in their respective team's profile. Risk being the enemy of capital, the teams' potential thus becomes more profitable through the elimination of any chance of losing, or at least of being relegated (which is synonymous with loss for the financial backers of spectator sport). Similar approaches seem to be emerging in other sports, including motor racing, table tennis, tennis and cycling.

Secondly, money leaves its imprint and marks with the violence of its power the very symbols of competition: the winners' trophies. It is no accident that over recent years sporting competitions and cups have gradually been rebaptised, as federal or institutional names have been replaced by commercial ones in order to offer sponsors and advertisers even more opportunities to make their mark: the British FA Cup became the Axa Cup; the Belgian Championship became the Jupiler League, and in rugby the European Rugby Cup became the Heineken Cup.

Thirdly, these new trends pose very particular problems which are likely to erode the most basic competitive principles of sport. In opposition to the traditional "may the best man win" ethos, the entrepreneurial-style management of clubs and teams opens the way to all sorts of abuses that will gradually undermine the logic of sport. For example, influential groups – whose extent and structure are not always transparent – may control competing interests. It is true that steps[32] have been taken in European soccer to counter the problem of groups having majority shareholdings in more than one team within the same competition, and some groups, including Canal Plus (majority shareholder in PSG and Servette Geneva), have been obliged to make choices (Bourg and Gouguet, 1998).

However, on the one hand the financial set-ups involved can be so impenetrable as to conceal various types of scheme, including the use of offshore companies and other tax evasion arrangements, and on the other hand certain groups, such as ENIC, once the majority shareholder in three clubs, have made no secret of their desire to embrace the sport market on a grand scale, and have taken appeals to the Court of Arbitration for Sport, citing the principle of free trade in Europe (Bourg, 1999).

---

32. UEFA ruled that no two clubs owned by the same natural person or legal entity could compete in the European Winners' Cup.

Yet, can the game still be fair if the same financial power more or less directly controls more than one participant in the same competition? This particular issue was the subject of recommendations by the European Council, expressed specifically in the Nice Declaration of 2000. Similar questions have to be asked when choices are made between players from the same "stable", favouring one at the expense of another on grounds unrelated to their actual sporting merits. Behind the Senna-Prost rivalry in Formula One racing, certain financial interests were at work, seeking to thwart the laws of uncertainty in sport. In the interests of conquering the South American car market, it was logical to give the Brazilian Senna the best cars, as French victory would not have had the same commercial impact. Schumacher's surprise victory in the Austrian Grand Prix in 2002 – when Barricello, after looking certain to win, allowed him to gain the upper hand – was dictated by similar principles: the Fiat Group, which had just floated Ferrari on the stock exchange, needed to reinforce their brand image by securing a win for their emblematic German driver. The same mechanisms work in cycling, where team members know that they personally are not in the race to win, but rather to support the designated victor – an individual being more effective than a group as a medium for conveying commercial messages (Chartier and Vigarello, 1982).

Placing money and brand image at the heart of competitive events in this way represents a major break with European tradition, in which, since the inception of modern sport in late-eighteenth century Britain, the first and ultimate purpose of competition has been sporting victory (Thomas, 1999).

Fourthly, the excesses of commercialism and free-market economics in sport has the potential to lead to the privatisation of public assets (Sobry, 2003; Fontanel and Bensahel, 2001).

In France today, the major sports clubs operate simply as big companies. Building on the Avice Act of 1984, the Professional Sport Act of 28 December 1999 (Law 99-1124) defined two new types of commercial status: the *"société anonyme à objet sportif"* (SAOS) [limited company established for purposes of sport] and the *"société anonyme sportive professionnelle"* (SASP) [limited professional sport company]. Apart from the fact that clubs with such status continue to receive public funding – placing the French Minister for Youth and Sport in a tricky position with regard to the European Commission and competition law – the legitimacy of allowing them to use municipally-owned facilities that are maintained and renovated with public money is surely questionable.

Many clubs use facilities that belong to the cities in which they are located (Sobry, 2003). The Vélodrome stadium in Marseilles, renovated by the municipality at a cost of hundreds of millions of francs when France hosted the 1998 World Cup tournament, offers a good example of this dubious practice. OM, the resident club, subsequently had all the advantages of a brand-new stadium at minimal cost. A public asset was made available to commercial companies and the sole quid pro quo was the fact of the city's name being kept or enhanced in the public eye through the organisation of a sports event. Members of the public may not be able to use the pitch but they are welcome to pay for a place in the stands. The point has been made that such cases of privatisation of a public asset ought to be scrutinised very closely, particularly if the clubs concerned are floated on the stock exchange (Fontanel and Bensahel, 2001, p. 182).

In conclusion, we need to acknowledge objectively that while money in sport may not be the root of all evil, it is increasingly obvious that it is helping to pervert the traditional image of sport. It has become the dominant force, and its excesses, which are in effect a form of violence, help to erode the credibility of sport and athletes and to diminish sports fans' enjoyment.

Something also needs to be said here about the way in which the world of sport and athletes themselves have embraced the logic of profit. From the case of the French women athletes who refused to share relay-race prize money with the reserve members of their team to that of the former French World Champion soccer squad imposing a charge of €10 000 per player on a public television company (shooting footage "behind the scenes" at OM) for the privilege of filming them in training ... money is spoiling the game.

The will to push oneself beyond one's limits – which underpinned the spirit of the modern Olympic movement – has now been seriously called into question. Among the many clear illustrations of this is the case of Ukrainian pole vaulter Sergey Bubka, who was regularly achieving heights of more than 6.20 metres in training yet succeeded in increasing his official best only centimetre by centimetre, pocketing a bonus of 150 000 French francs from his sponsor each time the record was broken.

The market has become the principle around which sport is organised, with profit the measure of performance.

Deregulation of the sport market: business v. ethics

From the Bosman ruling to flexibility

The Bosman ruling of 1995 signalled a fundamental change in the professional sport set-up in Europe. In the case of Belgian soccer player Jean-Marc Bosman the European Court of Justice (ECJ) interpreted Community law in such a way as to condemn two principles that had guided the operation of certain national football federations and of UEFA. The first of these was the arrangement whereby transfers of players from one club to another were restricted by the requirement that the club acquiring the player pay the old club a transfer indemnity for training or promotion. The second was UEFA's restriction on the number of foreign players permitted on a team. The ECJ decision introduced into sport the concepts of freedom of movement for workers (as set out in Article 39 [formerly Article 48] of the Treaty establishing the European Community) and free competition (Article 81 [formerly Article 85] of the Treaty), which had been impeded by the transfer fee system.

A number of comments need to be made on this important decision, which opened the world of football to the principles of free trade in the European single market.

The judgment had certain damaging effects (Manzella, 2002). By applying business principles in the world of sport it demolished rules about the use of foreign players at match level that had been imposed by national and international sports federations for technical and sporting reasons, notably the need to guarantee local training centres an outlet for their players in high-level competition. The rule that it set aside had also been designed to ensure a contingent of experienced players for national teams.

The ECJ decision ran counter to the principle of subsidiarity within the Community and repudiated the right of sport to make rules for itself at the basic level of what happens on the pitch. By encouraging a shift of power from the sports federations to the clubs and television channels, it threatened the pyramid structure of European sport. Because it offered the sports authorities no fall-back solution or alternative that might have permitted them to recapture the initiative, it undermined the system of rules around which sport is structured and thus constituted a body blow to its basic principles and its legitimacy.

The ECJ decided to apply an economic reading of sport, thus helping to obliterate its educational, civic and health aspects. Sport had become the preserve of wealth, and the principle of fairness and equal opportunity in competition was quite clearly denied.

The final effect of the decision was to initiate an uncontrolled process whereby more new business-based rules could be imposed on sport from outside. In fact the Bosman ruling was followed by decisions in other cases which had the effect of extending the principle established to nationals of countries outside the EU. One such case was that of Polish basketball player Lilia Malaja. The Strasbourg-based club Racing, which was already fielding a Bulgarian player and a Croat player, had not been permitted to sign the Pole. Lilia Malaja, basing her case on the Bosman ruling and on an association agreement between the European Union and Poland, applied for a player's licence and the status of EU resident. The Strasbourg Administrative Court initially rejected her application but it was approved on appeal to the Administrative Court of Nancy on 3 February 2000, and upheld exactly a year later by the Conseil d'Etat [the highest administrative court in France] after a legal challenge from the basketball federation. It is not hard to imagine the possible consequences of the decision, given that the EU has association and co-operation agreements with twenty-three countries in eastern Europe and North Africa.

From the perspective of the sports authorities (UEFA and all the national federations and leagues), the ECJ decision had a whole series of negative repercussions (Bourg and Gouguet, 1998, 2001):

- It threatened the personality, style and culture of football at national level – national soccer identity being denied by the turnover in players and the cosmopolitanism now dominating clubs and championships. In the 1999-2000 season Chelsea had twenty-six foreign players of fourteen different nationalities among its thirty-four professional players. At national championship level 41% of players in Belgium in 1998-99 were non-nationals, and in England in the 1999-2000 season forty-one nationalities were represented.
- It damaged supporters' ability to identify with teams and broke the teams' cultural ties at local and regional level.
- It undermined quality and homogeneity in the national team selection process, particularly by making it harder for young nationals to obtain a professional licence and at the same time increasing the number of championship players ineligible for selection.
- It increased inequalities in sporting terms by making it possible for some teams to recruit star squads, thus introducing competitive imbalance.
- It undermined player-training policies by making it impossible for clubs to recover their outlay via indemnity payments when players left at the end of their contract.
- It triggered an unbridled increase in salary costs, in which the negotiating power of star players and the numbers and influence of their agents (507 agents enjoy FIFA recognition) were also significant factors.
- It provoked an exodus of players from the least well-funded national championships to the richest.
- It tended to transform what had been a collective sport into an individual one by creating a commercial, careerist image of what it meant to play football (with the focus on actual or projected new sources of earnings such as image contracts, stock options or copyright fees on goals shown on television).

Ultimately the effect of subjecting sport to EU law has been to give primacy to free-market economics and to encourage the privatisation of clubs, which in turn has the paradoxical effect of weakening the very pyramid-based model of European sport that the EU institutions have defended.

There is no doubt that the Bosman ruling liberated players while at the same time liberating the appetite of the clubs and placing athletes on a sort of European carousel in the name of flexibility. Most significantly, it helped to make football a "two-track" sport (Lanfranchi, 2002, p. 23) and very clearly reinforced the demarcation line between amateur and professional. It accelerated the pace of transfers, put salaries on an exponential growth trajectory and accentuated inequalities between players.

One end result of the increased professional freedom has been to widen the gap between the highest and lowest salaries and to create more unemployment and job insecurity, particularly among young, unknown players. It has accentuated the partitioning of clubs and players and encouraged the emergence of new types of employment and employment contracts which stretch the limits of legality – for example, the pre-contract non-solicitation agreements offered to the youngest players, who thus commit themselves, in return for more or less official payments, to signing their first professional contract with the club in question. A more general effect has been to provoke a rash of schemes designed to enable clubs to hold on to their young players. In addition, the clubs have been obliged to find different ways of offsetting the loss associated with transfers: players may be asked to sign long-term contracts restricting their powers of negotiation or may be offered the option of early release from contract for a fixed fee under a cancellation clause. The new freedom has also necessitated the emergence of mechanisms such as revenue sharing and the capping of overall expenditure on salaries, which offer a degree of financial solidarity (Bourg and Gouguet, 1998).

We might be tempted to agree with Gérard Ernault that European Commissioner Karel van Miert's decision not to define football as a "cultural exception" to the EU rules, but to consider it as a purely economic activity, could well constitute a leading form of cultural violence (Ernault, 1998).

Athletes subject to influence

Sport is currently caught up in an economic whirlwind and – despite the example of a few brilliant careers – has lost control over certain aspects of the situation. For the great mass of professional and semi-professional athletes and young hopefuls, the deregulation process and the installation of business logic in sport, with the wave of media enthusiasm that has accompanied them and the markets they have created, leave the way open for all sorts of abuses and forms of violence.

In highly-paid sports like tennis the young athletes are particularly vulnerable to manipulation. This can take many forms, ranging from the control and pillaging of the athlete's financial resources by an authority figure or, at an earlier stage, the general influence exercised by such persons in the athlete's entourage over the course of his or her career and daily life, right through, in certain cases, to sexual pressures and abuse.

The story of Swiss tennis player Patty Schnyder, from Basle, formerly the eighth-ranked woman player in the world, illustrates almost perfectly the vulnerability of highly-gifted young sportswomen under the influence of people who are supposed to protect them. The young woman had great difficulty extricating herself from the clutches of her partner, obscure healer Rainer Harneker, a man in his 40s accused by the tennis player's family of having "bewitched" her. Harneker – who was labelled a "guru" by the press and had made Schnyder follow a strict vegetarian diet and undergo a particular form of acupuncture based on a theory developed by Baunscheid in the eighteenth century – was finally found guilty by a German court in 2002 of practising medicine illegally. Yet, following this outcome, the weight of influence on the young sportswoman seemed merely to shift as she became attached to a charismatic German detective assigned to watch her, a development that led to a family row involving allegations of embezzlement (*Le Monde*, 30 January 2004).

Because the financial stakes in sports careers can be so high, the most vulnerable athletes, particularly children and young women, can find themselves coveted, over-protected and preyed upon, family members being in some cases the worst offenders.

Different types of abuse may be committed within the family or immediate professional circle, and both athletes and sport itself are seriously exposed.

A recent tragic incident in the French tennis world demonstrates the extent of the violence that can be committed for the sake of money or kudos in sport. In south-west France several young people of both sexes were deliberately poisoned by the father of one of their rivals, who repeatedly added medication to their water bottles in order to impair their performance on court. This father-manager was trying to turn the careers of his own children – a son and a daughter (the latter a prodigy ranked number one in France in her category) – to his own advantage, without their knowledge and without the least respect for either sporting ethics or, worse, the lives of the children, teenagers and young adults whom he placed at risk. Worst of all, following the poisoning incidents one of the players concerned died in a road accident after falling asleep at the wheel (*Libération*, 11 August, and 6 and 7 September 2003).

Not only those close to athletes but also their clubs can be guilty of robbing or simply exploiting young people, as demonstrated by the case of young footballer Saliou Lassissi, who, after joining AS Roma in Italy, was reported to have received no money for six months (*Le Monde*, 27 February 2004). Saliou Lassissi, who had previously been based at the Rennes Stadium training centre in France, called on UEFA to withhold AS Roma's European licence for the 2004-05 season.

The phenomenon of exploitation has, as a rule, been aggravated by the rise of new intermediary professions (notably those of manager and agent), which are poorly regulated under both sports rules and European countries' national legislation. "The agent's job is expanding alarmingly" ran a headline in *Le Monde* in March 2002 (*Le Monde*, 17 and 18 March 2002). In that year there were ninety-four licensed soccer agents in France and 235 people waiting to sit the exam to obtain a licence. Omitted from these figures were other individuals without any recognised status in the sport, who nonetheless functioned as players' intermediaries (Bourg and Gouguet, 1998). *Le Monde* reported that wage inflation and the increasing number of transfers had helped to promote the idea that becoming a player's agent was an easy way to make plenty of money without too much effort (*Le Monde*, ibid.). An even more alarming aspect of this trend is the fact that, at the bottom of the scale, talented young players – who are being recruited at an ever-earlier age – find themselves handed over to people with little or no awareness of the responsibilities they have to their protégés. A veritable organised market is developing in Europe in this area, with young people from economically disadvantaged countries as its prime victims.

When it comes to the agency game, the big European soccer countries are the busiest: in 2002 the United Kingdom had the highest number of licensed footballers' agents (160), although Italy (with fifty-six agents at the same date) looked set to overtake it as almost 400 candidates were due to sit the federal licensing exam.

These few examples concisely illustrate the dangers and various forms of violence to which children, young people and women, in particular, are exposed in sport. Some years ago Council of Europe representatives tasked with studying sport and the abuses that took place in it had already identified these types of violence fairly accurately (*The Council of Europe and sport*, 2001, pp. 35-36), focusing specifically on the employment of young people in high-level sport (Recommendation 1292 (1996), CDDS (98) 90, Vol. 1, p. 195).

The Parliamentary Assembly of the Council of Europe declared that it was concerned at the involvement of young people in high-level sport at too early an age. It had looked at the different approaches to sport for young people, and made the point that while sport had a primary role in the mental and physical development of young people and should thus be an integral part of the general education process in a democratic society, elite sport, by contrast, was aimed exclusively at top-level performances that only very few could hope to achieve, and had its own further risks – which the recommendation proceeded to list:

– physical and physiological risks (such as the overloading of the respiratory, cardiovascular and neuromuscular systems);

– psychological risks (such as the strain caused by the "win at all costs" mentality and "dropping out" as a result of early commitment to intense training);

– reduced possibilities for children involved in intense training to attend normal school, especially during competition periods.

More recently, at a Multilateral Seminar on the Protection of Children, Young People and Women in Sport, organised in Hanasaari, Helsinki, from 14 to 16 September 2001 by the Council of Europe, the Finnish Ministry of Education and the Finnish Sports Federation, representatives of the twenty-three member states on the Committee for the Development of Sport (CDDS) discussed the key question of how to ensure that children, young people and women could be guaranteed human dignity and equal rights in sport.

The first point made in the seminar findings was that although the different regions of Europe had followed dissimilar cultural paths, their positions with regard to male and female roles and status "were now seen to be merging and factors such as lifestyle, urbanisation and living standards were more important in determining sexual mores than political regimes" (*The Council of Europe and Sport,* 2001, p. 35). In addition, the work of researchers and the evidence of athletes had made it clear that the world of sport, far from being a world apart, was one in which "mistreatment including sexual harassment and abuse of children, young people and women" was a fact of life (Council of Europe, op. cit.). The delegates therefore issued the following reminder:

> "With respect to the protection of children and young people in both recreational and high-level sport, it was agreed that the articles of the UN Convention on the Rights of the Child (which is an open convention and has been signed by all member countries of the UN except the United States and Somalia) apply also to sport"[33] (Council of Europe, op. cit.).

---

33. Under the convention, a child is defined as anyone up to the age of 18.

Specific concern was expressed about influence being exercised on the most malleable groups of athletes and those least able to defend themselves from the pressures applied in a sporting environment increasingly dominated by economic considerations. The main areas of concern were identified as:
- early intensive training, which could be seen as a form of child abuse (forbidden under Article 19 of the convention);
- physical abuse demanding too much from a young body during training and competition, which leads to health problems in later life;
- doping (incompatible with the right to health and protection from drugs, under Articles 24 and 33 of the convention);
- corporal punishment;
- incitement to aggression;
- child labour and economic exploitation, including trafficking and the sale of young players and athletes in several sports;
- the sexual integrity of the child (sexual harassment,[34] abuse and violence being prohibited under Article 19 of the convention);
- transactions and transfers of athletes amounting to economic exploitation of their talents (see Articles 32 and 35 on protection from slavery and trafficking);
- neglect of the right to education (as guaranteed under Article 28 of the convention) because of intensive training schedules.

The Council of Europe made the general point that sports federations and authorities should be more alert to such abuses, ensuring that children's rights were respected in sport. It urged that full and proper investigations should be carried out into all allegations of mistreatment, exercise of undue influence, or violence against children, young people and women in sport. It also drew attention to the need for preventive and protective measures such as independent monitoring of sports centres and institutions (p. 36) and for provision of support systems and follow-up for those reporting abuse, and called for consideration to be given to the possibility of drafting a specific European convention on the protection of children and young people in sport (p. 36).

Further recommendations concerned information and education, proposing, for example, that programmes be developed to teach adults (notably parents and trainers) to recognise behaviour indicating that children or young people might be suffering negligence, abuse or violence. A system of information

---

34. The seminar worked with the definition of sexual harassment given by the Netherlands Olympic Committee and Confederation of Sport: "Sexual harassment is any form of sexual behaviour or suggestion in verbal, non-verbal or physical form, whether intended or not, which is regarded by the person experiencing it as undesired or forced."

networking was also proposed in order to keep track of people with a record of violence, and particularly sexual abuse, who worked in sport and might have moved from one country to another (*The Council of Europe and Sport*, 2001, p. 37).

From another perspective, a further reason for exploring such issues and proposing general measures at European level is to achieve a situation in which young athletes, having received the right type of support, training and upbringing, might themselves achieve an impeccable standard of behaviour, thus helping to underpin sporting ethics, most importantly if they find themselves in the limelight of success. As things stand, more than half those questioned in an opinion poll commissioned in the United Kingdom by the *Sun* newspaper, found sports stars arrogant and spoiled, blaming their behaviour on the fact that they were overpaid (*Libération*, 13 October 2003, p. 27). Recently reported incidents of delinquency and what might be termed abnormal behaviour illustrate clearly how sport and the pressures that it puts on young athletes, combined with the impact of sudden wealth and the power associated with icon status, can lead to a loss of normal values on the part of athletes, who then get out of control, regarding themselves as beyond the reach of the law.

> "These gladiators in football boots – mostly very young, unpolished and naive, having left school at 16 – believe they have a licence to break any prohibition" (*Le Monde*, 12 and 13 October, p. 1).

Examples of such behaviour in the United Kingdom include an incident in which a drunken Newcastle United player was involved in a racist assault, for which he was subsequently fined; the case of two Leeds United players arrested on suspicion of rape; and that of a group of Premier League players convicted of gang raping an under-age girl in a well-known London hotel. There are also more and more cases of high-level athletes behaving aggressively, getting drunk and speeding. Marc Roche, writing in *Le Monde*, attempted to pinpoint why this should be so:

> "Passion, power, money, alcohol, drugs and sex: the perfect recipe for the most serious crisis yet to hit football. The key factor behind this disgrace is the unforeseen impact of money on a sport that has been hijacked by speculators" (*Le Monde*, 12 and 13 October 2003, p. 1, p. 12).

Marketing sporting prowess and managing the trade in athletes and players

Economic disparities between north and south and between east and west have contributed significantly to the emergence of a very real imbalance in the sport market in Europe. The first pre-requisite of the market is a market in sportspeople – in other words, a market in sporting prowess as embodied in individual athletes and players. The latter thus acquire value in their own right and are likely to be the object of takeover bids or financial bargaining between wealthy sports organisations or countries.

These inequalities are a distinctive feature of what is now referred to in some circles as a "planet sport" – an idealised image of a world without cultural or economic borders in which rationally regulated exchanges of persons and techniques are governed, more often than not, by money and in general by the economic clout of the richest and most influential nations, financial groups and clubs.

It is a phenomenon that affects all sports. It is estimated, for example, that between 1990 and 1997 some 1 500 athletes emigrated to the west from the Russian Federation alone. They included footballers (600), ice-hockey players (300) and handball and volleyball players (100), as well as some twenty coaches. Most of the Olympic sports have been affected by the trend. It was an enforced exodus triggered by the collapse of communism and the Russian Federation's opening up to the market economy. The demise of the state-controlled sport system plunged the entire sector into an unprecedented financial mire, forcing players, trainers and managers to submit to the laws of supply and demand. Sports clubs and federations chose to escape from penury by driving people into exile, agreeing to cash in on their best up-and-coming talent. "'Selling' these players has long been the main source of revenue for clubs in the former USSR" (Bourg and Gouguet, 2001, p. 90).

This system whereby the clubs live off their assets has gradually become institutionalised but it has a harsh effect on two counts. It weakens Russian sport by slowly draining its pool of potential champions, which in turn makes it less attractive to investors, while for the Russian athletes who come to offer their services in the west it means a loss of homeland, culture, bearings and roots. In some cases these "mercenaries" are required to change nationality, and indeed there can be a third form of violence involved in their enforced exile if their newly-acquired high profile exposes them to harassment.

The pressures that can be applied in such situations are illustrated by the case of Russian gymnast Dimitri Karbanenko, "a Russian athlete and a French champion" (*Le Monde,* 28 April 1998). In 1996, after his federation had excluded him in authoritarian and arbitrary fashion from the national selections for the Atlanta Games, the gymnast took French nationality – at the time an unprecedented step in his sport. His move marked the start of a trend, with Valery Benky, Sergey Kharkov, Dmitri Nonin and Sergey Pfeifer all leaving for the richer pastures of Germany. Karbanenko's story ended with a bitter settling of scores as his former coach and club boss Leonid Arkayev, resenting the gymnast's success and doggedly determined to get his own back, exercised a right of veto that allowed him to prevent Karbanenko from representing his new country within a year of naturalisation. At the same time, the language used in the case suddenly took on a humiliating and violent tone that was also tinged with a chilling commercialism as Arkayev spoke of "selling off" Karbanenko like a vulgar piece of merchandise, in disregard of all the rules of the sport (*Le Monde*, ibid.).

While such a market-trader's tone may be unacceptable, we should not be surprised by it for it broadly reflects the atmosphere in which all transfer dealings are conducted and it is employed by both the sports press and newspapers generally. Editors have no compunction about the regular use of implicitly violent headlines that dehumanise players, placing them on the level of commodities or machines, available for purchase at the right price. "Bordeaux splashes out on Brazilian Deivid in order to forget Pauleta" (*Sud-Ouest Dimanche*, 20 July 2003, p. 6), is just one recent example.

Documentary records of footballers' careers following transfer illustrate the alarming degree of abstraction that characterises such deals, even when the players at the centre of the haggling are very well paid. For the inherent violence here springs not from the fact that indecently large sums of money are changing hands but from the way in which human beings are treated as commodities. The Franco-German television channel Arte recently screened a behind-the-scenes documentary about OM.[35] Shot in fly-on-the-wall style, it revealed how transfer deals are commonly conducted. "The club wants to get rid of Bakayoko, the centre-forward who hasn't had a touch of the ball recently but still picks up his €130000 a month. He only wants to go to Arsenal, Real Madrid or Barcelona," club President Christophe Bouchet explains in a weary tone to a stupefied Piola (his managing director), who was reportedly trying to "offload" the player to a "second-rate Belgian side" (*Libération*, 3 May 2004, p. 34).

Still more worrying is the fact that the transfer business has gradually changed from a long-standing makeshift set-up to an organised but commercially deregulated system of selling players that treats players even more as objects to be haggled over. The rules governing transfers are nowadays framed by, and change in response to, the law of the market. European harmonisation in football – to take just one sport – is not concerned with players' social security status, with training or with bringing on young talent, but rather (and unsurprisingly) with the alignment of markets in the name of "healthy competition". Indeed, in France, the only real basis for the supposedly ideological justification of a winter "mercato" (the football transfer market) is an economic one. In 1998 the director of the French Union of Professional Football Clubs (UCPF), Philippe Diallo, convincingly summed up

---

35. *Allez OM*, a five-part documentary by Vassili Silovic, shown on Arte in France from 3 May 2004.

the reasoning behind what was an inevitable development: "Spain and Italy have a winter market, so for the sake of harmonisation France ought to get in step" (*Libération*, 26 and 27 December 1998, p. 16). Apart from reflecting the dominance of economic considerations, this line of thinking gives serious cause for concern inasmuch as it implicitly denies players any say in their circumstances, their future or the future of their sport – which seems destined, despite the efforts of UEFA, to become merely another form of business with players as the stock in trade (*Libération*, ibid.).

At the same time as Europe's clubs have been shifting their focus in line with the all-powerful market, the strategy of giving athletes new nationalities has proved to be another means of monopolising human potential in sport without according to the players concerned, or to their disciplines, the humane, supportive and ethical approach that ought to be fundamental in competitive sport. Thus when Turkey was prepared to "put €10 million on the table" (*Libération*, 15 and 16 November 2003, p. 30) for the naturalisation of Iranian Hossein Rezazadeh, it was not for reasons of support or co-operation, nor even a political response to oppression, but simply a way of boosting its successful weightlifting team's chances against Greece in the 2004 Olympic Games. Of course, other European nations are just as ready to haggle shamelessly for new blood in a whole range of sports: football, that great converter of nationalities, naturally tops the list, but the same thing happens in athletics, cycling, gymnastics and ice skating.

Every day, the gulf between the sporting nations and the nations that supply the athletes grows wider, as the power of money becomes more and more obvious. So marked has this exodus of sporting talent become that it was actually debated in the context of the World Athletics Championships in France in summer 2003 because 85% of the medals won went to the five richest countries on the planet (Dasque, 2003, p. 18). This domination has another obvious effect: because the winning countries are the wealthiest, they are capable of drawing in athletes from poor countries. At the same time and to a greater extent than other countries, they have the financial capacity to achieve their aims by unfair means. This was illustrated recently in the French football world when false passports were used in an attempt to get round the rules on the number of non-EU players allowed in championship squads (Genevois, 2002, p. 10).

In addition, familiar patterns are reinforced as sporting muscle and talent is displaced from east to west and from south to north – although the supply lines are complicated by the fact that the European club scene perpetuates certain specific inequalities of its own. In football, for example, globalisation has produced a very clear trade pattern: France gets its supply of new players largely from North Africa and trains them for the United Kingdom, Italy and Spain. Players from eastern Europe, on the other hand, are chiefly to be found in German and Austrian clubs (Lanfranchi, 2002).

This flow of players and techniques has consequences for the European nations involved, however, inasmuch as the footballers, when they return to play for their national sides, bring them the benefit of their experience abroad. France's defeat in the 2002 World Cup by a Senegalese team, of which almost all the members had spent time in French clubs may well represent an unexpected side-effect of the way in which European teams have hijacked African soccer: a case of "what goes around comes around".

Other trends that are seriously disappointing from a European point of view include the drying up of funds for professional cycling in Spain, forcing Spanish racing cyclists to look elsewhere for their living. "Spanish racing cyclists are the latest group to have to emigrate, as dozens of them face unemployment" (Libération, 8 September 2003, p. 26). A trend less in the public eye is the emigration of athletes in response to the profile that particular sports enjoy. Top-class French women handball players thus tend to move to Denmark, attracted by the promise of a high-level professional championship affording them recognition and reward – and the trend has had repercussions on the French national handball training system (Le Monde, 2 December 2003).

Some European nations – victims of their own success in training – now also find themselves preyed upon by bigger fish, one example being the mass descent of American scouts on INSEP [the French National Institute for Sport and Physical Education] in search of new basketball talent. (The angry reactions this has provoked (Le Monde, 15 April 2004) may seem somewhat puzzling, given that France applies the self-same policy in relation to other sports.) Young basketball players aged 15-18 are thus offered a golden future in the United States, and the success of the recruitment scheme has been enhanced by the "Tony Parker effect" since French-trained Parker shot to stardom in the National Basketball Association (NBA). Despite the existence of clearly worked out schemes for reconciling training and study, the young people recruited tend to prioritise success in what is a mass-audience sport: "At school they no longer want to work ... all they think about is making it in basketball as quickly as possible" (Le Monde, ibid.).

Ultimately those who suffer most from this trade are young players and athletes, including children, for they are being recruited at an ever lower age by unscrupulous agents who have no hesitation about leaving them to their fate, out of work and untrained, should the experiment fail to pay off.

The problem of monitoring and training players is certainly a major one in terms of the future of European sport, and the way in which it is resolved is likely to determine the direction in which sport moves: towards greater solidarity or towards a free market with no holds barred. The market in players and athletes has no answers to the legitimate requirements of the individuals concerned in terms of supervision, support, training, education and well-being. The disparities created by money in Europe are such that the professional football circuit is seriously considering delegating the training of its players to lower-ranked clubs or simply outsourcing it to southern countries, thus creating at yet another level a two-track system in European sport (Gouguet and Primault, 2003).

The Council of Europe addressed some of these aspects when it considered the various forms of abuse affecting children and young people in sport, notably in relation to "transactions and transfers of athletes" (*The Council of Europe and sport,* 2001, p. 36). Its programme of proposed measures included efforts to combat the exploitation of children and young people in sport, and to counter the exclusion of young people who failed to measure up to market requirements and the sort of psychological pressures that drove young people to extremes (including excessive training, use of drugs and sudden abandonment of their sport) (ibid.).

With regard to the problem of players given new nationalities, and with a view to regulating a thriving trade, whose first victims are young expatriated sportspeople and the countries robbed of their talents, one of the Council of Europe's proposals is the introduction of a minimum line-up of national players in club teams to guard against the "muscle drain" and support for national training centres (Council of Europe, 15th informal meeting of European Ministers responsible for Sport, CDDS (98) 90 Vol.1, p. 178).

A logical next step might be to impose a similar constraint on those with financial holdings in sport.

The dehumanisation of sport

In economic terms the profitability of competitive sport as an area for investment depends, to put it simply, on the winning of matches or events, as it is victory that ensures visibility in the marketplace. Once financial interests come to dominate, it makes business sense to increase return on investment by reducing the very uncertainty of outcome that is the lifeblood of sport.

The logical next step in the business-based approach is a process of driving athletes beyond their natural capabilities. The most obvious consequence of this today is the increased incidence of both over-training and doping, although there are also other related areas in which the side-effects of the commercialisation of sport manifest themselves more subtly, reflecting indirectly the "economically generated" violence that occurs in the sport world.

The first point to be made is that the steep rise in doping-related incidents has paralleled the relatively recent development of the drive for profit in sport. Among the various distortions resulting from this colonisation of sport – and of athletes' bodies – by business has been the emergence of a rationale for cheating, including a tit-for-tat extension of doping, justified by the need to "level the playing field". The most recent development in this regard has been a keen interest in the very latest research techniques.

Moreover, the organised way in which rules and sports ethics are breached has naturally generated its own forms of control and its own processes of innovation, which constitute new sources of coercion for athletes.

On the one hand, because both the competitive environment and the taboo nature of the subject have encouraged a "law of silence", those who speak out – whether former cheats who have repented, people concerned to stop cheating becoming the norm or simply sports purists – have had to face bullying, revenge attacks and harassment. On the other hand, because of the ongoing need to keep one step ahead of the opposition (who are seen as potential cheats), those who use and supply doping products have a constant interest in innovation, which nowadays can mean going beyond the familiar and relatively controlled territory of administering illegal substances, to experiment with biotechnology and gene therapy. The forms of addiction that have resulted directly from the spread of this new and dangerous rivalry in sport are a tragic illustration of the fact that dependency on a system dominated by its economic aspects comes at a price: the physical and psychological dependency that drives addicted athletes into a downward spiral which can end in death. The sad fate of Italian cyclist Marco Pantani who, according to the coroner's verdict, suffered accidental death as a result of an overdose of cocaine, tragically highlights just how real this form of violence is. The pitiful decline of soccer star Diego Maradonna only reinforces the point.

It is generally acknowledged now that a law of silence has largely shrouded the practice of doping in sports like cycling in Europe, but less attention has been given to the consequences of breaking this *"omertà"*. There is now a certain amount of evidence available, including the testimony of numerous European athletes, trainers and management personnel, which allows us to gauge the extent of the violence that has been covered up.[36] As a direct result

---

36. Good examples are the accounts given by racing cyclists such as Erwan Menthéour and Christophe Bassons, physiotherapists such as Willy Voet and sports managers such as Bruno Roussel (of the Festina team).

of contesting the systematic cheating imposed in pursuit of profit, whistleblowers have suffered forms of violence ranging from accusations of treachery, through harassment and shunning by former team mates and rivals to non-renewal of contracts, cool treatment by the sports press and, more generally, a cruel sense that their "coming out" has been misunderstood by the public (Raspiengeas, 2001; Bassons, 2000; and Roussel, 2001). The last of these effects has been experienced not just by people who have blown the whistle on doping but also by those who, for different reasons, have decided to unmask other abuses in sport. The case of French footballer Jacques Glassmann in the OM-Valenciennes bribery scandal of the early 1990s shows how a sportsman can be the victim of his own honesty, suffering different types of violence, not least a refusal of understanding or support on the part of a public anxious to minimise the impact of corruption (a symbolic form of violence) in order to sustain an unblemished ideal of sport (Bureau, 2002, p. 113).

At another level, the violent metabolic changes that athletes experience (and no one can yet measure just how serious they are) are a further reason for questioning the new resources available to those engaged in sporting and commercial competition, and the very real part they play in turning human beings into commodities. Already liable to be bought and sold unscrupulously, athletes are placed under additional pressure by a system that requires them to hand themselves over to it in a quite alarming way (with outcomes including uncontrolled experimentation, illness and premature death) and furthers a gradual dehumanisation of sport and athletes.

Genetically modified or cyber-athletes may still be projects on the drawing-board, but already, in the confines of laboratories, researchers are developing new forms of doping and artificial means of enhancing athletes' capabilities in order to stretch the generally accepted limits of the human body in sport.

A French specialist in the field, Doctor De Mondenard, talked recently on radio ("Là-bas si j'y suis", directed by Daniel Mermet, France Inter, 15 April 2004) about the latest strategies being developed to get round the rules of sport through the administration of banned substances.

Because the commercial stakes in sport have become so high, there is currently particular pressure to develop new methods of doping, which means that the substances used tend to be abandoned one by one as soon as the authorities find ways of detecting them. As a result, innovators in the field are looking to the still virgin territory of gene therapy. The idea is no longer to administer doping products (such as EPO or growth hormones), but rather to practise genetic engineering on athletes so that their own bodies will develop the capacity to secrete such substances in abundance. "The risk that we will one day see genetically modified athletes is taken very seriously, even though the techniques involved are still in their infancy" (*La Lettre de l'économie du sport*, 678, 2003).

Dehumanisation and a post-human era in sport are no longer merely the stuff of nightmares but scenarios that could well be realised in European sport in the future.

Sponsorship, and athletes as human billboards

As athletes become subject to the laws of the market they can also become vehement proponents of commercialism for they stand to gain in this exchange of services. The prominence enjoyed by rising stars of sport makes them the favoured target of companies competing for a high profile, and this places a new type of pressure on the athletes concerned. The constraints of commercialism come on top of the traditional pressures associated with stress in sport and, for athletes in competition, generate a state of tension in which they can easily lose their bearings. The obsessive placement and management of commercial logos – satirised in a television programme by Canal Plus based on the case of French athlete Marie-José Perec – is just one example of the new commercial pressure for visibility which is helping to transform sport, sportspeople and indeed the very spirit and values underpinning competition. Although other factors may also have been involved, Perec's flight from the Olympic Games in Sydney in 2000 and her subsequent exile are a clear case of an athlete being subjected to additional pressures as a consequence of sponsorship and the drive to obtain results not merely for the sake of a symbolic victory but in order to make commercial gain – with all the violence that implies.

At the same time as athletes are being turned into publicity tools, the very structure of European sport is undergoing a surprising and alarming change as it becomes increasingly concerned with branding. In athletics, for example, as recently as the early 1990s there was a limited number of big tournaments, the Olympic Games and the European and World Championships being the main ones. Then sponsors, agents and television channels began pooling their resources to stage their own tournaments, bringing together the finest athletes of the day. As the number of brand-name events increased, interest in the official competitions began to wane. The sports federations were weakened and star athletes were encouraged to stay away from certain international events in order to take part in the new, highly paid events in which they wore the colours not of their country but of their sponsors. One commentator noted that "the concept of the nation is gradually taking second place to that of the brand" and – a clear sign of the times – "in a new form of product promotion, the media are carrying a sponsors' Olympic medal table" (Bourg, 1994, p. 184).

The pressures induced by this new type of coercion have a knock-on effect right through to sports news, where they significantly compromise freedom of expression. The practices of controlling interview content, selecting particular channels and publications, and insisting on exclusive rights to footage constitute the new standards of communication with the media in the sport world, their purpose being to ensure that the messages which athletes deliver are associated with the sponsor's brand. There is of course an inherent risk that freedom of information will be manipulated, and there is no effective counterweight to this.

In fact, journalists who are normally swift to denounce censorship when they encounter it elsewhere in the course of their work, and notably in much more dangerous situations, are ready to bow uncomplainingly to the dictates of commercialism when athletes who have accepted their propaganda role insist on being filmed in front of advertising logos.

The logic of sponsorship, which has colonised European sport in a particularly brutal way over the last decade, is based precisely on this concept of visibility, with athletes as the advertising vehicle of choice in an almost carnal sense. The focus of criticism here must be the currently overriding principle of wealth creation, inasmuch as it tends to turn athletes and players into sales agents – a process that surely cannot be allowed to go unchallenged.

The violence inherent in the new commercialism is not so much that which results in athletes and players being paid indecently high salaries (though that too merits criticism) as that which requires everyone involved in sport (athletes, managers and spectators) to have a commercial profile.

The "athlete-as-sporting-product" has thus become a disturbing reality, evident in many ambivalent developments on the interface between mass-entertainment sports events and advertising. One such case was that of boxer Christophe Tiozzo, who was launched by Canal Plus in a flurry of publicity, managed by an entertainment professional and prepared for his fights in luxury hotels. This marketing strategy, encouraged by Tiozzo's initial successes in contests with inferior or past-their-peak adversaries, represented an attempt by Canal Plus to give boxing a modern image and sell it to a target audience, namely the channel's own subscribers.

A similar venture involved another boxer, Brahim Asloum, gold medallist at the Olympic Games in Sydney, whose high-profile television launch was orchestrated by the Réservoir independent production group under society television magnate Jean-Luc Delarue (Bénabent, 2001, p. 54). It was reported that after the boxer, under Delarue's tutelage, had negotiated the sale of exclusive rights to footage of his fights with Canal Plus, he made the "friendly" (i.e. unremunerated) gesture of agreeing to wear the logo of Réservoir group subsidiary Réservoir Sport on his shorts (Bénabent, op. cit.).

Similar considerations of image and marketing have recently affected a quintessentially British event, namely the annual Oxford and Cambridge Boat Race on the Thames, a national institution well over 100 years old. At the time of writing, the oarsmen were due to abandon their commercially neutral college stripes in order to give prominence to the logos of the event sponsors, coverage of the event having been taken over (from the BBC) by commercial station ITV, which intended to make full use of the teams in pursuit of its commercial aims (*Le Monde*, 1 March 2004).

As for "les Bleus" – the victorious French World Cup squad of 1998 – the once "perfect heroes" have been accused of shattering their own image and turning themselves into "over-exposed human billboards advertising French brands" (Bancel and Blanchard, 2003, p. 56).

Sports scandals in Europe

Mafia-type interests at work

Among the forms of violence that have accompanied the transformation of sport along free-market lines, the pressure of money and all the discrimination that goes with it are not the most alarming. That distinction goes to the intrusion into sport of mafia interests and the impact they have had on competitive events ever since commercialism came to pervade the European sport world.

In terms of the manifestations of organised crime in sport, some areas of Europe seem to be worse affected than others. Recent scandals have shown, however, that influence peddling, corruption and money laundering through sport are not confined, for example, to east European countries: they can raise their ugly heads anywhere in the continent, in any sport and at any level of competition.

One illustration was the scandal which hit the world of French ice skating at the 2002 Olympic Games in Salt Lake City as the French Olympic ice-dancing champions, the President of the French Ice Sports Federation (FFSG), Didier Gailhaguet, and French international judge Marie-Reine Le Gougne all found themselves implicated in different ways in a shabby deal "designed to ensure that Russian figure-skating pair Elena Berezhnaya and Anton Sikharulidze won a gold medal in exchange for the victory of the French ice-dancing team of Marina Anissina and Gwendal Peizerat (*Le Monde*, 7 March 2003, p. 23). It turned out that this amicable little arrangement had been more or less orchestrated by a notorious Russian mafia figure, Alimzhan Tokhtakhounov (*Libération*, 6 August 2002; *Le Monde*, 3 and 7 August 2002 and 7 March 2003), who, on his arrest in Italy on 31 July 2003 (*Libération*, 6 August 2002), was presented as the head of the criminal Mazutkinskaya organisation (*Le Monde*, 3 August 2002).

Even more alarmingly, Tokhtakhounov appeared to have constructed an entire web of contacts in the sport world, including such well-known athletes as the Russian tennis star Yevgeny Kafelnikov, who referred to him as a "good friend" (*Le Monde*, 2 August 2003). The links developed by Tokhtakhounov and his friends, all well-known mafia figures, also extended into the realm of football financing in Italy, the south of France and Monaco (*Le Monde*, 20 December 2002, 18 January 2003 and 19 February 2004).

A further cause for concern is the fact that certain areas of continental Europe seem more particularly affected than others by mafia activity.

In the Russian Federation, where – because of the country's political history and its unregulated conversion to the market economy – organised crime has found particularly fertile terrain, there is clear potential for infiltration of sports bodies by the mafia. Jean-François Bourg and Jean-Jacques Gouguet, quoting western experts' reports on the Russian economy, have estimated that 70-80% of private-sector companies in the country are under mafia control (Bourg and Gouguet, 2001).

That being so, sport – as a highly profitable sector – could scarcely hope to escape repeated exploitation, and there has already been considerable evidence in the sporting world of criminal organisations at work: a number of sports bosses have been murdered, athletes have been abducted and referees have been bribed.

The laundering of money derived from different types of trafficking and racketeering is another significant activity that has led mafia organisations to invest in sports clubs. The mafias have also worked at infiltrating sports federations in order to derive tax advantages (such as exemption from import duty on alcohol and tobacco). In theory the purpose of the tax breaks is to give sports organisations an alternative source of income to make up for a lack of support from the public purse. Siphoning off this supposed "subsidy" can be highly lucrative: in 1995, for example, the Russian ice-hockey federation realised profits equivalent to some €20 million from such sales. Mafia organisations have also invested in the production of doping products, setting up a veritable parallel economy, which received an additional boost when state-controlled drug supplies dried up while the demand for illegal substances for athletes competing at international level continued unabated. Among those employed in the illegal production chains are highly paid chemists.

All these abuses raise questions about the true nature of the criminal system that is spreading through sport like cancer. In fact, far from being content to function as a "service provider", the mafia has organised its operations on a solid market basis. In a situation now characterised by uncertainty – replacing the former determinism of state control in sport – the Russian sporting world may still be working towards a new organisational model (Bourg and Gouguet, 2001, p. 91), but the danger remains that mafia infiltration of sports bodies will increase through a "copy-cat" effect, placing European sport on a highly problematic course as the constraints of free-market commercialism are overtaken by murkier pressures from mafia quarters.

Corruption as a form of regulation

Paradoxically, the glorious uncertainties of sport now constitute a barrier to the efficient and profitable communications policies of the financial players who have chosen to invest in the sector in different ways (by forming sports companies, engaging in patronage or sponsorship or buying shares). This has produced a situation in which financial pressures accumulating from the pursuit of revenue, profitability and return on investment have led to the use of new methods that make success more calculable.

One such is the bribery of both players and referees in order to manipulate results and to secure by illegal means a desired outcome in what ought to be a fair contest between clubs. The victims of the swindle in such cases are the spectators and sports lovers, and money is once again at the centre of a vicious circle of corruption.

In France a number of high-profile cases have come to epitomise the damaging practice of match-fixing in soccer, chief among them the OM-Valenciennes affair and the scandal at Bordeaux under the presidency of Claude Bez.

In the case of the Marseilles club, it is clear with hindsight that in the run-up to the Champions' League final, the financial and media stakes were considered too high for the outcome of even an "easy" match to be left solely to the talents of the players. With their eyes on the prize of securing the French championship at the cost of minimal effort, allowing the team to prepare serenely for the Champions' League final against AC Milan in Berlin five days later, as well as the financial gain that would flow from a double success, the club directors resorted to bribery to eliminate any risk of things going wrong. Yet the strength of sport lies precisely in the uncertainty of outcomes, and it seems this principle was understood by Valenciennes player Jacques Glassmann, who blew the whistle on the affair after having been approached by the OM bosses (Bureau, 2002).

Similar practices had gone on at Bordeaux FC in the 1980s, when Claude Bez was president of the club. Under questioning, Claude Bez admitted operating a system whereby illicit payments might not have been enough to secure a win but they meant a defeat was not a foregone conclusion (Fontanel and Bensahel, 2001).

In fact, there have been similar incidents in different European countries, particularly in sports such as football that attract large television audiences. A very recent case occurred in April 2004, when Portuguese police made sixteen arrests in an investigation into influence-peddling among referees. Those implicated included league President Valentin Loureiro and the President of the Portuguese National Refereeing Council, Jose Antonio Pinto de Sousa. The lengthy inquiry was instigated after suspicions of match fixing had been voiced (*L'Equipe*, 21 April 2004).

Similar bad faith surely informed AS Roma's purchase of Christmas gifts (listed by the *Gazetta dello Sport* in January 2000) for refereeing officials. The two representatives of the football federation in charge of selecting referees each received a gold watch worth €13,000 francs; thirty-six referees each got a silver watch and watches were also given to linesmen (*Libération*, 10 January 2000).

The inevitable effect of corruption – which is more or less tolerated depending on the level at which deals are struck – is to destroy the principles of the game by doing away with supposedly fair rules of competition. Not only that, but it serves to replicate in sport the ever-present inequalities between those who possess the means to corrupt and the less fortunate who have their price. When a match is fixed, however, the greatest loss is always to sporting ethics – and it should be emphasised that football is not the only sport afflicted in this way.

It has to be recognised that the phenomenon affects all team sports, including those such as volleyball and handball that get less television airtime. For example, in both these sports professional clubs that compete internationally make compensatory payments to east European rivals in return for their waiving the right to a home match in two-leg fixtures – thus distorting the normal competitive process (Fontanel and Bensahel, 2001).

This sanctioned corruption runs counter to the most basic principles of sport and constitutes a complete modification of the rules. The strongest team in sporting terms will not necessarily win. The winner will be the club that manages to apply the most resources (financial resources and contacts) in pursuit of the result it expects.

The logic of regulating sport by means of purchasing power does not stop with bribery, however: it can be seen at work in a whole battery of financial fiddles and schemes for getting round the law. One notable example was the case of the footballers supplied with false French passports in 2001, an affair which, apart from its aspect of human exploitation, did little for the reputations of the clubs implicated (Saint-Etienne, Monaco, Metz and Nice). The deception – exposed by Toulouse FC, which called for the guilty teams to be dropped from the First Division – involved Brazilian, Ukrainian, Chilean and Argentinian players using false passports so that the clubs concerned could get round the quota rule limiting the number of non-EU players on a squad to three (*Le Monde,* 14 April 2001; and De Silva, 2002).

The interface between business and terrorism

The economic violence infecting sport in Europe has found a fertile breeding ground in terrorism. In some cases the link has been direct, with political demands attached to specific terrorist activities in a sports context, such as the ETA attacks in Madrid in 2002 before a match between Barcelona and Real Madrid (*Le Monde,* 3 May 2002). Much more commonly, however, mafia-type schemes play a part in the effort to fill terrorist groups' coffers.

A striking example of this type of collusion made headlines in France recently, with a case involving Charles Pieri, suspected leader of a Corsican separatist group. The interesting aspect of the case – still under investigation at the time of writing – was the way it highlighted the variety of abusive practices and insidious forms of violence that stem more or less directly from the application of commercial logic to sport.

Extortion "in connection with a terrorist enterprise" was practised against travel company Nouvelles Frontières, described by its own managing director as the "chosen sponsor" of the soccer club Sporting Club de Bastia (*Le Monde,* 6 February 2004), illustrating how – thanks to the cash flows generated by sport (in sponsorship and the sale and purchase of players) and particularly to the murky nature of such financial transactions – racketeering, political militancy and terrorism can become bedfellows.

Sporting Club, revealed in the course of the investigation to have been "strictly under the thumb of Pieri and his entourage since the early 1990s" (*Libération,* 16 April 2004, p. 15), was in fact functioning as a front, with cash being generated from "compulsory" sponsoring and excess commission charged on the sale of players. Press reports of the investigation revealed that money being charged in the name of hard-up football clubs was actually being siphoned off in the direction of Corsican separatists, and highlighted the extent of the losses entailed (*Le Monde,* 30 January, 6 February, and 17 April 2004; *Libération,* 16 April 2004).

Sport, money and terrorism were linked again, albeit at a different level, given the sums of money involved and the risk entailed, just as the world was preparing to turn its eyes on Athens for the 2004 Olympic Games. Such were the commercial stakes in the Games that the IOC decided to take out a new form of insurance. "The sudden terrorist threat after 11 September created a shockwave, and the change of thinking became inevitable after the attacks in Madrid" (*L'Equipe*, 21 April 2004).

Yielding indirectly to the terrorist threat, the IOC deemed it necessary to take precautions against the risk that the summer Games would be cancelled, and insured the event for €200 million – the first time in the history of the Games that such a step had been taken (*L'Equipe*, ibid.).

The circumstances of the decision illustrate, albeit indirectly, how the intricacies of politics and business can create a context for violence at two levels: the deadly terrorist violence expressed in the ambient threat of attacks during the Athens Games, and then the economic violence implicit in the fact that the desire to protect the Greek edition of the Games stemmed less from humanitarian considerations (although cancellation of the Games might have been interpreted in that light) than from an obvious concern for what was at stake commercially. The reality is that the organisers and the heads of the IOC are obliged to protect the financial investments of the event sponsors, for staging the Games without sponsors has become inconceivable. Surely the real violence that has been done to sport – preceding the unacceptable threat to human lives from a small number of terrorist groups – lies in this new form of blackmail and in the predominant ideology, now largely taken for granted by a majority of people, whereby commercial interests come first. This new form of terrorism (an economic terrorism measured in terms of investors' confidence or fears) had the capacity, for the first time in the modern Olympic era, to cause the Games simply to be cancelled. The only other possible explanation is that the United States, which triggered the loss of confidence by suggesting that its athletes might not go to Greece, saw the threats as a convenient cover for avoiding what are increasingly stringent anti-doping controls, and exploited terrorism and the fear of terrorism to avoid losing face.

Of course, attempted terrorist blackmail in connection with the Olympic Games is not new and nor has such blackmail been confined to the Olympics, as witness the threats that hung over the French team at the World Cup in Japan (*Le Monde*, 23 May 2002). Until recently such cases of attempted blackmail were based essentially on political demands, as in the case of the Black September attack in Munich in 1972. Today, however, it is gradually becoming clearer that they can also have a commercial dimension. When Sweden was bidding to host the 2004 Olympics, for example, its candidature was effectively scuppered by the threat of bomb attacks, sustained for several weeks by a group calling itself 'We Who Built Sweden'. The terrorist group was demanding that Sweden pull out of the contest to host the Games because of their exorbitant cost and the resultant threat to the national economy (*Libération*, 1 September 1997). In what was certainly a rare moment in the history of sport, commercialism was defeated by a force just as blameworthy as itself, namely a readiness to resort to indiscriminate violence.

Sport and business: a voyage through troubled waters

Business is business. While the current system of financing sport is a fact of life, it does not mean we should be any slower to criticise it if it falls prey to organisations or machinations that affect it in the same way as certain big companies are affected when their dealings cross the line into illegality.

Sport and money are now wedded together, for better or worse – and certain significant events in Europe in recent years indicate that we probably still have a long way to go before we see the worst.

The colonisation of sport by commercialism, in the form of sports financing and the malpractices that go with it, has done damage (on a scale we cannot yet properly appreciate) as we have watched, in scandal after scandal, the break-up of groups that simply treated sport as another sector of business activity and often, too, as a corporate showcase or badge of honour for company directors.

The already tarnished image of innocence has been slowly and insidiously blackened as abuses have accumulated and more and more scandals have come to light in which sport has been indirectly implicated as an economic pawn of sprawling commercial empires.

Take the example of AC Parma, which shot to the higher echelons of Italian soccer during the 1990s and was helped in its ascension by substantial financial backing from the Parmalat food group (*L'Express*, 8 January 2004). The scandal that broke in Italy after the group went bankrupt threatened, at the time of writing, to be severely damaging not only for Parma, but also for a number of clubs in other countries which depended to a greater or lesser extent on manna from the hand of the foodstuffs giant: Moscow Dynamo, Boca Juniros and Palmeiras São Paulo being just a few of them. The main lesson of the case has been that football and indeed sport generally, having become tradeable commodities and sectors for investment, are no longer protected from the shockwaves of financial scandals in the business world. Stefano Tanzi – son of Calisto Tanzi, who was imprisoned on 27 December 2003 for embezzlement and fraudulent bankruptcy in what the press was quick to dub a "European Enron" – quit his post as President of Parmalat on

9 January 2004. The financial backlash from the affair will have a severe impact on AC Parma and the eight other soccer clubs affected. Equally damaging, however, is the way in which the affair has cast Italian football in a shabby light, suddenly portraying it as a business in the clutches of some fairly unscrupulous people.

In France, the Fondo affair (although less money was involved) provided a further sad example of sport being exploited in a fraudulent financial scheme. The problems began when Ahmed Chaker, an unusual individual and a swindler on a relatively modest scale, used his network of contacts to help set up a financial co-operative under Italian law, naming the enterprise "Fondo". Over a number of years Fondo amassed funds in France, not only from small-scale shareholders but also from larger investors, including optician Alain Afflelou, at the time President of Girondins de Bordeaux FC, who was introduced to Chaker by the Bordeaux coach, Roland Courbis (*Le Monde*, 27 November 2003).

A long list of investors entrusted their money to Chaker, attracted by the promise of high interest rates and Fondo's potential as a tax evasion device. All of them were to watch their cash disappear into the fraudster's personal deals and investments – notable among them the purchase of Brest FC (*Le Monde*, 21 November 2003). The most extraordinary aspect of the affair was Chaker's ability to sustain his financial juggling act, riding a general wave of enthusiasm for soccer and using his status as generous sponsor of the Brest club to court new investors (*Libération*, 24 November 2003), whose money was immediately siphoned off.

Total deposits with Fondo were finally reported at €18.3 million, the lion's share of which went straight into the pocket of Ahmed Chaker via an offshore company. Brest FC, which had been instrumental in his success, subsequently found itself in deep financial difficulty, with its reputation sullied by the affair.

A scandal of a different type – though not dissimilar inasmuch as it centred on international financial circles and their capacity to corrupt sport – found echoes in Athens as the city prepared to host the 2004 Olympic Games. It was pointed out in the press that the Greek capital is home to a "clan" of shipping magnates, a collection of powerful families whose circle of associates includes the former proprietors of the *Prestige*, the dilapidated tanker responsible for polluting the French and Spanish coasts after it spilled its cargo of oil; and that the same families are among the financial backers of soccer club Panathinaikos (*Le Monde*, 22 November 2003). The club – associated with its backers via their investment and the importance they attach to a publicly visible and honourable link with sport – inevitably suffers a loss of esteem if it has benefited from investment that would have been better spent on maintaining oil tankers operating in European waters.

There is no doubt that European soccer is an attractive target for investors, but the sport's dependence on these flows of funds makes it increasingly vulnerable to the whims and nervousness of the financial world (the story, cited above, of Matra Racing and Jean-Luc Lagardère being a case in point). Because European football is on an economic roll, huge fortunes have been poured into it, some of them originating in relatively distant countries such as the Russian Federation and the United Arab Emirates.

The case of the Russian oligarchs is particularly interesting. It shows how sport can function as a judicious investment option (in political, cultural and economic terms) and how the foreign clubs that benefit from such investment can be financially buoyed up by the injection of new capital from eastern Europe.

One such investor is Roman Abramovich (aged 37 at the time of writing), listed as the richest man in the United Kingdom, where he has registered a holding company, Milhouse Capital, with its headquarters in Piccadilly. The businessman controls more than 150 000 jobs in the Russian Federation (where his fortune is the second largest in the country), notably in the oil industry as one of the main shareholders in Sibneft, the fifth-ranked Russian oil company.

Abramovich recently began shedding many of his Russian holdings and was reported to have left the country to set up home in the United Kingdom (*Le Monde*, 8 April 2004). The former close associate of the Yeltsin family also let it be known that he would not be seeking a second term of office as governor of the Tchoukotka region, a post he held at the time of writing (*Le Monde*, 5 February 2004). The Moscow twice-weekly newspaper *Novaya Gazeta* reported that, rather than spend his money on electioneering, he had chosen to buy Chelsea FC and to head west (*Courrier international*, 664, 24-30 July 2003, p. 26). Indeed, as demonstrated by the Yukos case and the imprisonment of billionaire Mikhail Khordovsky for tax evasion (*Le Monde*, 28 October and 21 November 2003), the current political climate in the Russian Federation is none too comfortable for the oligarchs, who have been the focus of attacks from a newly dominant group around President Vladimir Putin comprising generals of the Federal Security Service (FSB), the domestic secret service which Putin headed in 1998 and 1999 (*Le Monde*, 28 October 2003).

It would appear that London has become a "haven for Russian oligarchs" since Abramovich set a trend with his takeover of Chelsea in July 2003 (*Le Monde*, 31 October 2003).

His purchase of a majority shareholding in the British club for US$240 million made waves both in the United Kingdom and throughout the European football world (*Le Monde,* business supplement, 9 March 2004). It was a move that also drew heavy criticism from the director of the Russian Auditor General's office, Sergey Stepashin, who expressed surprise that a Russian businessman should spend so much money [Stepashin valued the takeover at US$300 million] to buy a football club in England. He announced that the Auditor General's office was to carry out an audit on Abramovich's oil company and would also look into the administration of the region of which he was governor (*Le Monde,* 5 February 2004).

Asked why Abramovich should suddenly have been moved to invest in British football, his former mentor, Boris Berezovsky (another Russian billionaire exiled in London, where he has property investments), interpreted the deal in a political light: "I think that when he bought Chelsea he knew what was going to happen to Khordovsky. Now, if his interests are threatened, Roman can defend himself by accusing the Kremlin of trying to get its hands on his club" (*Le Monde,* 31 October 2003).

Relations between Abramovich and Putin would not appear to have reached breaking point, however. Indeed, some political observers see the businessman as an astute advisor to the president. Abramovich certainly has Putin's ear and, tellingly, found himself in a position of strength when the Yukos and Sibneft groups were merged (he has a 26.1% holding in the newly formed group), his circumstances a contrast to those of former Yukos chief Khordovsky, who was by then languishing in jail (*Le Monde,* 8 November 2003).

Abramovich's new-found enthusiasm for British football has, in all likelihood, little to do with a love of the game. The Moscow newspaper *Moskovskiye Novosti* doubted the sincerity of the businessman's allegedly disinterested passion for sport, given that Abramovich "had no qualms about allowing Spartak Tchoukotka, from his own region, to go to the wall, despite numerous appeals for support" (*Courrier international,* ibid.).

By keeping his distance from the Russian authorities, Abramovich gives himself commercial and political elbow room while benefiting handsomely from his investment in a prestigious club and winning public sympathy within what is a highly popular sport in the United Kingdom – sympathy that he will no doubt turn to account should the need arise.

Chelsea as a club, meanwhile, benefits from the Russian billionaire's investment and has been able to sustain a high level of success and keep its high ranking in European competition. The only real question that the club management and players need to ask is how long Chelsea can remain an attraction for Abramovich and his capital from eastern Europe.

The recent failure of a bid by Russian oil group Nafta Moskva to take over AS Roma – the would-be investors having been deterred by numerous Italian police investigations at the club in connection with the *"calcio* affair" (*Libération,* 1 March 2004, p. 25) – suggests that the wind of investment blowing through Europe from the east and revitalising the soccer economy at a time of mergers may be about to drop, leaving the most popular sport on the planet, and those who earn their living from it, in dire financial straits from which it will be difficult to find a way out.

Media violence and manipulation through sport

The influence of the media in sport today – particularly the importance of television – is manifest. For almost a quarter of a century television stations in Europe have been instrumental in the spiralling commercialisation of sport, players' wage inflation and the rising cost of broadcasting rights for event coverage being the most obvious aspects of the phenomenon – probably because they receive most media coverage!

The distorting effects of the media-driven, free-market-based transformation of sport go much further, however, and the forms of violence and manipulation that result when sport is constrained by the dictates of television are not only commercial in character, although money is ultimately the focus of the exchanges involved.

The exploitation of sport, and of media coverage of sport, for political propaganda purposes is, for example, one avenue that needs to be explored in any consideration of the violence associated with the media's use of sport.

In addition, the free-market transformation of sport that has taken place since the 1980s – as the Olympic movement has embraced the corporate world, and the right to supply television coverage has been commercially marketed – has had a number of pernicious effects. Specifically, there is considerable imbalance in the amount of airtime devoted to different sports, and within the same sports to men's and women's events; commercial law has taken priority over the laws of sport, and disparities have become more marked; public events have been hijacked in order to market new visual technologies; bankruptcy in large companies has left sports teams bankrupt too; and sports federations have gradually seen their power decline as the power of media operators and sport sponsors has increased.

This chapter will therefore consider the whole spectrum of violence and manipulation in sport against the background of its commercialisation through the media in Europe.

Sport, the media and propaganda

Television has played a role in political propaganda almost since the time of its invention and certainly since it was first used on sports fields. Indeed, it is fair to say that since the inception of television the trio of politics, sport and propaganda has found a means of self-enrichment, with each element feeding off the others.

The use of sport as a political tool in Europe has centred around large-scale sports events – the Berlin Olympic Games being the prototype (Ricard, 1987).

On 23 March 1935, the world's first regular television service was introduced in Berlin, broadcasting on 180 lines at twenty-five images per second. In the United States, where radio was highly popular and developing, there was a reluctance to branch out into this new technology, but in Europe the Olympic Games of 1936 lent political legitimacy to television. The crowds on the streets of Berlin might have had no opportunity to practise sport themselves, but Hitler's regime gave them the chance – on twenty-eight screens placed around the city – to watch their athletes winning new honours in each day's events. It was reported that 150 000 people watched the coverage every day (Ricard, 1987, p. 81).

Two observations immediately suggest themselves here. The use of sport on television in this way represented a combination of two important factors, the violent aspects of which only become apparent under analysis and critical consideration. Firstly, in the business of political and ideological propaganda, the phenomenon of sport plus new technology was placed at the service of a political regime which had no scruples about using mass public interest in sport as a means of justifying its ascension and establishing its corrupt ideology. Secondly, as Jean-Marie Brohm has pointed out, the operation was also designed to provide an "opium of the people" (Brohm, 1992). The rallying effect of sport, technologically intensified through the televised image and multiplied many times over by the miracle of the screens, drew in ever-larger numbers of spectators, turning them into docile "viewers".

Has this function of popular distraction disappeared over time?

The question is easily answered when we recall the large public screens set up in France to relay coverage of the 1998 World Cup: the coverage was watched in this way over a number of weeks by tens of thousands of people (in addition to those who viewed the matches at home or attended the stadiums). Although, happily, there is no comparison between the politics of the ruling regimes in the two cases, sport continues to perform the same functions of occupying people and diverting their attention. The success of the 1998 tournament in France was undoubtedly a sporting success but it also had numerous political ramifications (as the government exploited the positive image of sporting winners and the victorious French team was held up as an example of integration through sport). Most significantly, this official exploitation of sports imagery for political purposes took place in a context of virtually saturation media coverage throughout the country, drawing in as many people as possible and harnessing the influential forces of the nation (including its intellectuals[37]) in a great popular communion, while at the same time the world of politics continued to function as usual, and political decisions, many of them unpopular, continued to be taken amid the general atmosphere of soccer euphoria.

On yet a third, "sport policy" front, closer to the sport set-up, we would echo Brohm's observation that television seems actually to impose sports imagery (presented in continually changing ways). There is no doubt that, beyond the straightforward promotion of sport, this constitutes a veritable reification of sport's standards and a sport-based perception of reality "made concrete and given direct expression in statistics, names, tables and technical terms as part of a valid system of evaluation and appreciation" (Brohm, 1992, p. 305).

We cannot disregard the fact that this culture – this normative perception of the world, of competition and of sport – is available for exploitation by political regimes of every stripe. Indeed, this is an area that demands serious critical consideration, exploring the way in which politics uses culture and the mobilising effect of sport. The phenomenon of politics modelling itself on sport, and using television and the control of imagery to do so, also deserves attention inasmuch as it is a form of "piggy-back" propaganda, with politicians harnessing the media in order to exploit sporting successes. The political concept of Forza Italia – the name of Silvio Berlusconi's political party in Italy – was, for example, drawn directly from an AC Milan supporters' chant, Berlusconi being involved in football club ownership. A political message is thus carried on the back of a sports culture, which has already been disseminated and inflated via television. The result is a kinetic effect in communication across Europe, linking political messages with sports culture, and entirely dependent on the saturation media coverage of events, a process in which the viewer finds it increasingly difficult to identify the different elements involved. One of the consequences of this televised sports-based propaganda is that the workings of sport and the workings of politics begin to overlap, threatening a real blurring of awareness which in turn threatens the workings of democracy.

Lastly, a word needs to be said about the way in which media coverage (and not just television coverage) of sport contributes to a potentially dangerous transformation of our perceptions, as the harsher aspects of sport are airbrushed out – notably through commercial propaganda and advertising – for the sake of "correctness" or "marketability".

---

37. The rallying effect was clearly apparent even in intellectual circles, notably in the number and tone of articles by distinguished writers (from philosopher Blandine Kriegel to Alain Finkielkraut and including many academics) published in *Le Monde*.

Eliminating the negative aspects (violence, cheating and manipulation) that give sport a bad image amounts to a form of brain-washing and the most perfect expression of it occurs in the messages conveyed by big brand-name companies that are either directly involved in sport or sponsor it on an ongoing basis. The sport-based message has to sell, which means it has to be positive. The sporting spirit is therefore embodied in what is an artificial and deceptive depiction of the world of sport and athletes: "The aim of this brain-washing, with a sports event as its driving force and flesh-and-blood focus, is to produce citizens of the planet – rootless, immature and uncultivated beings without any critical faculty – who will consume goods and services" (Coutel, 2003, p. 20). The advertising message becomes almost an alternative source of awareness, displacing any critical perception and helping to generate, in Europe and across the world, a shared culture of mass consumerism, the first victims of which are young people. With their natural affinity for, and desire to identify with, heroes and role models, they constitute an avid market for brand-name garments and new consumer goods.

The process of handing down values and a legacy of cultural models thus becomes obsolete as the ever-present media offer simple, sport-based, off-the-peg systems of perception, creating the illusion that the real world with all its tedium is merely a bad dream. "Just do it!" we are told.

One of the most basic forms of violence that the media system fosters in, by and around sport is undoubtedly this collective brain-washing or conditioning through imagery.

Inequalities in the allocation of airtime

There is no doubt that television has helped to democratise sport in Europe by bringing it to a wide audience. It has also changed its image by concentrating on certain specific sports that are regarded as more telegenic than others, or better value in terms of entertainment, and this in turn has boosted the financing of such sports as football, tennis, cycle racing and motor racing, at the expense of others.

In France, for example, although handball would appear to be a "sound investment" inasmuch as both the men's and women's national squads have recently been achieving excellent results, the sport is virtually ignored by television. Yet in the Scandinavian countries, including Denmark, handball is relatively successful on television.

Such discrimination is nothing new. In 1990, out of eighty-two sports federations in France, sixty received no media coverage. In 1992, according to a survey commissioned by the Conseil Supérieur de l'Audiovisuel (CSA) [France's independent broadcasting authority], French television prioritised four sports – tennis (with 454 hours of airtime), soccer (342 hours), motor sport (173 hours) and cycle racing (120 hours) – which together accounted for two thirds of all sports coverage, not including Olympic coverage and general magazine programmes (Bourg, 1994).

The principle of a hierarchy still applied in 1996, although the ranking order of the sports had changed. CSA statistics for that year show that soccer was over-represented (with 518 hours of airtime), as were tennis (260 hours), cycle racing (198 hours) and basketball (156 hours), the top four again accounting for two-thirds of all sports coverage not including Olympic coverage and general magazine programmes (Bourg and Gouguet, 1998). At the other end of the scale, volleyball was the "poor relation" with just 29 hours and 43 minutes of airtime, while all the remaining sports together shared 152 hours and 20 minutes of coverage.

The CSA figures for 2001 (Nys, 2003) show two clear patterns. Firstly, there was an overall increase in the amount of sport shown on television and, secondly, the hierarchy was still in place, giving just a handful of sports a television profile at the expense of the rest. Soccer led the way (with 756 hours and 32 minutes), followed by rugby (264 hours), tennis (185 hours and 56 minutes) and cycle racing (164 hours and fifty minutes). Lower ranked were ice hockey (136 hours and 13 minutes), American football (118 hours and 25 minutes), basketball (87 hours and 25 minutes), athletics (59 hours and 3 minutes), ice skating (56 hours and 3 minutes) and Formula One racing (55 hours and 51 minutes).

Within this pattern of disparity there are other inequalities, notably the difference in the amount of airtime devoted to men's and women's sports. A breakdown of airtime on French television station TF1 as far back as 1992 illustrates this discrimination, priority going to three "male" sports with high audience ratings: soccer, Formula One racing and boxing together accounted for 86% of the channel's entire sports coverage (Bourg, 1994).

This gender-based apartheid in the televising of spectator sport in Europe is hardly surprising, given that men and women are also very unequally represented in sport itself, in the presentation of sport, in the allocation of senior posts in European sports federations and, of course, in the control and presentation of sports programmes on television.

Generally speaking, the world of sport seems to be one where gender inequalities are alive and well (Davisse and Louveau, 1998).

Women are under-represented not only in sports management posts in Europe, where they make up just 15% of federation board members, but also in virtually all sport-related occupations, spanning both television and the sports press. It is estimated that although one third of press card holders are women, the proportion drops to only 5% among sports journalists (Davisse and Louveau, 1998, p. 135). The French Union of Sports Journalists, which had a total membership of 1 800 in 1997, counted only 90 women among that number. At the Atlanta Olympic Games only 10% of the journalists accredited to cover the events were female.

Attempts to produce sports magazines (*Sportives, Fémisport, Olympe,* etc.) for women – potentially serving as a career springboard for women sports journalists and offering an alternative to the male-dominated general sports press (the readership of *L'Equipe,* for example, is 93% male) – ended in failure, confirming the impression that sport is chiefly for men. The disparities on television only reinforce this prejudice.

In fact, the discrimination on television is the same: sportswomen, apart from tennis players, have a low profile, appearing on screen almost exclusively in the context of designated "women's" sports such as gymnastics and ice skating and only rarely in coverage of team sports such as basketball or handball. The women's Tour de France and other women's cycling races, as well as women's soccer and rugby championships, are notable by their absence from television screens both in France and across Europe generally. Airtime is dominated by the telegenic sports (soccer, rugby, Formula One racing and cycle racing) as practised by men.

Sports news is another area of television that remains a male preserve, on the one hand because it is controlled and presented almost exclusively by men, and on the other because it is received in homes as an audiovisual product, the consumption of which is determined by men's choices (Davisse and Louveau, 1998).

Sport, business and the media: the emergence of a "product"

Among the pressures and forms of violence inherent in the media and entertainment business, it is interesting to watch how sport is being transformed by the dictates of television.

The requirements of presenting sport as televised entertainment now determine how it is organised, distort its systems of rules and cause competitions to be reorganised to suit programming demands (De Brie, 1994). It has been officially recognised that sports schedules are adjusted in line with media requirements, just as rules have been changed in certain sports to increase the entertainment value of their coverage (Economic and Social Council, 2002, 1-3).

The nature of the market for sports broadcasting rights has various negative effects which it is reasonable to regard as forms of violence perpetrated against sport, athletes and those who watch sport. Organisations that stage major sports events group together to form cartels and are represented by the national leagues: as a result, the rights market is an imperfect one, far removed from the rules of pure competition as advocated by neoclassical economists (Fontanel and Bensahel, 2001, p. 179).

It is the end-users who foot the bill for the imbalances. The soaring cost of broadcasting rights (with the rise of encrypted channels and pay TV) is thus covered by subscribers, by the consumers of products advertised on television during sports coverage (as a steep rise in advertising costs has been reflected in higher prices for the goods concerned) and by everyone who buys a television licence (Bourg and Gouguet, 2001, p. 13).

A second negative effect is the potential distortion of spectator sport. Television changes the way in which sport is presented, reconfiguring it to suit its own requirements. There is no doubt that it has a powerful filter function which distorts reality, and the root cause of the distortion is the high cost of broadcasting rights. It is not hard to cite examples of how rules have been changed, for instance, to make sport more exciting on television: in tennis the tie-break means that matches can be shorter and the introduction of fluffy balls has made it easier to follow the play, as well as altering the nature of the game by slowing down the rallies. Archery competitions had to be completely reorganised to make them more telegenic and easier for viewers to follow. In motor racing, after a group of ten or more television stations threatened in 1992 to stop showing Formula One because the domination of the Williams-Renault stable was making race outcomes too predictable and thus reducing both suspense and audience ratings, the Fédération Internationale de l'Automobile (FIA – the world motor sport governing body) bowed to the pressure and reduced the speed of the fastest cars, effectively disregarding the Olympic principle of *"citius, altius, fortius"*.[38]

In volleyball the scoring system was changed on 1 January 2000, and the Mexican President of the International Volleyball Federation, Ruben Acosta, has since made a proposal – undoubtedly reflecting a wish to heighten the entertainment value of the sport by exploiting the players' physical assets – to make "bodies" the compulsory form of match kit.

Table tennis matches nowadays consist of eleven-point, rather than twenty-one-point, games and are played on blue tables with yellow balls – the sole purpose of these changes being to facilitate television coverage of the sport, which ranks third in popularity in Germany and Japan and first in China.

In the scramble for coverage – in which certain athletes are quite prepared to get involved – sports events can also suffer at a more structural level:

---

38. "Swifter, higher, stronger."

increasingly, for example, major sailing races are scheduled to finish in television prime time, and preferably during the main evening news programmes. In the 1990s there was a similar unsuccessful attempt by TF1 to change the projected finish times on the stages of the Tour de France so that they would coincide with the 8 p.m. news (Bourg, 1994).

Although this intrusion by television into the technical organisation of sport (a supposedly independent territory) may be alarming, it is certainly not a new phenomenon. In February 1990 Joao Havelange, then President of FIFA, caused shockwaves when he revealed a plan to increase revenue from television coverage of the World Cup tournament to be staged in the United States in 1994. The idea was to split the matches not into the two traditional forty-five-minute halves but instead into four periods of twenty-five minutes each in order to create more time for advertising. So far, soccer has managed to avoid this shake-up projected in the name of profitability, unlike American sport, where games are under the control of a television director and electronic systems remind referees and players about interruptions for advertising breaks.

Another aspect of television's intrusive effect has been its role in gradually changing the legitimate status of referees, challenging their spontaneous, on-the-spot and sometimes fallible judgment with the electronic eye of the camera, the precision of action replays and a multiplicity of shots and angles. It is a case of human arbiter versus machine, in which "the man in black is totally inferior technologically" (Blociszewski, 1996, p. 33).

A third type of negative effect has been quantitative rather than qualitative, involving attempts to boost the return on investment by increasing the number of profitable sports events. FIFA President Sepp Blatter, for example, called for the World Cup to be staged every two years rather than every four years, a proposal that was rejected because it cut across the interests of tournament organisers at continental level (notably those of the African Nations Championship and European Cup) and also – although this was not stated explicitly – the interests of the players, who would be placed under considerable physical pressure by the increased number of competitions. In some sports for which television has a particular appetite, even managers are beginning to realise the devastating impact of the coverage-centred approach, with its imposition of a crazily busy schedule for the teams. In France certain rugby teams have found themselves scheduled to play on the same day in both a Top Sixteen match and a European Cup semi-final, with another major fixture, this time in the French Championship, as little as a week later. "It is indecent and it is damaging to the players: the people who produce these schedules are morons": such was the comment of Toulouse Rugby Club manager Guy Novès (*Le Monde*, 27 April 2004, p. 25). Stade

Français coach Nick Mallett is on record with a similar view: "Everyone wants more matches but no one thinks of the players. They are not machines – and things have to change. Here in France we are courting disaster!" (L'Equipe, 3 May 2004, p. 18).

A fourth negative effect – stimulated not only by the pressures of advertisers' demands, television companies' jockeying for market share and club shareholders' and sponsors' investment in the profile they acquire when their teams are in competition, but also by the media companies' own investment of capital in clubs where they have made a role for themselves – is the way in which television encourages clubs and their shareholders to contest the pyramid model of sport in Europe (with its system of relegation and promotion) and to look instead to an American-style closed-league system. In such a system no one is relegated and the clubs share the visibility afforded by the coverage, thus meeting the requirements of sponsors and shareholders. Journalist Jennie James has referred in this context to "the Americanization of European football" (James, 2000, p. 52).

The fifth negative effect is the disconcerting impact of the cut-throat competition for broadcasting rights, which damages the perception of sport as a public asset. One example of this effect occurred when the live relay by a French public channel of an AS Monaco UEFA cup away match with Widzew Lodz on 21 October 1999 was suddenly suspended by Polish television just twenty-five minutes into play, in a dispute about competition and the breaking of a contract between J.-C. Darmon and CLT-UFA (Le Monde, 23 October 1999).

In extreme cases, the workings of the market for sports coverage, and the broadcasting monopolies acquired by television stations without much thought for the viewers, can simply deny certain spectators the possibility of following major events on television. The various forms of pay TV – encrypted channels, pay-per-view systems and cable networks – all play their part here.

In 2001, according to the agency Media Content, more than 2 000 television stations in Europe were fighting over rights to sports coverage (Pierrat and Riveslange, 2002, p. 22). Yet current debate about the rules of the market does not necessarily take account of the general interest. Sport, as a hugely popular form of mass entertainment, has fallen under the yoke of television companies and rights agencies and is gradually becoming a private consumer good available only in restricted contexts – and this is part of a pattern of discrimination in which a growing section of society finds itself more generally excluded from the everyday enjoyment of entertainment and news. To take one example of the trend, on 22 April 2004 viewers of the free public channels in France found to their dismay that they were to be denied coverage of a European Cup match involving OM, as the fixture was to be screened only on the pay channel TPS Star. News of the deal provoked an angry reaction, particularly in Marseilles, where viewers felt themselves deprived not just of the chance to watch their club but also of a piece of sports heritage and culture, and there was a general outcry at the hijacking of what most people still regarded as the "public domain" of recreation and competition.

One can only be dismayed by the commercial logic and the rigid profit-and-loss-based management approach underlying the decision to privatise the coverage in this case. It illustrates a new form of media-generated violence that is helping to drive a wedge between the concept of sport as a popular and accessible human activity and an inalienable public asset, and the competing vision of it as a carefully packaged product for privatisation, being bitterly contested by a few commercial groups.

Another example (this time from the United Kingdom), is that of the BBC losing out to private sector ITV on coverage of the Oxford and Cambridge Boat Race on the Thames. From 2005 onwards the public station will no longer enjoy the exclusive right to cover what is an archetypically British event hugely popular both in the United Kingdom and abroad (the race has a television audience of 8 million at home and 400 million worldwide): the BBC in this case is a victim of its charter, which prohibits it from giving excessive publicity to sponsors (Le Monde, 1 March 2004).

The problems which surfaced in France in relation to radio coverage of World Cup soccer matches demonstrated that, far from constituting an exception, the privatisation of public broadcasting "territory", as proposed in this case by Radio France boss Jean-Marie Cavada, was a hidden but growing form of violence spreading throughout the media generally. In this instance, however, the joint decision taken on 3 April 2002 by the French Ministry for Youth and Sport and Ministry for Culture and Communication – defining radio coverage as an aspect of public information that could not be interfered with by sports federations or event organisers (Le Saux, 2002, p. 153) – served to halt further speculative developments. Representatives of the radio stations involved in the dispute, who had formed an economic interest group entitled "Free Sport", had plans to set up an association for free sport and culture with a brief to campaign for free radio broadcasting rights throughout Europe.

The sixth negative effect (demonstrating another aspect of speculation at work) has been one of vertical concentration as major groups have sought to control and manage the entire sports production process from ownership of players and teams to ownership of the television stations that screen the matches. The best example of this disturbing trend towards monopoly is probably the bid by Rupert Murdoch in 1998 to take over Manchester United. BskyB, the satellite television station in which Murdoch had a 40%

stake, was ready to spend US$1 billion on the deal. The British Government found it necessary to step in because the proposed deal raised a fundamental question not only about sport but also about freedom and ethics. As one commentator put it, "Can a television station become the owner of a club whose matches it covers?" (Kadritzke, 1999, p. 22).

The seventh negative effect derives from the fact that media groups band together into pressure groups and engage in lobbying. The decision not to allow Greece to stage the centenary Olympic Games – despite a Council of Europe resolution – was a reflection of economic and media interests at work, backed by the clout of the big American companies sponsoring the competition. "Less obviously but just as effectively, lobbying by major sports sponsors guides the choice of cities to host large-scale events, and often the deciding factors have nothing to do with sport" (Bourg, 1994, p. 177).

Obviously, in order to understand where these pressures come from, we need to look at how the Olympic Games are financed and at the dominant role of the media and advertisers in that process. In 2004, the year of the Olympics' return to Greece, Athoc (the committee organising the Athens Games) had an overall budget of €1 962 million. No less than 37.5% of that was to be covered by the sale of television broadcasting rights, the organising committee thus receiving €736 million from the television companies covering the Games. International sponsorship rights were valued at a further €248 million. The collective economic weight of this input is huge and, along with other factors, heavily influences IOC decisions on where the Games will take place and who will be involved in organising them on the ground.

The importance of the media factor in the whole venture becomes clearer when we consider the possible consequences for Greece of failure to complete the necessary infrastructure for the Games on time. Setbacks experienced in the installation of systems by the television companies preparing to film the events had the potential to mar coverage of the Games, and prompt rights-holding companies to renegotiate their contracts with the organisers – a fearful prospect for the latter, given the importance of the broadcasting rights to the project as a whole (*L'Equipe,* 21 April 2004).

Disenchantment

When major groups and television companies go bankrupt, they pull down in their wake the sports teams that depended on their bounty to fund a salaries explosion triggered precisely by the boom in the television industry and the broadcasting rights market. The whole giddying process is a vicious circle, and the solidity of the system everywhere in Europe is currently proving to be illusory.

In the United Kingdom, for example, the collapse of ITV Digital added to the problems faced by football clubs. Newcastle closed the 2001-02 season with a net deficit of €4.8 million. Leeds announced a loss of €62.8 million. Barnsley, a Third Division club that had been playing in the Premier League in 1997, was simply declared bankrupt, as was Leicester City, with losses of close to €50 million. Chelsea, despite making a gross profit of more than EUR18 million, reported net losses of €160 million and was rescued only by the financial intervention of Russian businessman Roman Abramovich.

At the time of writing the German Kirch group was still being dismantled following its bankruptcy. The collapse of this group has huge economic repercussions, for the portfolio held by its sports-rights management subsidiary Kirch Sport – transferred to a consortium after the bankruptcy – included broadcasting rights for the 2006 soccer World Cup, for which Kirsch had guaranteed FIFA 1.5 billion Swiss francs (€1.03 billion), as well as Bundesliga matches and certain events in the world skiing championships (Nys, 2002).

More generally, as noted by Christian Bromberger, inflation in rights' costs and the trend towards bigger and bigger deals have all too often been accompanied by dubious practices and financial crime, notably in France, where there was a belated attempt to remedy the situation through legislation (Bromberger, 1996, pp. 37-40). Bromberger's analysis is largely shared by a French Economic and Social Committee report on the subject:

> "European football, with many clubs in debt, is courting financial disaster. Since Canal Plus hit problems and several media groups (Kirch in Germany, ITV Digital in the UK and Tele Più in Italy) went bankrupt, large sums of money are owed not only to the clubs but also to FIFA" (Economic and Social Committee, 2002, 1-11).

Two contradictory positions currently seem to be emerging. On the one hand the professional leagues assert that they can always attract fresh bids for television rights. The French professional football league, for example, projects its annual rights earnings at €450 million from the 2004-05 season onwards.

On the other hand, the television stations are reluctant to pay more than they are currently paying, in all likelihood having learned their lesson from the collapse of various European operators, and deterred by the difficulty of concluding agreements that will reconcile the public service obligations of national broadcasters with the commercial interests of private sector groups (Fansten, 2004).

At the most recent Sportel [the annual international market for televised sport], in Monaco, Etienne Mougeotte from the French station TF1 predicted that television channels would soon be spending less money on sport, a view supported by Frédéric Chevit, France Télévision's head of sport (Nys, 2002, p. 70).

The real victims of the high-level dealing on the sports coverage market are, at the end of the day, the viewers. Although television promises them the latest and best services, what they get remains subject to the uncertainties of international competition, with all its costs and with the inherent risk that – because of disputes between operators or decisions that side-step a public service sector increasingly hard pressed in the current fiercely competitive climate – sections of the viewing public will be denied access to event coverage.

Human bodies and violence
Difficulties of approach and angles of interpretation

When academics or other intellectuals engage in critical discussion of sport they tend to cite the works of philosophers, including the ancient philosophers, to support their own vision of modern sports. Writing quite recently, for example, Redeker (2002) argued that sport expressed in practice the theory of the sophist Thrasymachus, for whom justice was whatever the strongest decided it to be. Redeker did not associate any real policy with sport. By contrast, his theory was based on a critical definition of it as a technical mechanism developed at the time of the Industrial Revolution for pushing nature and human bodies to the fullest possible use of their energy and thus making them more profitable (Redeker, 2002, p. 36). In this approach the historical context out of which modern sports developed is rightly identified as capitalism. On the other hand, Greek sophism is not necessarily a watertight point of reference in terms of logic. Specifically, there are a number of dangers inherent in this "historical" perspective on human power and human violence.

Firstly, there is a radical difference between the ancient and modern contexts for physical activity. In terms of historical reality the social relationships involved are not comparable: the violence practised then and now differs in its significance. For example, the introduction of democracy in European societies – whether gradual or abrupt – brought a shake-up in relationships between social groups and this inevitably influenced developing cultures, including physical culture, within those societies.

Consequently, the conception of a balance of power based exclusively on Thomas Hobbes' "war of each against each" must always be qualified. Hobbes' theory, expounded in his celebrated work Leviathan (1651), has been taken up by many other writers. The image of Leviathan, a monster from Phoenician mythology also mentioned in the Bible, was chosen to represent the natural human condition (Hobbes, 1971). As Hobbes saw it, the violence of "each against each" was an original condition particular to living beings and thus to human beings. Redeker built on this concept, arguing that the immorality in sport and its decivilising character were revealed in more or less crude jousts or contests to designate the most powerful among us at a given moment or in a given sport (Redeker, 2002, p. 71).

> It is not our intention to explore this hypothetical violent state of nature. Instead we aim **to show how the violence associated with sport and that affecting the human body are, like other types of violence, an important indicator of current European culture in its different forms.** Such violence symbolises – and indeed is a dramatic reflection of – the tensions inherent in each society. Sport thus more or less faithfully mirrors social relationships and even social expectations. In this way, sporting encounters at European or, more broadly, international level constitute instances of cultural compromise in which violent forms of behaviour are both standard and at the same time liable to variation. Certain national teams are characterised, for example, as having an "iron defence" or being "tough tacklers", reflecting the values traditionally attributed to players from the respective countries. Far from being insignificant, such stereotypes merit analysis as components of social reality at national level.
>
> Appreciation of these public perceptions can provide insight not only into the mechanisms of sociocultural determinism, but also into the ongoing interpretations of reality adhered to by human groups, in this case the nations that make up Europe.

Such perspectives – which seek to be fresh and dispassionate – on modern sports and physical exercise readily demonstrate their hidden aspects, and the reality is that many forms of physical violence are generated in and around sport (Bodin and Héas, 2002, p. 100; and Bodin, 2003). Approaching reality (the reality of sport and other realities) in this way is not something new, either here in Europe or elsewhere in the world. It poses the more general problem of the stereotypes, and indeed value judgments, that we are all tempted to apply to events, especially those that make an impression on public opinion because they receive substantial media coverage (see below).

How Europeans approach sport and other forms of physical exercise

In any study of sport as a cultural practice we need to avoid bias and the errors of interpretation. One source of bias is our personal experience of sport, whether individually or collectively. On average, large numbers of people in European countries are involved in sport: according to estimates based on an opinion poll conducted in the late 1990s, roughly half the population of the thirteen states covered practised some form of exercise or physical activity (CSA-TMO, 1998).[39] The same poll showed sedentary lifestyles to be widespread: 46% of Europeans aged 18 and over played no sport on a reg-

---

39. http://www.csa-tmo.fr/fra/dataset/data9897/actu19980317.html (consulted on 14 September 2001).

ular basis. Another poll conducted in the same year yielded similar results: almost one European in two did not play sport regularly (i.e. at least once a month), the Russian Federation being the country with the lowest level of participation (INRA poll, 1998).

For a section of the European population, however, sport or other forms of physical exercise have become quite routine. For at least ten years, men and women in northern Europe have been recorded as practising such activities relatively assiduously and regularly throughout their lives: "[in 1991] Swedes devoted half an hour a day [to physical activity], and Finns and Danes approximately a quarter of an hour, in contrast to the five or six minutes spent on it by the French, Spanish and Greeks" (Thomas, 1993, p. 21). Thomas mentions, in this regard, initiatives taken by the Council of Europe since the 1970s on the basis of work done by Castejon Pas in 1973 and Rodgers in 1977. Their criteria enabled comparisons to be drawn for the first time not only between the different European countries but also within countries. From the data gathered, both on specific indicators over a number of years and on a range of indicators at given times, we can determine whether particular countries are becoming more or less "sporty".

Enthusiasm for sport has to be considered in context. In 2002 the European Union conducted research into the situation in present-day Europe with regard to physical exercise.[40] Between 57.4% and 60.7% of the respondents said they had engaged in no "vigorous" physical activity during the preceding week. Differences in the results here are probably influenced by social perceptions: it is preferable not to admit to leading a sedentary life (which is viewed negatively in most countries), or at least not in response to a researcher's first question. But "moderate" physical activity was also not particularly popular: 40.8% to 47.1% of respondents said they had not engaged in any activity at this level. The study showed the divisions produced by the classic sociological variables: on average more young people than older people were involved in sport and more men than women. While two thirds of Europeans said they did not practise "vigorous" physical activity, half said they practised no such activity at all. Among the fifteen countries of the EU there were cultural differences in people's readiness to declare their involvement in physical activity: the largest numbers of assiduous sportspeople were to be found in the Netherlands, Germany, Luxembourg and Finland, while Spain and Italy were the least "sporty" countries. In contrast to the simplistic north/south divide, Greece (with a higher level of activity than the rest of southern Europe) and Ireland (with a lower level of activity than other northern countries) were atypical.

---

40. Special Eurobarometer 183-6/Wave 58.2-European Opinion Research Group EEIG.

Interpretive bias is even more evident in the many depictions of sport and other forms of physical exercise in the media, as the activities themselves are one step removed and subject to ad hoc processing by the media. In this way, sport is part of our lives by proxy: the images of sport, like the commentary, are presented as entertainment. Depending on the era and the media, champions have tended to be presented in a way that promotes respect for others (whether athletes or not). Yet sometimes the factor with which people (especially young people) identify is the acknowledged power – or indeed violence – associated with high-level athletes (Messner et al., 1999). Not everyone who wants to be a hero will become one, and it is not enough simply to take first place in one's event. Heroes are recognised as such by their fans, their peers and entire nations but they are not necessarily regular winners. Racing cyclist Raymond Poulidor [the "Eternal Second"] is an example. In many cases, heroes represent the people from whose ranks they have emerged, or whose values they stand for. They embody the highest levels of self-denial, suffering, effort and hard work, and all this helps to build the hero myth (Bodin and Debarbieux, 2003; and Duret, 1999).

The subjective and biased temptation to blame sport for transmitting, if not actually fostering, human violence is nowadays stronger than ever as sport seems to be both omnipotent and omnipresent. "Florence Griffith Joyner and Lance Armstrong are present to a degree in all of us. We all receive a continual transfusion of sport" (Redeker, 2002, p. 75, p. 86). The omnipresence of sport in our European societies, suffused as they are by the mass media, is manifest, and it is therefore no surprise that authors like Redeker should see it as such a strong influence on all of us.

Physical injuries and accidents in sport: media images and reality

In our developed societies the media have become an important sector of the economy as well as a daily source of news and entertainment for people in most European countries. There are radio and television stations, magazines and newspapers devoted wholly or in part to sport and other forms of physical exercise (*L'Equipe, L'Equipe TV*, and Eurosport being just a few examples). Different sports receive particular attention according to the predominant cultural tastes in the different countries: in one it is football, in another skiing, in another basketball or rugby. We intend to look, in this context, at the importance accorded to sport and specifically to the forms of violence inherent in it or perpetrated by it.

The mass media and the violence associated with sport: are these forms of violence emphasised or overlooked, prevented or intended?

What aspects of sport do we see in the media and what place is given to accidents and more generally to injuries caused in or by sport?

Media coverage of sport gives us an oblique understanding of sports events and, more broadly, of sport as a phenomenon. Real power is exercised through the choice of images and the words used, as well as the presentation of the images, and all these things can radically alter the impact of a given act, violent or otherwise and irrespective of whether its consequences are healthy, damaging or, indeed, fatal. Drawing on examples from several European cultures, we hope to demonstrate the complexity of the way such sports accidents are approached. From our piecemeal sources we do not aim to provide a comprehensive picture, but rather to suggest some avenues for further exploration with a view to achieving a more realistic, less idealised understanding of violence in sport, and thus of what is a deeply paradoxical aspect of modern sport.

Does violence invite further violence?

Numerous surveys and studies have highlighted the paradox between the media's emphasis in sports coverage on all forms of confrontation and violence, and the cruel reality (evident at least in the more objective studies) of the bodily injuries caused in sport despite the pervasive presence of medical personnel (Bodin and Héas, 2002; and De Mondenard, 2000). The main point here is that the violence portrayed in the media does not automatically have the influence that some would ascribe to it. In any event, seeing or hearing violent acts does not impel people to commit violent acts in the direct way that has often been suggested.

Influential images? Manipulation or mutual influence?

Media images are regularly blamed for various things: for manipulating us without our knowledge and indeed for inciting us to violence by presenting scenes of violence to the most susceptible among us (including children). Discussion of the relationship between society and images often centres on the apparently widely held notion that consuming violent imagery leads to more violent behaviour. Many researchers have explored the question and have pointed out the difficulty not only of measuring the relationships involved – the extent of the media's negative influence on aggression, its effect in desensitising very young people to violence, or its instigative capacity – but also of assessing existing regulations on the subject, or proposing new ones (Vedel, 1995).

We believe the key to the influence of images on our everyday lives is to be found in the sociology of suggestion, both heterosuggestion and autosuggestion (Héas, 1996). Suggestion pervades what we do every day, both at work and for recreation. It is a factor in any attempt to analyse the question of violence and the associated pain that athletes inflict on themselves in training and competition. This highly complex question of influence relates more broadly to the notion of the free will "granted" to people generally and specifically to those taking part in surveys.

Advertisements sometimes attract especially virulent criticism for being particularly representative of the influences at work in our image-centred societies and indeed in the consumer society in general (Debord, 1967; and Barthes, 1973). We are told that advertisements incite us (directly or otherwise) to purchase specific products or services, by placing before us evermore attractive possibilities. For advertising imagery does not merely show us the goods or services that are on sale: it presents them to us in staged settings, sometimes involving people who have nothing whatsoever to do with them. Different types of sport have become significant frames of reference for advertising, and more generally for all the information we receive through the media today.

Advertising professionals and their clients sometimes use human beings in morally suspect situations involving sexual allusions or explicit sex acts, the equating of people with animals or objects, and suggestions of injury or violence. Lobby groups and indeed government reports have attacked this type of advertising (Grésy, 2002), urging that it be withdrawn and that those responsible for it be systematically prosecuted. Advertising imagery is considered particularly persuasive, and therefore more liable to influence people. Suggested approaches to the problem include organising the advertising industry and requiring it to take greater responsibility, and educating ordinary people about advertising.

What conclusions have been drawn when advertising imagery has been analysed from different academic perspectives?

The first point to be made is that not all advertising images are "unacceptable" or morally suspect. Most images that we see are attempting to influence us in less brutal, more subtle ways. Images of women, for example, are not necessarily degrading, but they do reflect dominant cultural models such as male superiority, and the case they help to make is sometimes more concerned with female athletes' appearance than with their technical performance (Héas et al., 2004). The great majority of such images are not at odds with the established order and, while we may criticise that fact, they have to be seen as apologetic rather than revolutionary.

Moreover, the suggestion underlying advertising images is actually based on the factors in purchasing of which we are least aware: the colours, symbols and forms of language used. Such images can thus reinforce consumer loyalty to given products and services in the short term. Their influence over the longer term has not, however, been conclusively demonstrated. Even among children – who are regarded as more susceptible – advertising does not appear to revolutionise purchasing behaviour, much less desires and aspirations (Guichard, 2000). The seductive effect of advertising would thus seem to be largely superficial, or at least less radical and enduring than its detractors have claimed. Consumers, for the most part, are not duped by image-driven product presentation. The impact of such presentation is symbolic, in the literal sense, which does not mean, anthropologically speaking, that it has no influence – quite the contrary. Symbols convey essential aspects of culture, including messages that can have educational or indeed therapeutic purposes. The force of symbolism is acknowledged in myths, and advertising (indeed imagery generally) contributes to myths. But what about violence?

Do violent images encourage violent action?

This is not a new problem. Dagnaud reminds us that as long ago as the late 1920s the famous Payne Fund Studies (named after the organisation that sponsored them) established a correlation between juvenile delinquency and frequent cinema attendance in the United States.[41] Many studies (for example Goldstein and Arms, 1971; and Green and Quanty, 1977) concluded that, far from provoking catharsis, the spectacle of violence fuelled aggression. The development on a wide scale of new information and communication technologies led to powerful social and institutional pressures for action, for example from family associations, governments, the courts and media watchdogs (Maigret, 2003, p. 57). Meanwhile certain groups opposed – and continue to oppose – controls over the images conveyed by the new technologies.

Nonetheless the influence exercised by violent images of all kinds (from ritualised and codified combat in the case of sport and other forms of physical activity, to the murders perpetrated in many television films) does not automatically and necessarily accentuate actual violence. The research sometimes gets bogged down in complex mathematical calculations, only to end up referring to predispositions to violence and a likely genetic basis for such behaviour (Slater et al., 2003, p. 716). By contrast, the long-term effect of such images "tends to be that of casting a shadow over the world. The depiction of violence apparently tends to inhibit viewers rather than inciting them to aggression, making them more fearful and insecure"[42] (which is not to say more violent towards others). "If indeed one influence of the media is to stimulate anxiety, why would that influence necessarily be translated into violence?" (Maigret, 2003, p. 57).

Then there is the problem of defining violence, and more specifically violent imagery. Is a punch to the face in a boxing match more violent than a film scene in which the hero does not hesitate to insult everyone who crosses his path?

To summarise, research now tends to emphasise that images, violent or otherwise, can have an influence, and particularly that violent images conveyed by the media are never received in a neutral way. Studies have highlighted the fact that spectators/viewers – especially sportspeople or people with a knowledge of sport – are not inert in the face of such images. In order to avoid making ridiculously simplistic judgments about particular programmes or sports broadcasts we need to know details of their context, both generally and in relation to the game involved. It is a fact that the media can be convenient scapegoats for wider and more deep-rooted social problems. "Pointing the finger at the media can also be an easy way of excusing loss of

---

41. Quoted by Molénat (2003) in "Les écrans rendent-ils violents?", *Sciences humaines*, special issue No. 43, December/January, p. 62.
42. Baton-Hervé E., (2000), *Les Enfants-téléspectateurs. Programme, discours, représentations*, Paris, L'Harmattan – quoted by Molénat, 2003, p. 63.

parental authority within the family and the use of television as a babysitter" (Maigret, 2003, p. 59).

It should also be pointed out that a number of interesting initiatives have recently been taken with a view to providing real education about violence, in the media and elsewhere. The European Union's Daphne Programme (2000-03) was specifically directed at children, teenagers and women. In 2001, for example, under a project entitled Action Teenagers Against Violence (ATAV), the Italian organisation Women on Work (WOW), in partnership with Greek, Spanish and Romanian associations, enabled young people to confront the many forms of violence in contemporary society. Other initiatives – for example by the Leeds Animation Workshop (LAW) in the United Kingdom in 2000 – have been more concerned with the symbolic violence accentuated by the perpetuation of stereotypes, including gender-based stereotypes (see below).

Sport as the "opium of the people": a modern version of the circus?

We need to move beyond the type of superficial and apocalyptic, indeed nihilistic, analysis that dismisses sport as a temple of capitalism, with television – "a machine for spreading wasteland" – as its closest ally (Redeker, 2002, p. 71). This philosophical and to some extent sociological perspective is heavily influenced by the nihilism of Nietzsche: "the wasteland is growing" (*die Wüste wächst*). From this perspective, sport offers no insight at all into the reality of those practising it or those watching it and much less does it facilitate any broader political awareness. Certain radical strands of critical sociology have explored how spectator sport has the effect of depoliticising the masses. Brohm, with his *Sociologie politique du sport* (1976), was one of the main instigators in France of a movement critical of sport. His work brought sharply into focus a certain sociological approach to sport and other forms of physical exercise that has recently been described as "Nietzscho-Freudo-Marxist" (Duret and Trabal, 2001, p. 14). Other authors have drawn heavily on his theoretical framework in developing their own understanding of the subject (Caillat, 1996; Vassort et al., 1999; and Vassort, 1999).

American writers have given a special place to this same approach, which they classify as a "conflict theory" (Morgan, 1994; Coakley, 1994; Vogler and Schwartz, 1993; and Hoch, 1972), based on inequalities that are either economic (concerned with disposable income, acquired or inherited wealth and power) or cultural (concerned with access to higher education or to cultural facilities such as museums and galleries). Most conflict theories are based on analyses of social class or the relationships between social classes.

Structural violence in modern society

Critical analyses of modern society divide it structurally into those groups which manipulate (the powerful and wealthy) and those which are manipulated (the mass of ordinary people, the poor, and stigmatised individuals or groups, such as women, the sick and the injured). Within this framework, sport is seen as an institutional means of controlling the "lower ranks" – a means of oppression, in fact, under the cover of emancipatory values. Sport functions as opiates in the same way as the ancient Roman games did, curbing revolt and keeping the oppressed masses happy at relatively little cost. Major clubs and their affiliated training centres can be seen as having a special role in the controlling process, for it is there that young athletes are first approached, rightly or wrongly, as potential members of a sporting elite. They go on to become role models for others not fortunate enough to have benefited from sport as a springboard to social recognition. The profits amassed by those who run the clubs and their accredited sponsors, and the contracts that impose obligations on the athletes (rather than those who manage and control them) constitute the framework that dictates how sport functions.

Vaugrand recently summarised the main features of conflict theories as they have been applied to sports in France (Vaugrand, 1999), highlighting four main conceptual approaches to what he terms "critical theory of sport", each of which relates to a specific form of violence. The four key ideas are:

- the structural identification of sport with capitalism, the professionalisation of sport and leisure activities in general being merely a logical extension of the effort to extract profit from them, and consequently from various forms of exploitation of human beings (see below);
- the "ideological state apparatus [of sport]"[43] confirming the domination of a particular social class, namely the bourgeoisie;
- sport as the "opium of the people", or what we have called the hypnotic effect of sport (Bodin and Héas, 2002), which tends to depoliticise the mass of ordinary people;
- the iatrogenic aspect of sport, in the sense of a perverse, damaging and, indeed, reprehensible effect of intensive competition and its consequences.[44]

It is the last point, in particular, that we intend to consider, although the other aspects underpinning the overall theory also have to be borne in mind. The iatrogenic aspect of sport is the violence inherent in it, including even its "accidental" consequences.

---

43. A concept developed by Althusser.
44. Vaugrand, 1999, p. 171, quoting Brohm, (1987), "La iatrogénèse sportive. Contre productivité et effets pathogènes de la compétition sportive intense", in De Mondenard; and *Quel corps?*, *Drogues et Dopages*, Chiron, Paris, pp. 19-50.

These conflict-based approaches offer a great deal of insight into state and commercial sport systems in general (see below). On the other hand, they are less useful in relation to non-competitive or community-based sport – where the focus is not on commercial considerations. In 2001, the centenary of the introduction of the French "Law of 1901",[45] there was debate in France about the place of the associations covered by this law, and more broadly about the voluntary sector in general and the non-profit-making economy,[46] which directly related to the problems outlined here. It became clear that sports currently in the process of being commercialised and marketed also, and perhaps most importantly, represent territory in which people are mutually supportive and open to debate, if not to democracy.

Are accidents – and especially deaths – in sport a thing of the past?

The beneficial effects of sport would seem to outweigh all others (Bodin and Héas, 2002). They are numerous and we do not have the capacity here to list them all, much less to analyse them. Important among them are muscle-building and lung activation, helping to counteract the negative effects of contemporary – and especially sedentary – lifestyles (see below), as well as the enhancement of self-esteem and peer-group integration (De Knop and Elling, 2000). The advantages deriving from participation in sport are communicated and reinforced via what is a veritable "ideology of health" (Lorant, 2000, p. 150). The effect is to stigmatise Europeans who do not attend to their own physical or mental health, especially people who are not physically active (it is interesting here to note the bias in many surveys resulting from the fact that sedentary people feel guilty and this affects their answers). Newspapers and magazines, as well as the relevant institutional bodies, generally disseminate a message of health promotion through physical exercise (Travaillot, 1998; and Bodin and Héas, 2002). As a result, most Europeans find themselves in a pro-sport social climate, even though there is another side to the coin and one that is often underplayed. The Internet offers some revealing examples in this respect. Entire web pages are devoted, for example, to "minor accidents in sport". With an overall view to prevention, such accidents – most of which are "not serious" – are presented as the price that athletes pay for mistakes in training, technique or choice of equipment.[47] Such is the force of this ideology that the ill effects of sport can be presented as "different manifestations of one and the same disease [sic] –

---

45. Setting out a statutory framework for non-profit-making associations, which are the legal model in France for most sports and other clubs.
46. Lipietz A., (2001), *Pour le tiers secteur; l'économie sociale et solidaire: pourquoi et comment,* Paris, La Découverte/La Documentation française.
47. Based on an article in the review *Valeur mutualiste,* October 1998, by Dr D. Gloaguen, http://www.mariedefrance.qc.ca/cmfweb/secondaite/eps/sant%C3A9/esspog0.htm (consulted on 16 September 2003).

over-exertion".[48] Over-exertion is thus depicted as a real disease of our times (see below), just as physical inactivity is!

Sports accidents do happen – and are even documented

In this chapter we want to explore what is sometimes presented as a blind spot, namely "the unfamiliar area of accidents due to the practice of sport" (Lorant, 2000, p. 145). We intend to confine ourselves to discussing "straightforward" accidents, but what follows must be read in the context of the preceding chapters on other forms of violence in sport because the damaging consequences of sport include not only violence inflicted on the body but also psychological violence and undesirable or unintended side-effects. (Bodin et al., 2001). Before addressing the main theme we will develop the ideas contained in the preceding paragraphs by outlining the complex impact of physical exercise, intensive or otherwise, with reference to a number of cases selected at random, before looking at national statistics which will take us beyond individual examples.

Alarming data on sudden death among athletes[49]

The year 2004 has been remarkable for the high death toll among athletes at an elite international level, especially in Europe. The first quarter of the year alone saw the deaths of a Latvian basketball player (Raimonds Jumikis, aged 23), a Hungarian footballer (Miklos Feher, aged 24) and an Italian cyclist (Marco Pantani, aged 34). In 2003, three professional racing cyclists died: Frenchman Fabrice Salanson (23), Italian Denis Zanette (32) and Spaniard Jose Maria Jimenez (34). The mass media engaged in a seemingly endless series of investigations into this spate of deaths. Yet their astonishment bemused sports specialists and experts, most of whom are well aware of the damaging effects of sport at both elite and amateur levels.

Many writers, including medical practitioners, have highlighted the mixed and sometimes tragic consequences of practising certain sports, especially in competition. In 1995 a number of American studies showed that the immune systems of marathon runners were weakened during and immediately after the effort of competing: "Athletes competing in endurance sports have an increased susceptibility to infection ... in the days following an intense and prolonged effort such as that of a marathon" (Nieman, 1994, quoted by Legros, 2000, p. 130). The studies were reported and their findings sensationalised to a greater or lesser extent in the European press, with headlines

---
48. http://www.bmlweb.org/sport_enfant.html (consulted on 16 September 2003).
49. Subject of an article by Oliver Toscer in *Le Nouvel Observateur*, No. 2050, 19 February 2004, p. 69.

designed to shock in one way or another: "The fatal marathon?" or "Marathons and the immune system".[50] Yet the same studies show that runners' bodily defences are clearly strengthened in the longer term. A separate study quoted shows that, because levels of cortisol are raised during effort, marathon runners lose 15% of their memory capacity. Experiments on rats also show that high levels of cortisol alter the brain's hormonal balance and cause it to age more rapidly. Extrapolations from experiments with rats to conclusions about human beings are clearly open to criticism, but experiments have also been conducted on marathon runners during competition, and these shed more light on our theme. It would seem – without prejudging the subsequent consequences of such adaptation strategies – that people who practise sport regularly, and particularly elite athletes, cope with pain more successfully than others (El Ali et al., 2000).

In France, the condition known as spondylolisthesis [vertebral slippage][51] has been the subject of much debate. The widespread incidence in certain sports (diving, ice skating, judo and gymnastics)[52] of the stress fracture that causes the condition came to light as a result of the Lussac case, (despite manifest and reported pain, gymnast Elodie Lussac took part in a competition in November 1994, just before the world championships in Dortmund).[53] It was suggested that the young gymnast concerned was less a victim of fate than of a foreseeable affliction. "There was nothing unusual about her accident, it was perfectly predictable, and all 'baby champions' run the same risk".[54] In most cases the fracture itself is not painful and therefore goes almost unnoticed. "The arching of the spine required on apparatus such as the beam is beyond the physiological capability of the adult body and it grips the lower vertebrae like a vice. As things currently stand (in terms of techniques, the system of judging and attitudes to the aesthetics of gymnastics and sport generally), so long as forced arching of the spine is an integral part of [competitive] programmes, then with few and dangerous exceptions high-level gymnastics can be practised only by prepubescent ... athletes". Not all observers would lend their weight to such an unequivocal indictment, as other findings – including those of Cottalorda in 2002[55] – are less alarming. This specialist in children's surgery refers, without naming it, to a study conducted over a fourteen-year period on a population of eighty-four athletes

---

50. Holzey Christiane, "Marathon immunitaire", *Science et Vie*, No. 940, January 1996, p. 29.
51. The word comes from *spondylo* (vertebral bone) and *listhesis* (slippage).
52. According to Dr Bacquaert, sportspeople are twice as likely as those with a sedentary lifestyle to suffer from a vertebral stress fracture: http://www.irbms.com/Com_pb3.html (consulted on 20 April 2004).
53. She was Junior European Champion in the same year.
54. Dr C. Daulouède, "La poupée de porcelaine", *Sport et vie*, No. 29, pp. 12-13.
55. http://www.chu-rouen.fr/ssf/pathol/traumatismeduauxsports.html (consulted on 26 April 2004).

competing at international level and training for twenty hours a week. His conclusion is seemingly irrefutable: "There is no reason to limit the sporting activity of a child suffering from spondylolisthesis". Other types of fracture are also associated with early and intensive training. In the United States, fracture of the tip of the humerus is so common among young baseball players that it has been nicknamed "Little League elbow" or "Little League shoulder" (Vogler and Schwartz, 1993, p. 76).

In another example of the way in which certain sports are indicted, an AFP (Agence France Presse) report in 1999, claiming that the cyclists in the Tour de France had a five times greater risk of death than the spectators,[56] shook that French national sporting institution to its foundations. The report quoted an extract from research by Dr De Mondenard – into the health of 2 363 racing cyclists from western Europe who had competed in the Tour de France since 1947 – which had been validated by the biostatistics department of the Institut Marie Curie. The findings were complex. On the one hand the cyclists seemed to enjoy a relatively high level of protection:

> "They seem healthy, with an overall mortality rate between the ages of 25 and 54 that is clearly below average: 100 deaths as against 137 in a similar sample of the population generally. [On the other hand], there is a problem with mortality due to vascular accidents. The only explanations for the increased mortality here are the practice of cycling at a highly competitive level and the widespread use of scientific doping."

The term "scientific doping" may offend certain sports administrators, who would prefer to talk of "biological preparation" or "hormonal compensation" (see below). More recent studies, particularly from a historical perspective, have shown how the Tour de France and the highs and lows experienced by the cyclists have helped to forge a French national identity (Bœuf and Léonard, 2003). This type of effect may explain the impact of scandals in internationally regarded sports events which are symbolic of their host nation.

It is striking, however, that while there would currently seem to be an increase in the incidence of sudden death among athletes, the media are discriminatory in their coverage of the deaths and thus of any suspected doping. Cycle racing and numerous other high-energy sports are singled out for blame, while the media neglect or appear to neglect the fact that sudden death (along with many other negative effects) is associated with the use of erythropoietin (EPO) (De Mondenard, 2000), and there is no serious discussion of the vitamin injections given to soccer players at Juventus Turin or of the proven cases of doping in tennis.

---

56. AFP, 7 January 1999, available at http://www.actu.lokace.com/contenu/dos3

The examples mentioned are typical in several respects:
- they received extensive media coverage;
- they have only very recently been followed by radically new measures to protect the athletes at risk;
- they continue to be seen largely as isolated bad examples rather than evidence of practices that are inherently dangerous.

As we shall see in a further chapter, most European countries tend to react in a very similar way to cases that highlight the extent of doping among the sports champions of the day.

Accidentology: a convincing body of data

Individual incidents like this in Europe have shocked a public that is largely uninformed or, more insidiously, misinformed (which takes us back to the function of sport as the "opium of the people").

Hard data on the risks associated with specific sports do exist, however, and are generally available. In what follows we will quote from an ongoing Canadian study (the results of which are available on the Internet) covering all types of everyday activity, rather than simply sports. Some of its findings in the specific area of sport are interesting in that they indicate just how detailed systematic accident data can be.

An example from outside Europe

The Canadian Hospitals Injury Reporting and Prevention Program (CHIRPP) issues regular reports (and continually updates its web pages) on injuries associated with various everyday activities, including some sports. Its statistics are accurate and easily accessible to both sportspeople and others. They are essentially concerned with young people involved in sport because they are drawn from a network of paediatric hospitals in Canadian cities. Consequently, the data do not properly reflect the rate of accidents among adults or, indeed, the death rate because they do not cover those young people who die before they reach hospital.

One example of the CHIRPP findings, from June 1995, is an exhaustive study based on data for 1994 and covering 123 063 treated cases (with no age limit specified). Eighteen categories of injury are reported, six of which relate specifically to sport and other forms of physical exercise: horse riding, jet skiing, use of playground apparatus, in-line skating, rugby and trampolining. More children had accidents in playgrounds (4 261 cases treated) than during horse riding (1 179) or when playing rugby (839). The sociological interest of the data lies in their detail. The summary of in-line skating accidents is a good example, particularly as European data are available on the same sport and for the same period.

The study found that most in-line skating injuries (62.3%) involved children between 10 and 14 years of age and that 66.5% of those injured were boys. Injuries occurred most frequently in summer (37.8%) and in spring (36%), and between the hours of 4 p.m. and 8 p.m. (41%). The part of the body most commonly affected by all types of injury was the forearm (30.5%), and 17.7% of the injured children had been wearing some form of protection. As a proportion of all the cases covered, in-line skating accounted for 0.6%.[57]

Although the data gathered were of a general nature and not specifically concerned with sport, they were very precise. They included, for example, a breakdown of the circumstances or factors contributing to accidents, and it is worth giving an example of the detail recorded. The data specify, for instance, whether the person fell because of surface conditions (e.g., rocky, slippery, rough), 5.2%; because of a stunt or difficult manœuvre (e.g., use of a ramp), 5%; because of being pushed by another person, 0.8%; because of malfunction of the in-line skate (e.g. loose wheel), 0.8% etc. Even more detail is supplied (naturally enough) about the medical nature of the injuries incurred, including grazes, bruising or inflammation of the finger, hand, face, toe and ankle etc., dislocation or partial dislocation of the forearm, finger, hand or toe. It has to be said that many less wide-ranging sociological and ethnological studies fail to produce such a precise level of observation in relation to aspects of sport.

Information gathered in France about rollerblading accidents between 1986 and 1994 closely parallels the Canadian findings inasmuch as 50% of the accidents involved young people aged between 10 and 14 (EHLASS,[58] 1996). The most frequent type of injury was to the wrist, and 37% of the accidents occurred in street settings (e.g., on roadways or pavements or in pedestrian areas). The 932 cases reported over the period involved a disproportionate number of girls. While this finding cannot be extrapolated to the country generally and much less to European level, it is worth noting as atypical. There is no parallel finding, for example, in the EHLASS data on accidents in paragliding, windsurfing or karting (a particularly male pursuit) or on those which occurred in playgrounds or at school.

Clearly, accidentology is a specific branch of research in certain countries. Apart from its obvious uses in traumatology, it can help to explain how

---

57. Source: CHIRPP data summaries, all ages:
http://www.hc-sc.gc.ca/hpb/lcdc/brch/injury/irils_f.html (consulted on 28 September 1999).
58. In April 1986 the European Council set up a system of accident reporting and surveillance for non-public situations. It is entitled the European Home and Leisure Accident Surveillance System (EHLASS).

certain accidents may occur quite commonly and thus be familiar within a particular country, while remaining exceptional events in the lives of individuals.[59] It makes it possible to go beyond the approach whereby sports injuries are trivialised and the consequences of certain forms of physical exercise are overlooked, predictable though they are.

Here it is worth quoting a contemporary example of the value judgments underpinning the very notion of what is predictable in terms of sports accidents. A French physical education website categorised types of accident as follows: "foreseeable [e.g.] when a 40-year-old does ten 400-metre laps on a track, keeping pace with the other runners, and then has a heart attack; [and] unforeseeable, e.g. when a player is tackled during a soccer match"[60] (sic)! The perception of a difference here in terms of predictability is highly subjective: involvement in one specific sport can often impede understanding of sports in general.

The examples of France, Switzerland and Sweden

What, then, is the situation in Europe in those countries that have accident data systems? Does this type of data gathering offer a solution to the apparent problem of lack of awareness about violence in sport? And what other types of survey exist?

At European level there are various data-gathering mechanisms, including the European Observatory on the Prevention of Risks (OEPR, from its French initials) and the EHLASS accident monitoring system mentioned above in connection with rollerblading accidents. They enable us to form an accurate picture of sports accidents as a proportion of accidents generally. As a rule, accidents are grouped in three categories: traffic accidents, occupational accidents and accidents in everyday life. The last of these includes accidents in the home and at school as well as our particular area of interest, sports accidents. Between 1986 and 1997, head injuries, different sports and leisure pursuits and games generally accounted for 48% of accidents (compared with accidents in the home, which represented 46% of the total). Once again, young boys were the main victims of sports accidents.

Overall, sports are thus a major cause of injury, particularly for certain categories of people, notably young men who, of course, are the most active in terms of sport.

---

59. http://www.securite-routiere.org/Connaître/statisti.html (consulted on 14 October 2003).
60. http://universtaps.free.fr/nouvellepage68.html (consulted on 14 October 2003).

Study by the French National Sickness Insurance Fund

The argument that there is a blind spot, or lack of accurate data, where accidents directly associated with sport and other forms of physical exercise are concerned has been invalid at least since 1999, when the French Caisse nationale d'assurance maladie (or CNAM) [National Sickness Insurance Fund] published the results of a wide-ranging study. The CNAM's approach was quite particular inasmuch as it is the body responsible for the system of reimbursing medical expenses occasioned by accidents and injuries generally. The large-scale study emphasised not only the high incidence of sports accidents (across the age range they are the second most common type of accident in everyday life after accidents in the home, and the most common type among people aged 10 to 24), but also their nature and cost. What follows is based on data from the OEPR website and *La Lettre de l'économie du sport*, which asked the CNAM to supply certain detailed findings. A file summarising the various results and posted on the Internet is revealingly entitled *"Les accidents de sports sont trop frequents"* [Sports accidents happen too often].[61]

It is worth bearing in mind some aspects of the methodology used in the CNAM study, which covered the years 1987-94. The data were gathered by post from a representative sample of people insured under the general social security system (217 432 households with a total of 606 716 individuals). It was based on two questionnaires, one on the socioeconomic characteristics of the household and the other on accidents that had happened to each member of the household over the preceding year (excluding traffic and occupational accidents). It would seem that "the last twelve months" is gradually becoming the accepted period of reference in most studies of physical behaviour, and indeed consumer behaviour generally (Bodin and Héas, 2002). Working on the principle that respondents are likely to report neither the most minor accidents nor those that occurred least recently, the CNAM estimated that its statistics fell short of the reality. Eventually, in 1996, having noted little change in the results from one year to the next, the CNAM wound up the survey.

From the results, it was estimated that 8% of the French population suffered an accident in the course of their daily lives in any one year and that, particularly among younger people, many of the most serious accidents were caused by sport.[62]

---
61. No. 472, Wednesday 3 March 1999.
62. http://www.cepr.tm.fr/fr/observatoire/statAVCmaison.html (consulted on 14 October 2003).

- Between 1987 and 1994 there were 46 000 home and leisure accidents, including 6 600 sports accidents (14.4%). The risk of an accident in sport is thus approximately 11/1 000. More than half the accidents were caused by a ball sport (soccer, 35%; basketball, handball and volleyball, 10%; rugby, 6%; and tennis, 5%), while skiing accounted for 10% and cycling 4%.
- Three quarters of the accidents were suffered by men and boys.
- The risk of accident is fairly low among children aged under 10, and then increases up to the age of 24 (when it is 26/1 000).
- Falling is the main cause of accidents (57.2%, compared with 40.9% due to being struck by or colliding with a person or object),[63] especially among those at the lower and upper ends of the age range.
- The part of the body most affected was the lower limbs (hurt in 58.5% of the accidents, compared with 35% for injuries to the trunk and 25% for injuries to the upper limbs).[64]

What were the effects of the accidents?

The list of sports injuries in descending order of frequency was as follows: sprains (25%),[65] muscular lesions (23%), damaged tendons (22%), bruises and pulled muscles (10%), torn muscles (10%), and fractures (5%). The main causes of sprain were jogging, tennis and ball sports. In 13% of cases, the victims of sports accidents had to be hospitalised, and 22% (with a predominance of skiing injuries) needed physiotherapy. Absence from work, averaging thirty-two days, was necessary in 25% of cases (and some accidents, notably in gymnastics, skiing and horse riding, necessitated longer absences, averaging forty-two to forty-six days). Clearly the accidents cost society a great deal of money. The average cost of a sports accident in France at the time was €837.36, compared with €1 057.77 for an accident in the home. In absolute terms and extrapolating to national level, accidents in the home were the most costly (€1.8 billion), ahead of sports accidents (€0.45 billion) and leisure accidents (€0.25 billion).

---

63. Similar proportions were recorded in the EHLASS survey carried out in the United Kingdom in 1998: falling, 57.6%; being struck by or colliding with a person or object, 34.7%. *Home and leisure accident reports, summary of 1998 data*, Department of Trade and Industry, 2000. http://www.dti.gov.uk (consulted on 20 April 2004).
64. Source, CNAM 1999. A later survey (CNAM/Inpes 2000) showed the atypical consequences of the recent craze for skateboarding and other roller sports: here it was the upper limbs that were worst affected (63.6%), especially the wrist and forearm (45.4%).
65. EHLASS found that, between 1986 and 1995, 30% of sprains occurred in sport.

Supplementing these data, the French National Observatory on Safety in Schools and Higher Education Establishments (ONSES) publishes an annual report on accidents exclusively within schools, and therefore including those occasioned in physical education (PE) and school sports (as opposed to sports generally). Close reading of the report throws up a paradox: "Among student activities, PE is the main source of accidents (with eight deaths recorded), while the second source is the movement of students between classes (on corridors and staircases) .... At secondary level, where PE is taught as a more formal and institutional subject with specialised staff, the accident rate is very high. This is where most accidents occur" (Lorant, 2000, p. 146). While this information is interesting, it is insufficient because the causes of accidents in PE are not explained. Which young people are most prone to injury: the most active in sport, or the least "well prepared"? If it is the most active, then could over-training be a factor? If not, should we look for the causes in factors such as unbalanced diet, stressful lifestyle, or perhaps even a lifestyle in which risk-taking is admired? Or do the findings simply reflect less typical forms of behaviour, for example, behaviour involving a greater degree of violence towards the self and others?

The French "Baromètre santé jeunes" [Youth Health Barometer] for the period 1997-98 offers some ideas here: "Young accident victims are significantly more likely [than others] to consume alcohol more frequently, to smoke tobacco regularly and to have smoked cannabis at least once. It is reasonable to suggest a causal link between the consumption of these substances (which can lead to reduced vigilance) and the occurrence of accidents".[66] Sociological readings of the findings are not straightforward: "The French study (Arènes et al., 1998) also shows that young people from households in which the father is unemployed have a significantly higher incidence of accidents than others."

From these surveys we have a clearer picture of the objective consequences of sport and other forms of physical exercise, taking account both of the way they are practised (factors such as the use – or not – of protective gear, the setting, the age of those involved and the nature of the supervision) and of their purpose (competitive or recreational). The surveys have also led to practical proposals. In March 1999, following on from its own study, the CNAM in conjunction with the French Health Education Committee (CFES) launched an awareness-raising campaign, using television advertisements and brochures to promote the use of protective gear in sport for the 10-24 age group, particularly in non-competitive contexts. The data collected in the CNAM surveys, which drew on

---

66. Quoted in *Traumatismes et accidents chez les jeunes (13-18 ans)*, http://homoepages.ulb.ac.be/~ndacosta/prome/sano22.html (consulted on 14 October 2003).
67. http://www.doctissimo.fr/html/sante/te.../sem02/0823/sa_5829_sport_chiffres.html (consulted on 16 September 2003).

a very large population sample, were subsequently used over a number of years by other organisations involved in information and accident prevention.[67]

So have we moved closer to a real understanding of the "sports accident" as a phenomenon?

The first point to be made is that these detailed retrospective statistics may under-estimate the incidence of sports accidents. From the information on where accidents occur we can estimate that sport and recreation probably account for a quarter of all accidents. Roughly half of all accidents at school (4.5% of the total) happen during PE, and when combined with leisure accidents (8%) and sports accidents as such (14%) this gives us 26.5%, not counting accidents that happen at home – in gardens, for example, during casual games of football, ping-ping or boules.

In considering these statistics, compiled more or less systematically as they are, and ultimately under-analysed, one is inclined to urge particular academic vigilance with regard to two common types of bias.

The first is the high risk of introducing value judgments, or indeed a degree of paternalism. In attempting to counter "sociocultural imbalance", for example, there is a risk of drawing simplistic conclusions: "The most accident-prone young people are the most violent and those living in situations most characterised by violence. Sport can help them to deal better with these different types of violence". There is a risk of focusing too closely on a single main causal factor, (e.g. the socio-occupational circumstances of parents, or thoughtlessness on the part of either those practising a sport or those with a caring role). One paediatrician has commented, for example, that: "All the risk factors – both human and material – for accidents are to be found in lower-income families. Repeated accidents must be interpreted as alarm calls, signalling personal or family difficulties".[68] Prioritising a particular point of view often reflects a degree of self-interest – which brings us to the second possible form of bias.

This involves the ways in which physical education or sport and recreation can be used as tools for particular ends. "Beyond the policy choice of seeking to improve a nation's health, we need to question the missionary approach of certain institutions and their representatives at every level, where the will to do good, to help others and to be altruistic can be a means of assuming power or control over others" (Lorant, 2000, p. 150). Surely, at a time when the new, modern Olympics have just taken place in the historically significant location of Greece, this is a point that needs to be underscored.

---

68. Professor Chevalier, Head of Paediatrics at Ambroise Paré Hospital, quoted in *Accidents domestiques: les chiffres*, June 2002:
http://www.doctissimo.fr/html/sante/tex5640_accidents_domestiques_chiffres.html
(consulted on 19 April 2004).

Sport does harm, particularly at certain periods of a person's life, and the effects can be lasting. Some physical practices that are clearly counter-productive seem to attract approval from those who practise sports (including those who have suffered accident or injury) and/or from their families. In attempting to tackle these problems and paradoxes, comparing the situation in different countries will help us to address the specific issue of violence in sport more rigorously.

Sedentary Switzerland?

There are other countries that pay particular attention to accidents in sport and elsewhere, and have decades of experience in documenting them. The Swiss Accident Prevention Office, for example, has operated since 1938. Its focus in recent years has been determined by the following assessment: "Almost a million people are the victims of accidents every year, three-quarters of them on the roads, in the context of sport, at home, in the garden or during leisure activities, and a quarter at work. As leisure time expands the number of accidents will undoubtedly increase".[69]

It is for this reason that economic forward studies attempt to predict the direct and indirect harm caused by accidents and their cost to society as a whole, both in relative terms (physical activity as opposed to sedentariness) and potentially (considering the possible gains if people were more active). The Swiss Federal Office of Public Health (OFSP) has, for example, published data on the economic impact of the relationship between health and physical activity (OFSP, 2001).[70] On the basis of its analysis it states: "The beneficial effects of regular physical activity are widely documented in scientific publications[71] [and our] findings show that the physical activity practised by a majority of the population currently leads to the avoidance of 2.3 million cases of illness every year as well as at least 3 300 deaths and 2.7 billion Swiss francs in direct treatment costs". The authors acknowledge that physical exercise, and particularly sport, exposes people to "risks that also have economic repercussions. Every year around 300 000 accidents are caused by sports [as well as] some 160 deaths, with 1.1 billion Swiss francs in direct treatment costs". Logically, therefore, the work of the OFSP has to be supported by measures to control the risk of accidents in sport.

Switzerland continues to issue information about the benefits of sport and to encourage it as a form of preventive health care, for recent statistics show that the nation is becoming more sedentary. It would seem that sedentariness

---
69. http://www.bpa.ch/portrait/qui_est_le_bpa.index.html (consulted on 18 September 2003).
70. OFSP Bulletin 33/01 of 13 August 2003, published on http://www.admin.ch/bag
71. Van Praagh and Duché, 2000, and Lorant, 2000, are highly sceptical about the academic objectivity of such assertions.

has been identified as the evil to be tackled, and a methodical approach to combating physical inactivity is called for. Health promotion programmes follow one after another, although the OFSP study admits to significant bias in some respects, notably stemming from a hypothesis that runs counter to the fundamental tenets of sports sociology, namely the credulous assumption that "the proportion of active and inactive people in the Swiss population is the same right across the age range". Given that most European populations are ageing and that sedentariness is more widespread among the elderly, the OFSP estimates must be seen at best as optimistic. The study details the risk factors for people with a sedentary lifestyle in relation to specific illnesses: 1.84 for cardiovascular problems; 1.90 for colon cancer, and 2.00 for osteoporosis (the respective risks of death being 1.43, 1.88 and 1.68). "Doing nothing" would seem to have become a mortally dangerous pursuit[72] and to say that activity (both physical and mental) is prized would be an understatement.

Whereas Switzerland is trying to combat the "evil" of sedentariness, other countries are much less afflicted by the image, or reality, of ageing.

Sweden: Europe's "sportiest" country

As mentioned above, people in northern European countries seem less resistant to sport than their southern counterparts: more of their week is devoted to physical activity, which they practise more regularly and over a longer period of their lives. Sweden, in particular, stands out: with just 19% reporting that they practise no form of sport on a regular basis, the Swedes have the greatest enthusiasm for sport in Europe (CSA/TMO, 1998). The differences between the Swedish statistics and those for countries such as France or Russia are significant. Specifically, sport in Sweden seems to be practised regularly rather than "vigorously", according to the latest available large-scale study for Europe. Sports activity there would seem to be largely recreational, and indeed the Swedes do less "training" than people in many other countries (EORG, 2003, 23). What then is the situation in this pro-sport country with regard to sports accidents and injuries?

Some clues are available from a local-level study (De Loes, 1990), the conclusions of which include a reference to the scientifically-proven benefits of sport and physical exercise, notably in protecting against coronary disease and mental illness. The author goes on to highlight Sweden's "relatively high consumption of health care, entailing substantial costs" in relation to motor

---

72. A similar approach was adopted in Canada after a medical association documented 21 000 premature deaths due to inactivity (Katzmarzyk et al., "The economic burden of physical inactivity in Canada", *CMAJ*, No. 163 (11), November 2000).

sport, riding and snow sports such as downhill skiing. Sports accidents were the reason for 3% of consultations at the hospitals and clinics which took part in the survey. Drawing on reference studies, De Loes argued that the actual figure could be much higher, in the order of 9%. A great deal of emergency treatment generally was administered to the victims of sports accidents and this applied particularly to orthopaedic treatment (where more than half the patients in some units had suffered sports injuries). Soccer, as the most popular sport was, unsurprisingly, responsible for the greatest number of accidents (68 out of 162). The average number of medical consultations required per accident was 1.9. The proportion of patients hospitalised as a result of a sports accident was less than 1%, and the average length of stay in hospital was four days (much lower than the corresponding figures for France). On the question of the cost of sports accidents, the study is less convincing, because of the limited size of the sample and the difficulty of comparing health care systems and systems of payment for treatment.

All these data would seem to be significant in terms of policy choices in the different European societies. While we are not in a position to list all the aspects of economic and legal policy to which sports accidents are relevant, it should be noted that legislation is in preparation, or in some cases already on the statute books, requiring that the responsibilities of people involved at different levels in various forms of sport be clearly spelled out. Because sport and other forms of physical exercise entail risk-taking and present dangers, many countries have been quick to class the financial burden of the treatment required under the heading of costly emergency expenditure (in France, for example, provisions on mountain and air-sea rescue were extended in 2002 to other sports activities). Much of this type of legislation emphasises the responsibility borne by the individuals most directly concerned – i.e. those who practise sports – and it therefore requires them to cover part of the cost of emergency treatment, whether through special insurance or otherwise.

Does this widespread preoccupation with accidents mean that we live in high-risk societies? And what other forms of violence do we risk in sport, apart from accidents?

Addiction, sport and human bodies: strong political and social implications for Europe

There seems nowadays to be greater openness about addiction in sport than there once was. Since the late 1990s, doping scandals in particular have sparked widespread public debate and controversy about the status of various champions or teams and indeed about the legitimacy of specific sports (cycle racing in Europe, for example, and American football and baseball in the United States). The sudden and sometimes unexplained deaths of well-known young champions have reinforced the impression that certain practices have been going on largely behind the backs of the public, if not of major event organisers.

Opinion polls record reactions ranging from indignation through disillusionment to resignation. Reaction to the 1998 Festina scandal in the Tour de France was fierce: 52% of respondents said they were shocked that well-known figures from the worlds of politics, sport and entertainment had recently admitted to taking drugs (Ifop, 1998, for *Santé Magazine*). In relation specifically to sport the reaction was similar if not stronger: only 26% of respondents said they had not been at all shocked by revelations of drug-taking among racing cyclists; 84% agreed with the assertion that doping was unacceptable because it compromised the image of sport in the eyes of young people (Ifop, 1998, for *France Soir*, 20 July). In the immediate aftermath of the scandal, reactions thus seemed unanimous. A few years later, however, when doping in sport had become more visible (or at least less hidden), the public attitude seemed to be one of disillusionment. The major difference seemed to be that for more than two-thirds of French people (and sports fans showed little more optimism than others in this respect) the image of high-level sport had been ruined. There was no doubt that, by 2005, practices which people regarded as entirely on a par with doping would be widespread in the world of professional sport (Sofres, 2001, for *L'Equipe*). In response to the further question of using genetic science to enhance physical performance, the reaction was overwhelmingly negative: "All applications [of genetics] intended to produce fundamental changes in physiological characteristics or to improve performance were massively rejected: 73% of those questioned said 'no' to their use in prolonging athletes' careers (as against 25% in favour); in relation to the goal of improving stamina, 77% were opposed (as against 22%); for enhancing performance the rate of rejection was 82% (with 17% in favour); and for muscle-building in athletes it was

84% (as against 15%). Clearly the public is not attracted by the concept of sport as circus, offering a series of encounters between 'superhumans'". There would thus seem to be a certain discrepancy between the ideal and the reality.

A great deal of academic attention in Europe has been devoted to doping: numerous colloquies and seminars have been held and many publications have been produced. Indeed, in terms of recommending action, Europe has been in the vanguard: the Council of Europe was the first to pass a resolution on the subject (Resolution (67)12 on the doping of athletes), in 1967 (see below), recommending institutional, regulatory and statutory measures to control the violence which the different forms of doping represent. Nonetheless, there are problems inherent in approaching a social phenomenon that involves personal habits, particularly illegal habits (even if they are also group habits). People and organisations commonly decline (explicitly or otherwise) to reply to questionnaires (they refuse to take part, fail to distribute forms or do not collate results). This makes reliable data – in terms of sample size, for example – much harder to come by, although in the case of nationwide studies the information that is gathered is at least realistic (Laure et al., 2004). Similar difficulties affect attempts to collect data on such issues as homosexuality in sport (see below).

Looking beyond addiction as a medical problem

The issue of addiction is a familiar one that has been widely documented in different regions of the world. We intend to look both at the concept of addiction and at the current systematic use of doping, for both are significant.

The concept of addiction has received increased attention in recent decades, at the same time coming to be regarded as a medical problem.[73] "We can trace very clearly in the literature of psychiatry and psychoanalysis how, in the mid-1970s, concerns about depression and about addiction developed in parallel" (Ehrenberg, 1999, p. 141). Depression has been depicted as a major modern disease and as the rejection of an inherently contradictory imperative: to improve one's performance continually in every field of life while at the same time remaining relaxed (Ehrenberg, 1998, and see below). The connection between over-training and symptoms of depression, such as loss of self-esteem, has been specifically acknowledged, for example in soccer (Cascua, 2001). By contrast there is no such specific recognition of links between the depression that is "normal" in adolescence and the incidence of

---

73. Addiction was a concept in mediaeval justice, under which individuals incapable of paying their debts were required to work them off and thus became, to some extent, slaves (*Science et Vie*, No. 960, September 1997, p 112; Yvorel, 1991).

drug-taking (Peretti-Watel, 2003), and this demonstrates both the complexity of the phenomena with which we are dealing and the danger of slipping into value judgments that stigmatise a section of the population on the basis of what is essentially piecemeal information.

The practice among psychiatrists and doctors of using the term "addiction" rather than other expressions such as "drug-taking" or "use of doping products" reminds us that there are underlying institutional issues at stake. Since 1964 "addiction" has also been the term of choice for the World Health Organisation (WHO), being regarded as relatively non-stigmatising. The fact that societies today, especially in Europe, characterise certain types of behaviour by athletes and others in this way can be considered from a Foucauldian perspective in terms of the regimes to which human beings are subject, and more specifically "micro-powers" or "bio-powers" (Foucault, 1963, 1976, 1984). Medicine and its many allied disciplines, including psychology, nowadays exercise a significant level of surveillance of our most minor deeds and acts, and in sport this situation seems to be particularly accentuated.

Of course, medicine enjoys a great deal of legitimacy even though its various undesirable effects are now widely acknowledged – one such being the incidence of hospital-acquired infection, a recent outbreak of which in the French Clinique du Sport received much media coverage. It is also appropriate in this context to mention the fierce criticism directed at the medical personnel of some sports bodies. Among the problems highlighted by the Festina scandal in 1998 were shortcomings in the training and skills of the medical and paramedical personnel who work with professional cycling teams, and most particularly shortcomings in terms of self-regulation (through a professional code of conduct) and outside supervision.

Addiction or a personalised biochemical approach to human beings

As psychomedical phenomena the most obvious forms of addiction are those to such substances as alcohol, tobacco, pharmaceutical products in general and doping agents in particular, or other dependency-inducing drugs. These are known as "directly psychotropic" addictions.

Studies of addiction in the world of sport have focused to a remarkable extent on the life stories of particular well-known athletes – great and unusual figures (Heinich, 2003) – and academics have documented the ends of high-level athletes' careers (Chamalidis, 2000, p. 139; and Messner, 1992, p. 111). When such people leave the limelight they lose the social interaction associated with sport (as former comrades become estranged), public prestige is revealed for what it is (in some cases a mere veneer), supporters gradually turn to other heroes, and fan clubs disintegrate. Many former champions seem at this point to "give in" – to chronic inactivity or one of the many forms of addiction, for example. This perspective on the use of doping and other substances is a limited one: firstly because it fails to distinguish between substances that have different effects in terms of dependency, or indeed whose effects may be unknown (Fost, 1990), and secondly because it is simplistic. An addiction-centred approach emphasises the alienating and dispossessing effects of substance use, and downplays its collective aspect, except in terms of its consequences as regards sociability.

Yet taking pills or administering substances by injection is not a purely individual, or even an essentially individual, act. To read it as such is to misinterpret basic tenets of the sociology of deviance (Becker, 1985). Addictions are cultural practices in their own right and to lose sight of that is to overlook many aspects of the question.

There is no doubt that leaving the limelight of sporting glory is a very difficult transition for many athletes, who – whether seeking a form of substitution or attempting to carry on as before – react by turning to substances that apparently offer to recreate the pleasures, and more generally the sensations, that they previously derived from sport. It is clearly important to make this point.

At the same time, if we acknowledge that ending a career in competitive sport is like leaving a demanding job (whether paid or not), then sport can be considered a habitual, everyday activity. People retiring from other types of activity suffer a similar process of personal and social "bereavement": the diary is suddenly empty and normal everyday interaction has to be rethought in order to make it dynamic and capable of replacing what has been lost. Michel Platini summed it up when he said: "I died at the age of 32, on 17 May 1987" – thus equating the end of his professional football career with a symbolic death.

We therefore want to highlight other forms of addiction that are less obvious but just as significant. The use of substances is not, in fact, the only means of enhancing one's relationship with the world (and, in the sports context, one's performance) or indeed more broadly of altering one's mental and physical state (Héas et al., 2005). Clearly we also need to look at quasi-obsessional daily pursuits that involve a high expenditure of energy or respiratory hyperventilation – in other words, behavioural forms of addiction – and at the use of non-psychoactive substances that work indirectly by stimulating the body to release its own chemicals.[74]

---

74. http://hedomania.freee.fr/glossaire/addiction.htm (consulted on 13 December 2002).

Addiction in sport: hypercivilised or uncivilised?

The concept of addiction has undergone a noticeable shift in recent years: "less emphasis is placed on substances and more on compulsive behaviour and sensation-seeking. Anything can become addictive ..." (Ehrenberg, 1999, p. 141). For example, if mental and physical hyperactivity is interrupted or greatly diminished, athletes are left in a biological and psychosocial void and may have difficulty in coping.

These indirect addictions raise the basic anthropological questions of self-control and the control of others, and self-governance and the resultant ability to govern others (and vice versa) (Foucault, 1984, p. 116; Haroche, 1993, p. 54; and Héas, 2004).

The question is directly linked to that of interaction between individuals and groups and to the phenomenon of recognised or unrecognised prestige as a vector for social relationships. The theory generally accepted today is that self-control (and thus enhanced prestige) is socially required to a greater extent where social relationships are interdependent and mitigated by the legitimate authority of institutions specialised in all forms of control (Elias, 1973, 1994). In this context, addiction, whether to psychotropic substances or forms of behaviour, can be seen either as a hypercorrect habit from a sports perspective – as the athlete, following the advice of a peer group, strives to maintain control over his or her actions and kinaesthetic sensations – or as a deliberate releasing of controls. In the latter case the athlete plays along with the idea of the sport as a world apart, in which behaviour can be less controlled than it is elsewhere in society. Comments by athletes themselves highlight both these facets of their active life. Bodily exuberance and verbal exuberance are presented not only as valued, stimulating and virtually obligatory forms of group behaviour but also as extreme forms of expression for celebrating physical accomplishments, or indeed asserting one's existence as an athlete, as in the case of sportswomen in certain male-dominated pursuits (Héas et al., 2004).

Depending on our approach, whether from within a particular sport group or from the outside, we will categorise one and the same practice differently along a continuum ranging from adaptation to deviance. This individual and social approach will itself evolve through time and depending on the location of the activities considered: the use of a particular substance or device will be frowned upon in one situation and regarded as normal in another. The very notion of a dividing line between practices that amount to violence against oneself or others and those which are respectful of the self and others is inappropriate. Any form of behaviour observed or signalled emanates from a particular and thus specific sociocultural configuration. Analysing it is a complex business and requires us to relativise.

For example, even at modest levels of practice, certain sports require an exemplary degree of self-control, which can lead in the longer term to highly restrictive forms of behaviour. "I was 12 years old. The illness (an eating disorder) manifested itself gradually. I got involved in sport and started paying great attention to what I was eating .... There were times when the scales ruled my life" (Bourdeux, 2003). The practice of dieting to stay within a certain weight category is a case in point. It is very common for sportspeople to restrict what they eat – between a third and two thirds of them do so – and it can sometimes result in apparently sudden death (Eitzen, 1999, p. 66). It can also be part of a health-conscious lifestyle, amounting in some cases to a form of asceticism which is pursued day after day even when it is no longer essential to the life of former athletes. When people leave the world of sport behind more or less definitively, their former routines cease to have any value and become socially inappropriate and overtly damaging.

Prevention and treatment of dependency in sport

This more sophisticated approach to doping and addiction helps us to identify the different types of dependency at work in sport and elsewhere. As well as controls and advice, in different forms, for athletes and sports organisers, treatment and social support are gradually being developed. To address the complexity of addiction, a variety of initiatives have been taken in different parts of Europe.

In France several new clinics specialise in sports-related forms of addiction, and specialist groups of practitioners have also been formed. Examples include the Antennes médicales de lutte contre le dopage, or AMLD, [Anti-doping outreach units] set up in 2001, the Centre d'accompagnement et de prévention pour les sportifs, or CAPS, [Athletes' support and prevention centre] founded in 2000, and the Montevideo Clinic, which opened its doors in 2003 (Maitrot, 2003, p. 74, p. 82). Analysis of cases referred to units not specialising in the treatment of sportspeople also reveal the widespread nature of addiction and its pervasive presence in sport at every level. In 1999 a survey was carried out that offered (belated) insight into the links between sport and addiction to various substances: "13.9% of respondents had practised sport for more than two hours a day over a period of more than three years, 10.5% had already taken part in a national or international competition and 13.1% had used doping agents. The sports most frequently implicated were soccer (14.3%) and cycle racing (6%)".

These professional athletes were thus in contact with what has been termed "the dark side of sport" (Bodin and Héas, 2002, p. 100). But this notion needs to be approached with circumspection. F. Nordmann, for example, a former swimmer and a patient of the Montevideo Clinic, has supplied a more prosaic and perhaps more useful definition of doping: "The best way I can explain doping is the 'has to' syndrome [a notion borrowed from a mother whose injured daughter had been advised by Nordmann to take complete rest]. She was practically castigating me when she replied, 'That's just not possible, sir. She has to swim this weekend!'" (Maitrot, 2003, p. 84).

The next point to be made concerns the standard-setting, axiological climate apparently predominant in certain European countries: a climate that advocates reason and denounces excess. While it is not in itself a novelty, historically speaking (Héas, 2004, p. 69; and Foucault, 1984, p. 66), it has been particularly in evidence in recent times.

Are we trying to make physical activity too "reasonable"?

As noted above, health promotion is everywhere today. In the sociocultural context that is tending to become the norm, excess of all kinds has been increasingly stigmatised. Consumers who over-indulge in products and services available for satisfying their desires risk the disapproval of family and colleagues. Governments are gradually putting in place systems of communicating, preventing and analysing risks that are directly or indirectly related to sport. The sanctions applied by anti-doping committees are part of this trend towards health monitoring and the control of people's behaviour (although the latter remains largely ineffective). Instructions not to use this or that product or not to behave in this or that way are legion. The public-health statistics referred to above are reproduced freely in the mass media in campaigns to curb personal habits. The precision of risk analysis lends a moralistic, if not soteriological,[75] tone to campaign messages. "People end up believing that moderation in all things is the key to avoiding premature death [and] former hedonists are becoming old fogies" (Fohr and Monnin, 2004, p. 11, p. 18). As anthropologist V. Nahoum-Grappe puts it: "There is a religious aspect to asceticism and prescriptiveness". What is new, however, is not the salutary nature of certain practices nor the missionary way in which they are presented, but rather the fact that they have been taken up on a massive scale.

Physical temperance as a mass pursuit

Other studies of physical practices have already highlighted the way in which some of them, such as relaxation and different forms of yoga in vogue in Europe in the 1980s and 1990s, were taken on board in this type of soteriology (Héas, 1996, 2004; and Perrin, 1986). The practices in question came out of a counter-cultural movement in the late 1960s that coincided with the importation of the Californian Human Potential Movement and with a reassessment of ancient practices from both the western world and the east

---

75. Soteriology is the doctrine of salvation.

and Far East. Massage, deep-breathing routines and relaxation techniques gradually acquired new social legitimacy as they offered people a whole range of sensory experiences and benefits, real or imagined, in terms of vitality with due regard for the self, others and nature.

The notion of not taking risks has come to be valued as these practices have spread steadily over thirty years – with the formation of national federations and European-level teachers' organisations providing professional codes of practice, standard methodologies and respected institutionalised training programmes (Héas, 1995, 1996, and 2004). Previously confined to more privileged sections of the population, such practices have now become widespread and thus more democratised. They all promote sustained attention to the body for the purposes (explicit or implicit) of achieving a better quality of life, learning to relax and take care of oneself, staving off the ageing process and generally preventing "wear and tear". Tens of thousands of Europeans come together every year in a plethora of classes and courses. And as relaxation has become a leisure activity it has also become quite a lucrative occupation: people skilled in bodily practices – who previously operated on the fringes of institutions such as hospitals, schools and sports clubs, sometimes on a voluntary basis – are now fully involved in health, education and physical exercise programmes.

The injunction to relax physically and mentally and what is a real social need for relaxation seem, paradoxically, at odds with the cult of performance and activity that is equally promoted in the same European societies. There is an apparent choice between gentleness and pain. Yet that choice is illusory, for all the practices in question – whether high-risk or low-risk – entail forms of violence such as the dependency that is induced between teachers and students, or the pressure on both to achieve results. In particular, there is an increasingly pervasive ambivalence between the notion of respecting one's "own" pace and the suggestion that one should keep up with others. Like any paradoxical injunction it creates uncertainty which can be disconcerting, and indeed a source of anxiety, for individuals and groups.

Relaxation and risk-taking: a modern and paradoxical form of violence

The way in which the physical models associated with the practices in question have been disseminated to people everywhere via the mass media is probably unprecedented. This ongoing imposition of norms – on the one hand through the media and advertising and on the other through senior figures in charge of sport – potentially invites a reaction. Both those groups of people in Europe closest to the forms of cultural behaviour being advocated and those most removed from them are likely to reject such mass programming en bloc. One form of reaction is already happening, in the shape of risk-taking behaviour on the part of the "heirs" of privilege.[76] By pitching themselves against the elements (in mountaineering or on the high seas, for example) they take risks in order to bring meaning to lives that they regard, consciously or otherwise, as monotonous and lacking any real challenge or harshness because the constant concern in the modern urban environment is to offer squeaky-clean comfort, safety and ever-present physical support (provided by new information and communication technologies, motorised transport, moving walkways, lifts etc.). Technology is becoming a standard of life, and contact with the world and others is frequently indirect and mediated by the available technological tools.

Using different risk-taking practices, young people from disadvantaged backgrounds also seem to need to go through the ancient anthropological process of seeking out the fundamental limits of the human being: driving too fast and/or taking mood-altering substances are aspects of an individual and collective quest for direction. A state of giddiness is sought because it identifies instability and, by extension, possible footholds and points of support. Losing one's bearings in a controlled way becomes the key to finding out what life is actually about. Risk or risk-taking confers meaning on one's existence.

Older Europeans who practise certain extreme sports, such as motor or motorcycle racing, off-piste skiing, solo rock climbing or ultra endurance,[77] have to subject their bodies to a remarkable degree of actual or potential violence, immediate or deferred. The risk of sudden death (or the increased likelihood of death in the case of ultra endurance) has become an element of key importance for some athletes in Europe and throughout the world. This desperate quest for meaning in modern life inevitably leads to forms of addiction or – to put it differently – to forms of psychosocioactive dependency.

Is the sedentary lifestyle on the way out?

The values currently being disseminated promote hyperactivity in physical pursuits and sports as a means of combating the sedentary lifestyle of some European countries (Switzerland, mentioned above, being a case in point). The ritualistic, anthropological bases for this denunciation of sedentariness can be explained precisely with reference to relaxation practices, in which physical immobility and rigidity symbolise death and people are therefore exhorted to movement and to suppleness in all areas of modern life (Héas, 2004).

---

76. A similar social phenomenon was observed among the nineteenth-century bourgeoisie, whose children (and potential heirs) placed too much importance on consumerism in general and travel in particular, in opposition to their parents' attitudes (Schumpeter, 1942, quoted by Herpin, 2001).

77. The term now commonly applied to series of traditional practices (e.g. swimming, cycling and running races) which athletes undertake consecutively either without breaks or with measured breaks. Such events include, at the upper extreme, the multi-day deca triathlon.

Doping as a behaviour pattern: alien or familiar?

In the sociocultural context described we should seek to approach the various forms of addiction from this more complex and non-partisan perspective. In other words, we need to take an approach that is more anthropological than sociological, eschewing official or moral reproach and simplistic value judgments, and ignoring the inevitable rumours that spread when rules are broken with ease in milieus such as that of sport.

The use of doping agents and the virtually omnipresent suspicion that they are being used are prominent factors in the approach to sport in many European countries. Resistance to genuine spot checks – where no one is given advance notice that drug testing will be carried out – is no longer confined to particular individuals or bodies within the sports system. Instead it has become the subject of what can be bitter negotiations involving representative bodies, host countries and/or event organisers and participating countries (Maitrot, 2003, p. 93). International institutions, event organisers and competitors henceforth have to accept a mutual understanding not only in relation to behaviour in sport but also with regard to drug-testing practices, whether or not all parties find them tolerable. The conflict between the official imposition of controls on the one hand and attempts to avoid controls on the other is increasingly becoming a basic feature of sports events. At stake are not only sporting outcomes (e.g. whether a team or competitor is eliminated or progresses to a further round) but also, and more prosaically, the direct and indirect financial consequences of the way in which national event branding is developed or enhanced. There are innumerable examples of conflict in recent years over values and standards: in the soccer World Cup in France in 1998, in the Six Nations Tournament and the 1999 Tour de France, to name but a few. The overlapping and sometimes contradictory interests of the different parties involved make it extremely hard to assess the phenomenon of doping, which involves identifying the boundaries between what is acceptable and what is accepted, and between forms of preparation and training and the taboo area of artificial aids. What is called doping today may be standard practice tomorrow.

Are both sport and doping modern imperatives?

The very existence of these multiple interests and of the negotiations that precede sports events makes the actual competitions more pressured. The only factor that seems to have remained unchanged down the years is the prestige to be gained in the competitive arena. And here we need to exercise the vigilance of the historian, for it is hard not to slip into naive optimism or at least a degree of nostalgia.

In ancient Greece there were various series of games. Each city (many of them the port cities) apparently organised its own: as well as the Olympic Games there were games at Delphi (the Pythian Games, initiated in 586 BC), Corinth (the Isthmian Games, dating from 582 BC) and Argos (the Nemean Games, started in 573 BC). And all this pre-dated the golden age of the ancient Olympics – from around 500-450 BC (300 years after the Games first came into existence). This development of the games organised by different cities was not problem-free. The various games embodied and facilitated attempts to gain or maintain political and commercial domination. The different peoples were concerned with promoting their own particular currencies, their raw materials and, in some cases, their institutions or more generally their way of life or world view (the particular alphabets and languages used being tools in this process). Similarly, financial and other games were a preoccupation for the ancient cities just as they are for our modern societies. For example, the democratic Athenian law-maker Solon (640-558 BC), whose policy it was to reduce the tax burden on poorer people, put a 500-drachma ceiling on winnings from games (Thomas, 1992). Recent archaeological studies have highlighted the amounts of money to be won at the ancient games, and also the quantities of wine consumed in the arenas.[78]

There is no doubt that doping has a long history. It is not our intention to explore that history in detail. The sports system itself was probably becoming more complex at the same time as different practices were coming into use and others were being dropped more or less arbitrarily. None of this is new. What is newer is the spread – gradual at first and now more rapid – of a single model of what it is to be a sportsperson: namely to enjoy international recognition and to be paid for what has generally become a job, albeit a prestigious one in which the work has high added value (see below). Sporting performances and their settings are today largely standardised, thus facilitating comparison among them, and sportsmen and sportswomen therefore appear in principle to enjoy greater basic equality. As a result, confrontations between them tend more and more to have an international if not almost "universal" dimension. It is a process that inevitably elicits a quite out-of-the-ordinary level of risk-taking.

Sport, economics and the quest for power: warfare by another means?

The systematic doping practised in former East Germany was another facet of the violence perpetrated in the name of defending a nation or an established political system and represents an aspect of sport's apologetic function (Bodin and Héas, 2002). The facts have now been established through access (albeit partial in some cases) to archives, and through evidence from both

---

78. Article from Archaeology, quoted in *Le Nouvel Observateur*, No. 2059, 22 April 2004, p. 89.

former top athletes and former coaches. Moreover, we hear world records in certain sports being described – notably by those champions of sports apologia, the television commentators – as being "from another era" or "unattainable"! Of course the involvement of states in the preparation of those who represent them is peculiar neither to sport nor to the countries of the former eastern bloc. Stigmatisation is a common response to difference – to those who have another cultural point of view or who disregard what are considered normal practices. It has been directed, for example, against the practice of body-building for sports that require technical finesse, or against slow-paced training if the norm is rapid, repetitive workouts.

Not only that, but other sensitive activities, such as the physical and psychological preparation and deployment of combat troops, involve sustained recourse to chemical substances. Under the cover of state secrecy, such activities – whether of a systematic or a one-off nature – conceal practices the consequences of which are unknown or may even be hushed up. In the fields of artistic and creative endeavour, drug use is much less taboo and, indeed, is sometimes sought as an aid to creativity or a spur to inspiration. Are many people genuinely offended by this, and does it really tarnish the reputation of those authors or artists recognised as drug users, if their works continue to be admired long after their deaths?

In sport these precisely programmed and orchestrated practices have involved, and probably continue to involve, serious forms of violence: dangerous experiments with the molecular composition of drugs or with combinations of drugs, temporary or permanent side-effects that are more or less incapacitating in future life, injuries, accidents and premature deaths. While these forms of violence would seem to be directly physical in their effects, they inevitably have wider repercussions on the lives of athletes and members of their families. Another legitimate source of concern is the fact that they resemble in many respects the types of orchestrated violence practised against some Third World peoples. Evidence that has come to light of certain practices in less advanced countries suggests a strong similarity between the most disinherited peoples of the world and athletes – take, for example, the use in certain southern-hemisphere countries of human guinea pigs for the rapid testing of new substances or new medical "solutions" without the burden of ethical regulations that apply in the developed world.[79]

However, the question of doping and other forms of addiction also raises the further question of its indirect and symbolic consequences.

---

79. *Manière de voir*, (2004), No. 73, February/March.

Finding an approach to doping between control and negotiation

In certain cases where athletes, having "repented" of their past actions, have elected – either at the end of their careers or more rarely following a decision to leave the sport world of their own free will – to tell the truth about doping as a habitual practice, resistance to openness about what actually goes on is sometimes reminiscent of the mafia. The fact that athletes attempting to sound the alert can find themselves ousted from a team, or indeed from their sport, raises the issue of freedom of expression and action, and thus of what democracy actually implies. What existing or potential safeguards can guarantee freedom of expression and action in these cases, and how can such controls be applied in real situations?

Laws and regulations on the control of doping in Europe

While addictive practices and doping are not new, they appear to keep one step ahead not only of recommendations designed to alert competitors, event organisers and the public in general to such systematic practices, but also of supranational harmonisation measures. The recommendations have constituted regular reminders about the systematic use of doping in particular sports or particular countries. The harmonisation measures have been framed with a view to avoiding policies as regards regulations or criminal law that are of dubious fairness and may even be contradictory in relation to one and the same form of behaviour, which may be categorised here as deviant, there as criminal and somewhere else as harmless.

Pioneering legislation was first enacted as early as 1965 in French-speaking Belgium and France. In France it is doctors responsible for the care of professional racing cyclists (in the Tour de France and Tour de l'avenir) who seem to have originated the first attempts to combat doping in "their" sport – attempts subsequently replicated for sport in general. It was at the doctors' initiative that a European colloquy was organised, on the basis of which the French law of 1965 was drafted. It is important to note this, for it underscores the point that "while a doping culture does exist in cycle racing [the particular sport in question here], there is also an anti-doping culture, and that should not be forgotten".[80] The struggle between the two cultures continues today as cyclists and event organisers try to evade anti-doping measures decided elsewhere. There is a real danger that the status quo will simply be maintained (with doping acknowledged and more or less camouflaged by certain advocates of the sport) if, on the one hand, decisions are not democratically taken and uniformly applied and, on the other, sports events are

---

80. From an interview with P. Laure, author of *Le dopage*, published in 1995, available on the Internet at http://perso.infonie.fr/arthur73/universitaire.html (consulted on 6 January 1999).

effectively monopolised by particular interest groups. At any time, under the cover of increasing rest periods for the benefit of the athletes, the controlling bodies – by deciding to limit the number of competitions, thus curtailing certain events – can effectively exclude both particular practices and particular organisations as they wish.

Since its inception in 1949, the Council of Europe has pioneered the fight against doping. As long ago as 1963 it described doping as the intention to increase the output of the human body in athletic performance through the administration of substances alien to the body or of any physiological substance in abnormal quantities (Dugal, 1990). A broader warning against doping was issued in 1967 with Resolution 67 (12) of the Council of Europe, inviting the member states to introduce anti-doping regulations. The resolution was passed at a time when Europe's collective conscience was beginning to be stirred by widespread media coverage of doping problems (Council of Europe, 1999).[81]

The primary purpose of such initiatives was to control practices taking place at elite level and to alert public opinion in Europe more than it had been alerted by the press reports of the day and behaviour and reactions on the ground – which included refusals to undergo testing, strikes, and cases of athletes being taken ill, dropping out or, indeed, dying in competition. The IOC eventually followed the lead given by the Council of Europe and certain international sports federations (notably cycling's governing body) by adopting anti-doping rules for the 1968 Olympic Games in Mexico.

The Council of Europe's second avenue of approach found expression in the wider context of the European Sport for All Charter (see Resolution (76) 41), Article 5 of which stipulated that methods should be sought "to safeguard sport and sportsmen from exploitation for political, commercial or financial gain, and from *practices that are abusive or debasing, including the unfair use of drugs*".[82] While it is the last point that interests us here, it should not be allowed to obscure the wider issue of the abuse of sport or debasement through sport, including the exploitation of human beings.

Against this background, negotiations between sports bodies and supranational institutions gradually moved in the direction of setting up national anti-doping committees, a move that had become theoretically if not yet politically possible. The European Anti-Doping Charter for Sport – introduced in Recommendation R (84) 19, adopted on 25 September 1984, provided for the problem to be tackled on a wider front, urging research and education measures and an injection of public funding. While the charter was not legally

---
81. Study of national legislation on sport in Europe, Council of Europe (1999).
82. Emphasised by the author.

binding, it constituted a step towards the signature in 1989 of the Anti-Doping Convention (ETS No. 135). The convention was innovative in that it was potentially applicable in every country, within Europe and beyond it. In force since March 1990, it aims, among other things, to make it harder to acquire and use drugs such as anabolic steroids (which are singled out), and it supports the introduction of testing for drug use both during and outside periods of competition. The latter practice was current in a number of countries, including Sweden, where most testing took place outside the context of competitive events (Dugal, 1990). It was not until September 1995, however, that the IOC and the European Community decided jointly to spend more than US$2 million on combating doping involving the injection of growth hormones, a practice known to have been going on since the 1980s. Indeed, some observers had gone so far as to accuse the IOC of having done nothing for fifteen years "while athletes who had been prepared with not only growth hormones but also cortisone, EPO, testosterone and other undetectable substances stepped up to receive medals in many events" (De Mondenard, 2000, p. 268). And what is one to think of the IOC awarding the Gold Olympic Order of Merit to Honecker, former Chancellor of the German Democratic Republic, where doping was institutional in the state system?

Litigation

The question of litigation in this context is a timely one today. Depending on the relationships between sports movements (associations, federations and private companies) and the administrative authorities in the different European countries, dispute resolution can take quite different forms.

On the one hand, for a long time disputes about rulings in the world of sport could not be handled by the ordinary courts. This applied in relation to disciplinary measures in Finland, the United Kingdom and Denmark in 1999. Rulings by sport bodies are not subject to review by the civil or administrative courts in all Council of Europe member states, and in those that have such a system the approaches vary. (In the United Kingdom in 1999 it appeared that sport's "independent" status was about to be reviewed.) This inconsistency within Europe still continues to impede the recognition that "sports scandals" affect, first and foremost, citizens who are free and equal in the eyes of the law.

On the other hand, litigation has not been exclusively concerned with people who practise a sport occasionally or regularly and who, in the course of competition or play, suffer injury and have to take as much as several weeks off work. In cases involving repeated accidents, or indeed proven instances of doping, who is responsible and who should bear or share the resulting costs (of hospital treatment, for example, or treatment for drug addiction)? Should it be the keen, if imprudent, athlete, or the association that encouraged him or her to resort to doping or indeed the national federation? Or should action be directed against the political authorities responsible for the location where the accident occurred, or where the drug use was alleged? A range of individuals and bodies are implicated or affected here, including employers, insurers and members of local and national authorities.

In 2000, the single issue of financing mountain rescue was approached in many different ways across Europe: in France it led to a bill giving local authorities the power to require that persons rescued after accidents as a result of sport or leisure activities should contribute to the rescue costs (Amoudry Report to the French Senate, 267, 1998-99). As the issue was being debated in France, rescue was still being provided free of charge in Spain and Italy by, respectively, a public service in the form of the Civil Guard and the National Alpine and Cave Rescue Corps, a joint public and voluntary-sector service.

In those cases where local authorities (at *Land* or canton level for example) provide the rescue service for victims of sports accidents, the costs tend to be shared between these bodies and the state, with a contribution from the principal beneficiary, namely the accident victim. In Belgium, before recent changes in the rules, sportspeople who suffered accidents received no reimbursement of their medical costs (even for a stay in hospital), nor any incapacity benefit for periods off work.[83] Henceforth, injured sportspeople are to be reimbursed by Belgium's mutual insurance funds, with entitlement from the day following an accident.

At a more general level, not all Europeans are equally satisfied with sports and cultural provision and with what is undertaken at local level. Women and older people are the most likely to express dissatisfaction with local authorities' provision for sport and recreation (EORG, 2003, p. 29). This is probably a reflection of the inequalities that affect all Europeans in relation to sport. The values and standards promoted through sport and recreation focus on adults and on the male sex (see below).

With regard to doping, no cases may ever come before the courts in situations where athletes' representatives or event owners carry sufficient clout in terms of market share or audience ratings. The NBA (see below) has, for example, such negotiating power that it has managed to veto certain controls on the consumption of alcohol and marijuana (Eitzen, 1999, p. 63). That

---

83. Law of 24 December 2003, Section 233 (*Moniteur Belge* [Belgian Official Gazette], 31 December 2002; Implementing Decree of 12 May 2003, *Moniteur Belge*, 26 May 2003). http://fr.indicator.be/personnel/archive/articles/WAAC-PEAR_EU100201.html (consulted on 14 October 2003).

being so, we can hardly be surprised at young players, most of whom use both the drugs in question, finding themselves involved in violent incidents both during their sporting careers and after they are over.

Thus, while the courts and legislative bodies have made significant progress, the sternest critics argue that the law as it is framed and applied merely reflects the consensus of the day and not the objective (and violent) reality experienced by the men and women involved in sport at all levels (*Revue critique du sport,* No. 5, 1997, p. 4).

Violence directed at minority groups

In the light of what we now know about practices in the world of sport and their sometimes tragic outcomes in terms of human dignity, what might have been regarded as radical criticism thirty years ago seems eminently realistic today.

Given that such practices amount to violence against thousands of people, it is inevitable that regulations and, indeed, the force of the law will sooner or later be brought to bear not only to defend the interests of all the individuals involved but also to uncover, and if possible change, sport-related social situations that are potentially alienating or even debasing. Almost thirty years ago the Council of Europe took a stance against such potential forms of alienation (Resolution (76) 41, Article 5).

The offence of "failure to assist a person in danger" may well prove to be the chink through which the light of legal clarity finally penetrates the social configurations of the contemporary sports world (Maitrot, 2003, p. 217).

Work and reason over-valued

On the face of it, the situation in sport is not substantially different from that in other sectors of business and industry. The consequences that people suffer, in terms of injuries, accidents, doping and addiction in the broader sense, are aspects of the ordinary world in which we live and thus of human activity, especially work.

Sports activity is increasingly regarded as activity first and sport second (Laure, 1995). Like any activity, it involves individuals in contained groups (family, neighbourhood, club, association, private company or government department), but it also involves them in larger groups (on the scale of localities, regions, nations, Europe and the world as a whole). It thus offers some insight into the way these various groups function collectively – and they are becoming less and less capable of functioning in isolation from one another. Increasingly, therefore, we need to regard sport as a "regular" human and social activity.

The twentieth century saw a number of significant developments in the field of occupational and labour law. Without attempting to detail these, if we compare the evolution of work and the evolution of sport we observe a divergence (at least in terms of the pace of development) and to some extent a contrast.

On the one hand we have the activity of work, which has gradually been shaped by negotiated agreements and by laws that impose restrictions (on the employment of the very young, on night-working, on the number of hours people may work without a break and on the organisation of working time). Associated with all this was the development of specific professions (notably occupational medicine and factory inspection) responsible for monitoring – and in come cases imposing drastic controls on – physical working conditions (especially in relation to safety). More recently the remit of inspections has been extended to cover work-related mental conditions. Accidents and deaths at work are a fact of life and their incidence continues to be under-estimated (ILO, 2003).[84] Discussions and studies of both harassment and occupational stress have also contributed to the process of developing case and statute law and more generally of raising awareness in European and other industrialised countries (Aubert, 2003; Hirigoyen, 1998; and Leymann, 1996). It is reported that 12 million people were victims of harassment in Europe in 1996.[85] Indeed, despite a significant overall improvement in working conditions in European countries, a growing process of "taylorisation" would seem to have affected certain conditions, particularly in the service sector and in the employment of young people "who can (once again) be exploited" (Brochier, 2001).

On the other hand we have sports activity, which has also been streamlined to an increasing extent, but for which communities have been much slower to assume collective responsibility, for example, in relation to the safety of the individuals involved and the pressures they suffer. For many years sport was regarded – wrongly – as an activity apart, with its own particular internal ways of working. Over the last few decades the anti-doping measures described above have constituted remarkable intrusions into the sports system, or systems. It would seem that, by comparison with other areas of activity, notably paid employment, the (sometimes conflicting) interests involved in sport have only very recently received proper acknowledgement.

There are still relatively few groups defending the interests of athletes or groups of parents of sportspeople (on the model of school parents' associations), never mind athletes' trade unions, and those that exist have little influence. The high profile of certain successful organisations, such as the ATP representing professional tennis players, or the NBA representing basketball

---

84. In its most recent report – quoted in *Le Monde diplomatique*, June 2003 – the International Labour Organisation (ILO) estimated that work kills around 5 000 people per day.
85. Survey of working conditions in Europe in 1996, reported in *Le Nouvel Observateur*, No. 171, January 1999.

players in the United States, obscures a multitude of less well-organised, less reported sports and physical activities, or at least activities in which those centrally involved (the players or athletes) seem less able to secure representation as distinct interest groups (Duret and Trabal, 2001; Bodin and Héas, 2002, p. 25; and Héas et al., 2004).

To make this point clear it is necessary to outline the sometimes very different ways in which developments in sport as a social phenomenon have been analysed. Historians and sociologists, in particular, can be divided into those who contend that sport is a new phenomenon in modern societies and those who argue that it is much older and has made a comeback (Bodin and Héas, 2002, p. 45). The latter regard sports as practices that came down from our ancestors or whose roots lie in the far-distant past. The opposing school of thought situates the arrival of sport in relation to the various revolutions (political, economic and technical) of the seventeenth and eighteenth centuries, and sees it as a product of these changes. Within this school of thought there are two main strands: in one, sport and recreation are regarded as political and even democratic phenomena; in the other they are seen as phenomena shaped more by economic forces. From the former perspective, choice and freedom with regard to physical practices and forms of expression are seen as indicators of democratic progress. For the latter, the division of labour and the commercial relationships in sport are bound up with the triumph of capitalism from the nineteenth century onwards. From both perspectives the rationalisation of behaviour and thought patterns is regarded as an extension of scientific research into the application of the body's movements. Considered in this way, developments such as the improvement of performance and the extension of scientific knowledge about human functioning are culturally logical and consistent. Modern sports and the process of enhancing bodily and human performance cannot be regarded as exceptional phenomena or marginal forms of behaviour. On the contrary, we see them as clear windows into contemporary European societies.

Early and intensive training, and the power of dominant social and cultural thinking

In considering the pace of physical and sports education we need to look both at appropriate thresholds (from when to when) and at levels of intensity (involving not only frequency of practice but also the very definition of physical activity), and this, once again, means approaching sport and recreation as cultural activities in the fullest sense of the term.

The point here is that cultural activities are influenced by dominant codes and perceptions. Certain violent actions are not necessarily regarded as such, depending on the context in which they occur. This was the case for long decades of the twentieth century with regard to child abuse and, more generally, children's pain and suffering.

> **A historical vignette**
>
> In 1879, pathologist Dr Ambroise Tardieu published a description of infant subdural haematoma: it was generally a very serious condition, if not fatal (being, in fact, most frequently diagnosed in post-mortem examinations), and associated with it were various unexplained fractures. The clinical description was that of an idiopathic syndrome (a "stand-alone" illness existing independently of any other morbid condition).
>
> It was not until 1966 that Professor Neyman put forward a new definition of the syndrome – namely "child abuse". Until then, the notion of parents' ill-treating their own child had been so unthinkable as to skew the clinical "reality", effectively in disregard of the evidence.

While "child abuse" as a medical concept was quite explicit (perhaps even too explicit) it was not easily accepted. Even today there is resistance to the idea in some quarters, and a self-serving silence on the part of certain people in charge of associations or federations is a cover for intensive physical practices that can amount to abuse. We have already considered the abusive aspect of doping, but parents can (by proxy) also require of their children a level of sustained effort that is nothing short of diabolical. Yet children's sport and recreation have been the subject of academic research, international declarations and reports to national governments and European institutions, all of which have led to fresh warnings and to the introduction of precautionary principles and statutory measures to protect certain categories of individual (see below).

At least as long ago as 1980 American doctors were warning that the syndrome of child abuse had assumed a new form, namely abuse through sport, with society's approval.[86] In France this problem was first addressed under the heading of *"entraînement physique intense chez les enfants et les adolescents"* [intensive physical training involving children and adolescents] (Delmas, 1981).

Children's sport and recreation became a focus of academic studies and reports, all of them highlighting the dangers of early and intensive sports training. The current threshold levels are generally considered to be six or more hours training per week in addition to school sport for a child aged 12, and eight or more hours training for a 14-year-old. Major awareness-raising

---

86. *Medical world news,* 24 November 1980.

efforts have been urged (Personne, 1987, 1993), on the basis that the public knows too little about the risk of damage caused by sport.

In France, the Mouvement Critique du Sport [Critics of Sport movement] estimated that in 1997 early and intensive training was a problem for 15 000 – 20 000 children (*Revue critique du sport,* No. 5, October 1997). Information on the situation in France includes, for example, data on champion athletes of the future, of both sexes. In 1987, out of eighty-eight "pre-Olympic" athletes, eleven had undergone an operation that year and had been told to quit training for at least twelve months. The medium-term effects of their training regimes were already largely apparent: 50% of them had chronic tendon lesions and 39% had osteo-articular lesions (among competitors in the jumping sports the figure was 93%).

Even as a veil of silence is drawn over certain phenomena, such as repeated injuries among young athletes, and athletes' dropping out of competitive sport after operations necessitated by over-training, high-level sport continues to impose new physical and physiological pressures (talented youngsters are being identified and trained at ever-younger ages, training time is being increased, recuperation periods are fewer and shorter, and the number of events in a season is growing). There are new psychological pressures too (stress, the sense of a duty to get results, pressure from the intimate circle of parents, coaches and club bosses, and the problem of young people abandoning their studies) and all of these affect not only the young athletes' immediate performance but also, and especially, their future as human beings (Di Megglio, 1999; and Palierne, 2003). It is fair to regard what takes place here as symbolic violence practised by sports institutions in the process of producing a national elite, and in some cases it can jeopardise the employment chances of former high-level athletes. Indeed, so many sportspeople abandon their education that our own research has been confined to those who have "succeeded" (Papin, 2001; and Creuzé, 2003). On the basis of isolated observations of small sample groups, it should be possible to study individual career patterns, taking account of factors such as the duration of training, how long ago it started and whether or not the athletes were warned of the dangers involved. A further question is whether or not the athlete still has options by the time he or she and his or her family have a proper understanding of the short-term and medium-term risks.

With regard to children the situation is complicated by the general social bias in favour of all forms of sport and physical exercise, and particularly competitive sport. Positive prejudices of this kind are sometimes relayed through those in charge of sport. For example, records of marathon times are kept, albeit unofficially, for boys from the age of 4 and for girls from the age of 6, (the official age at which records begin to be kept in athletics is 16). In certain cultural settings, including in the United States (where muscle development and performance are highly prized and action is a key feature of films and video games, for example), doping as an everyday phenomenon is less shocking: the average age at which people first take anabolic steroids is reportedly 8 years in the United States (in France it is between 12 and 14 years).[87]

Demystifying sport and enforcing laws and rights

There is no shortage of relevant regulatory and statutory provision. The problem is rather a cultural one, concerned with the dominant social perceptions of the day – and that is why it is important to demystify competitive sport for the very young and to enforce the existing legislation. As Clastres put it, having described various policy steps taken in connection with the Declaration of the Rights of the Child and noting how poorly the policies were applied in some cases, "Children have rights – even if they have a talent for sport". Below is a non-exhaustive list of current rules and recommendations, going back as far as the late eighteenth century to the period of political revolution that triggered radical changes – initially for men:

- 1789: the Declaration of the Rights of Man and of the Citizen (a Declaration of the Rights of Woman and of the Citizen, championed by Olympe De Gouge in 1791, was soon forgotten, as was the possibility "offered" to women of involvement in politics and specifically of exercising political rights);

- 1924: the Geneva Declaration of the Rights of the Child acknowledging the need for children to enjoy special protection;

- 20 November 1959: the United Nations' Declaration of the Rights of the Child indicating that "the child, by reason of his physical and mental immaturity, needs special safeguards and care including appropriate legal protection, before as well as after birth";

- 20 November 1989: the UN Convention on the Rights of the Child, signed by 191 member states, with the notable exception of the United States, instituting the right to protection from "all forms of physical or mental violence, injury or abuse, neglect or negligent treatment, maltreatment or exploitation" (Article 19) and the right to "enjoyment of the highest attainable standard of health" (Article 24). Article 24(e) requires the states parties "to ensure that all segments of society, in particular parents and children, are informed, have access to education and are

---

87. Dr P. Laure cites an international survey carried out in 1997, in *Journal du dimanche*, 9 September 1998, quoted by Ehrenberg A., (1999), "Du dépassement de soi à l'effondrement psychique", *Esprit*, January 1999, p. 136.

supported in the use of basic knowledge of child health and nutrition ... and the prevention of accidents";[88]

The observance of Article 31, requiring the states parties to "recognise the right of the child to rest and leisure, to engage in play and recreational activities appropriate to [his or her] age and to participate freely in cultural life and the arts", is a matter for speculation. Article 32, meanwhile, is concerned with protection "from economic exploitation and from performing any work that is likely to be hazardous or to interfere with the child's education, or to be harmful to the child's health or physical, mental, spiritual, moral or social development". Article 33 refers explicitly to the illicit use of narcotic drugs and psychotropic substances. Each one of these articles, therefore, can in its own right be applied to sports, and other articles are also applicable, even if they are less explicit (Article 36, for example, affords protection "against all other forms of exploitation prejudicial to any aspect of the child's welfare" and Article 37 prohibits "cruel, inhuman or degrading treatment").

– 12 October 1995: the Lisbon Manifesto groups together recommendations on fitness testing, which had been the subject of evaluation since 1990.

Since 1982 children's sport has been one of the themes addressed by the Committee for the Development of Sport, which has warned against what we would term an "adult-centred" approach. Urging that priority be given to children's own goals and standards, rather than pushing children to do what adults wished – with possible adverse effects on their development – the committee stated in 1998 that: "Adult sport should no longer be the only or dominating didactic model: diversity of pedagogical approach should be maintained" (CDDS (98) 90 Vol. II, p. 23, p. 33). More recently, fitness testing has begun to be used among groups other than young schoolchildren, notably the over-75s.

In 1996, in the wake of the Elo Report, the Council of Europe made a number of recommendations on high-level sport, calling among other things for competitions to be staged at reasonable intervals and for the introduction of lower age limits (between 16 and 18 years) for international competitions. Looking beyond the application of regulations and legislation, the Council also underscored the importance of reaffirming basic traditional values in sport, namely fair play and sportsmanship, as well as the key role of the voluntary movement.

In 2001, as part of an effort to provide a framework for sports development in the spirit of the European Sports Charter, the 1992 Code of Sports Ethics

---

88. We would venture to hope that this text will serve as one source of such information.

was revised. Building on the concept of fair play, as enshrined in its title motto "Fair play – the winning way", the code (appended to Recommendation R(92)14 rev of the Committee of Ministers) sets out to "combat the pressures in modern day society". In a related initiative, efforts were under way in 2004 to set up a European children's parliament.

What values ought to be rehabilitated?

The answer to this question is not obvious, for seeking to return to the traditional foundations of sport could be a utopian or even a dangerous ideal. The notion of fair play, for example, is not historically neutral: it originally concerned a certain section of the population in the late nineteenth century, so seeking to apply it today on the basis that is traditional is a debatable undertaking. Moreover, is fair play actually compatible with sport at competitive level? With reference to the issue of doping, we might well conclude that it is not. Everything today, and not just in high-level sport, would seem to be geared to obtaining results in the form of social recognition, for the players and athletes, club bosses and sponsors, as well as return on investment for parents and sponsors. The tension here is the eternal one between doing (in this case playing a sport, in order to win or simply for recreation) and being seen to do (achieving the status of champion and the adulation that goes with it and earning vast sums of money) and the latter appears increasingly often to be the priority, not only when people choose to practise a sport but also when they resort to doping (Bodin and Héas, 2001, 2002).

Introducing a code of ethics is a laudable step, albeit a common one nowadays and in some cases compulsory. In fact, the existence of such codes has become a selling point for certain sports and activities. In pursuits such as trekking a traveller's code is used: this draws on a certain ethic of tourism but also lends legitimacy to a practice that can attract censure, for example from environmental pressure groups (Héas et al., 2001). Recommendations on what constitutes reasonable practice vary significantly, as we have seen, depending on their economic and cultural context. Perceptions of what is excessive, as opposed to moderate, are continually evolving in our societies and that is why we believe ongoing vigilance is needed. As a necessary minimum measure, annual reports on the application and observance of existing rights and codes should be widely disseminated.

At the same time we must be careful not to confuse what are quite distinct problems. The need for ongoing vigilance (under the ILO Worst Forms of Child Labour Convention of 17 June 1999) with regard to child labour cannot be equated with what we advocate here in relation to sport and other forms of physical exercise. Excessive efforts demanded in sport are not comparable to the workload of child slaves. As we suggested earlier, in a brief reference to the etymology of the term "addiction", the concept of "working to pay off debts" probably covers more insidious practices in European countries, notably in the world of sport. Nonetheless, certain transactions involving minors in sports such as soccer require us all to be watchful, and demonstrate the need for both public and government opinion to be mobilised at short notice.

Yet, here too, a single set of circumstances provokes different reactions. The case of a young Italian player bought by Torino (Turin) in 1999 is a telling one.[89] In response to this commercial transaction, some (notably Arsène Wenger, manager of Arsenal since 1998) could not see what all the fuss was about, while others (notably Strasbourg coach Claude le Roy) saw it as an example of a "new slave trade". The former argued that Europe was effectively a single market in sport and compared the travelling times from French and other European cities. "If the kid had opted to go to Rennes or Monaco, no one would have had a problem. Yet in Monaco he would have been further from his parents than he is here in London, where he will be living with his grandparents. You cannot talk on the one hand about European integration and, on the other, squeal every time it is put into practice". Somewhere between the two viewpoints, others (notably doctors) raised the question of the risks to the young player. Some of the metaphors used here were quite breathtakingly patronising, however. Referring to the boy at the centre of the "sale scandal", one paediatrician employed Heath-Robinson-type terminology to outline the risks he faced, referring to his muscles as "strings" and his tendons as "nails"; "If he is made to play with 15-year-olds, who are going through puberty and developing their muscles, he is going to take a few knocks, and the nails won't hold" (M. Binder, paediatrician at the Clinique de Sport, Paris, at the time).

Child abuse and the ill-treatment of children did, nonetheless, come to be more widely recognised in the developed countries at least from the nineteenth century onwards. Not infrequently were they regarded as phenomena that occurred exclusively within families or in the immediate social circle of the children concerned (at school, for example), those responsible being classic authority figures such as teachers. Sports and other forms of physical exercise were all too rarely included in attempts to monitor and prevent violence through the relevant institutions. They seem to have been systematically ignored in educational support initiatives involving protective and preventive measures. The third study day staged by the organisation Defence for Children International focused, for example, on the theme of children's rights in the family and at school.[90]

---
89. *France Soir*, 6 February 1999.
90. http:// www.globenet.org/enfant/intro.html (consulted on 22 April 2004).

The situation today is considerably more serious than it was in the 1980s, and even then alarm calls were occasionally issued by members of the sports elite. Sebastian Coe (speaking at a press conference at the French INSEP in 1982), for example, said that to begin training too early was to cage and brainwash young people and to leave them open to physical deformities and skeletal damage. As the appropriately named review *Sport et vie* [Sport and Life] commented recently, "there is an urgent need to wait!"[91]

Two widely received ideas need to be combated. The first is that early specialisation is preferable and profitable. There are players and athletes (some, as adults, currently at the peak of their chosen sport) who, as teenagers, refused to specialise. The 17-year-old Michael Stich, for example, had a choice of turning professional in either tennis or soccer. The second false idea is that young athletes need to be pitched against the best as part of their learning process. French skier Destivelle did not begin competing until she was 24 years old. Racing cyclist Tony Rominger first took to the saddle competitively at 21, to avenge a slight from his younger brother. The world's most successful woman racing cyclist, Jeannie Longo, was 17 before she began to compete, and she continued downhill skiing until the age of 23, after having "sacrificed" skating, tobogganing and swimming. Now aged over 40, she is still a professional competitive athlete. All these examples undermine the policy of identifying top athletes at an early age and requiring them to specialise (in whatever sport and whether the emphasis is on energy or on aesthetic achievement) in order to obtain the best results. Not uncommonly, the success of athletes who "ought" to have retired gives the lie to this form of eugenics in sport. Yet another factor may be that, as well as having longer potential careers before them, young athletes offer the "advantages" of being more dependent and submissive than their elders.

Since 1991, the International Federation of Sports Medicine (FIMS) has advised against early specialisation. In 1997, at the IOC's 4th World Congress on Sports Science, certain doctors and psychiatrists working with athletes (including Professor D. Hackfort, Germany, and C. Carrier, France) proposed approaches that had been tried and tested at high-level training centres. The FIMS argued that, in the long term, an athlete who had not been successfully "socialised" through interests other than sport would find it all the harder – for neuro-psychological reasons, but also for physical and hormonal reasons (though typically there was no mention of environmental factors) – to cease being a slave to sport when his or her career was over (Carrier, 1992).

---
91. *Sport et vie*, No. 44, p. 50.

The search for alternatives to the habits of a life in sport, and particularly for other strong sensations, all too often leads to dangerous substitute habits such as drug abuse, bulimia or alcoholism.

The Mouvement Critique du Sport takes a particularly radical approach, arguing for the introduction of specific sports legislation (paralleling labour law). The fact that sports medicine is a recognised branch of medicine is, in the eyes of the MCS, all the proof necessary that sports cause physical injury and illness. Recent statistics on the experience of professional footballers in France highlight the fact that, after injuries, they are not given the recommended time for healing and physiotherapy (Rochcongar et al., 2004) and the findings also confirm data from other European countries, including Sweden and the United Kingdom, on the frequency of injuries (although the research methods and indicators used were not the same in all cases). Efforts thus need to be directed at preventing not only total lack of exercise but also excessive exercise, for both can cause tremendous damage, in some cases very rapidly.

Real violence and symbolic violence: the gender factor

Real and symbolic forms of violence feed into each other, and making the distinction between them is a matter of analysis and didactic approach. Real violence can lead to symbolic violence and vice versa. Moreover, real violence is not necessarily the more difficult to overcome, and – crucially – the two forms often occur together. In our discussion of addiction we made the point that dependency on substances or forms of behaviour was likely to have as its corollary a significant degree of stigmatisation, in itself a symbolic form of violence. An example is the situation of the dependent person craving a drug and repeatedly having to ask for it from someone else (especially hard for the athlete who enjoys celebrity status). Another example is that of a seriously-injured male champion having to be looked after, washed and fed by female carers, if he was someone known for extramarital escapades or macho behaviour. The problem is that of how to become anonymous again when one is a national or international star.

It is impossible to dissociate symbolic violence from social situations in sport that are imbalanced, and indeed more broadly from disparate or unequal situations in both sport and society generally. We see this particularly clearly when we approach sport from a perspective of male/female, or majority/minority differences. The problems thus concern not only the way people relate to the opposite sex but also cultural, ethnic and religious interrelations, and there does seem to be a tendency in sport today for people to close ranks within their own communities. While this is not something new, it has become more marked in recent years. Approaching sport in this way also means looking at relations between the able-bodied and people with disabilities (or people with reduced mobility and/or mental handicaps).[92] In what follows we will highlight certain particularly recurrent forms of symbolic violence.

These different forms of real and symbolic violence, complex as they are, have been the chosen focus for research into certain physical and sports-related habits in modern society (Bodin, 2003; and Elias and Dunning, 1986). Recent studies demonstrate that we each have our own social construct for the word "violence". "The ways in which we categorise violence are also preconceptions that we need to deconstruct" (Welzer-Lang, 2002). It would seem that, socially, men's definitions of the word range much more broadly: there is a "continuum of physical, psychological, verbal and social violence, associated with the notion of intention". For men, there is thus a wider social variety of violent acts. This "bare" (although by no means insignificant) fact means, in turn, that men are more likely to be involved in multiple forms of violence and that their violence is generally more likely to be directed against women – a point borne out in numerous reports and studies (e.g. Méda, 2001; and ENVEFF,[93] 2001). A partial study carried out in Sweden, the results of which were published in 2000, is informative here: the number of reported cases of assault and battery rose by 50% in six years, and sex crimes increased by 80% over ten years. In 1997, more than 19 000 Swedish women reported that they had been subjected to ill-treatment, "in 78% of cases by a man known to the woman, and a woman is killed every ten days".[94] The French ENVEFF study highlighted the extent of the many forms of domestic violence against women, an area in which violent acts often go unreported. On average, roughly one Frenchman in ten is responsible for conjugal and/or domestic violence – the inverse of the more familiar statistic that one French woman in ten is a victim of domestic violence. The implicit victimisation in the latter expression is, in itself, symbolically harmful. Since the publication of such findings, European public opinion (at least in France, Italy and Catalonia)[95] has come down in favour of widespread information and awareness-raising campaigns in relation to violence against women (60.8% of respondents thought these were required).

A number of "stars" from the world of sport have been involved in violence against women and we want to mention some of these cases briefly. In

---

92. Since 1980 the Council of Europe has set up a number of pilot projects to promote sport for people who are mentally handicapped (CDDS (98) 90, Vol. II, p. 84).
93. "Enquête nationale sur les violences faites aux femmes" [French national study of violence against women].
94. From an article published in the review *Femina*, No. 13, 26 March 2000, http://www.sos-sexisme.org/info/suedoises.html (consulted on 26 April 2004).
95. Sampling procedures for these studies were not specified. The research was carried out by Women's Rights Information Centres.

Europe this type of violence has not received a great deal of media attention, whereas in some countries acts of domestic violence by sports champions have been very widely reported and commented on by the media (with, in some cases, live television coverage of trials) and been documented. On this side of the Atlantic three names are particularly notorious in this respect – those of Simpson, Tyson and Pippen. Apart from these private "scandals" that become public because a crime is committed, there are telling statistics that need to be confirmed through research on wider sample bases: for instance, certain major sports events (such as Super Bowl Sunday in the United States) coincide with the dates for the highest number of calls to the emergency telephone line for battered women. Is the situation in Europe comparable? We are not aware of data having been gathered systematically here, and the research that has been done is insufficiently compelling.

Yet the information is enough to indicate the sharp cultural divide that appears to exist between male practice and female practice. On the one hand, the fact that men are particularly involved and recognised in an activity where violence is codified does not prevent them from using force in other situations. On the other hand – considering the problem from the sportswoman's point of view – by stepping outside the sphere traditionally allocated to women (i.e. the home and "female" pursuits), with their very real cultural boundaries, women as a social group can find themselves marginalised in a way that entails violence both real and symbolic. They are in a minority on the "foreign" territory of male-dominated sport and it thus becomes socially and culturally "logical" that they should be excluded, and radically excluded in some cases (Héas et al., 2004).

Where and when are women involved in the practice of sport?

It is well recognised that women and girls in sport experience social domination, especially by men (Bourdieu, 1990, 1998). The statistics speak volumes, for women are heavily under-represented, with fewer women members of clubs and the main federations, fewer sportswomen at the top level and fewer women competing in what are regarded as the major sports events. They therefore receive less media coverage. Apart from the Olympic Games and certain other sports meetings or events with an unusually high level of female participation, women are scarcely seen in television coverage of sport, other than in traditional niche areas such as figure skating and gymnastics. This lack of visibility is a key additional form of violence in a real sense. We are not familiar with sportswomen and their exploits – or, indeed, simply what they do. In the male-dominated world of sport and the sports media, it is thus hard for female players and athletes to achieve recognition (Bodin and Héas, 2002).

Certain countries have taken remedial measures and made legal provision for women to have a greater place in the sport world generally, as players, managers and coaches. This process, which is seen in France as part of a wider "positive discrimination" movement and elsewhere as "affirmative action", involves a multiplicity of local and national initiatives. In America its effects seem limited, to say the least, given that it began there in the 1970s.

A critical factor dictating the terms of both men's and women's involvement in sport (or indeed cultural activities generally) is the amount of time they can organise to suit themselves – and the fact is that the burden of work in the home and family still falls almost exclusively on women. The statistics are irrefutable: in France, there is a core of domestic tasks 80% of which are still done by women (CNRS, 1999).[96] Moreover, parenting is reckoned to require on average thirty-nine hours a week, with women doing two thirds of it and men one third (Méda, 2001). While we are often told of the phenomena of "new fathers" or "new men", the differences persist although there is a significant distinction in this regard between certain northern European countries, excluding Ireland, and countries like France, Spain and Italy. In the former there seems to be greater elasticity in the way the burden is shared between spouses and/or parents.

Advancing towards parity

Various bodies and interest groups in Europe are committing themselves to the achievement of parity generally, and specifically to parity in the world of sport and recreation. Since the mid-1970s, the European institutions have issued directives and established committees to promote equality between women and men: notably Directive 76/207 EEC of 1976 and the Council of Europe's Steering Committee for Equality between Women and Men (CDEG), set up in 1979 and strengthened in 1992.[97] Equality is the ultimate objective and parity is a means of achieving it, not only in the key fields of politics, administration, education and training, but also in sport and recreation.

One strand in the process is an effort by authorities and associations to achieve a better balance in the way in which people spend their "social" time, dividing it between work, parenting and recreation. Care provision, not only for children but also for elderly people and people with disabilities, has gradually been transformed in order to lessen the burden on women of parenting and domestic responsibility. In March 2002, for example, the

---
96. Quoted in the *Le Nouvel Observateur.* Des Déserts S., (2001, p. 14), "Le retour des pères", No. 1914, July.
97. Mission des affaires européennes et internationales, MAEI 2, fact sheet "L'égalité entre les femmes et les hommes au CE", January 2003.

European Council called on the EU member states at its Barcelona meeting to take measures along these lines, tailored to today's needs, by 2010 in order to facilitate women's access to both employment and leisure activities.[98] There is a clear political will, nationally and at European and world levels, to promote a "culture of equality". The movement towards parity received a particular boost in 1995, the International Year of Women, notably from the 4th World Conference on Women, held in Beijing, which had a unifying effect and launched the process of gender mainstreaming. This involves taking account, as a matter of course and in all policies and activities, of the differences in women's and men's circumstances, situations and needs.

One of the aims of such initiatives is to tackle the clear problem women face of lack of time, compounded by their limited scope for organising what free time they have. Women with rigid working hours are less likely to play a sport. The specific problem they face is that of taking time for themselves. The social image of the woman taking care of other family members is a powerful one. In keeping with this, women who go out to work are also more likely to play a sport than women who stay at home, even though, on the face of it, the latter have more time at their disposal. The most striking difference between men and women with regard to sport, however, is apparent at weekends, when (in France) more than 40% of men are involved in some form of sport or physical exercise, as against 26% of women. Overall it thus seems to be easier for men to fit together free time, family time and time for sport. Clearly it is socially difficult for some women to get out of their own homes in order to do something purely personal without having to look after others.

On the basis of these observations and the Elias-style approach described above, we are entitled to ask whether European society is in fact becoming more female-friendly. There are contradictory answers to this question, which can be summed up as follows:

– on the one hand, yes: we see more and more women in areas that were previously a male preserve. This means that women are exerting influence in new situations, new roles and new areas of work and responsibility. There are ongoing initiatives and studies in this area: governments, for example, are publishing numerous reports on the subject,[99] and schools are also actively addressing it;[100]

---

98. Grésy, Zimermann, Pareschi (coord.), *La Charte de l'égalité entre les hommes et les femmes, la France s'engage*, March 2004, p. 166.
99. For example, "Les enseignants chercheurs à l'université, la place des femmes" ["Woman's place among university research fellows"], March 2000.
100. Radier V., (2001), "Carrières scientifiques: osez mesdames!" ["A scientific career: take the plunge, ladies!"], *Le Nouvel observateur*, No. 1912, June, pp. 132-134.

- on the other hand, no: what is happening is an alignment around male values. Women have achieved a higher profile in certain areas of society (including business, politics and sport) at a cost to themselves (in that they have had to adopt prevailing male habits, they are under increased mental pressure and they have to manage a double workload). The fact is that, by and large, women still carry the prime responsibility for the same areas of life: motherhood, caring and parenting. A recent study offers insight into this situation by distinguishing for the first time between housework and parenting, notably ferrying children back and forth and helping them with schoolwork. On average women spend an hour a day longer ferrying children, as well as two hours twenty minutes more on housework (Barrère-Maurisson, 2001).

Physical and cultural devaluation and transformation

At a more general level we need to note the perverse effects of certain situations in which women and girls find themselves in the world of sport today.

In non-female sports federations – those dealing with sports with a strong male tradition such as wrestling, soccer, boxing and to a lesser extent cycling – the first phase of women's sport, which lasted for several decades, commonly had an air of parody about it. In the late 1970s, would-be wits were still comparing women's events to "pedigree-cattle shows", for example (Héas and Bodin, 2001). Even today women's events are sometimes used as crowd-pullers before the first games of the season – a sort of taster for the real (i.e. the male) event. At a further level of machismo, such "entertainment", already dubious in itself, has been turned into a sort of soft porn: examples include women's mud wrestling or boxing, in which the competitors are scantily clad or topless. This sexualisation is even more common in activities that have a female social connotation. The terms in which these are advertised say it all: erotic dancing, for example, "easy on the eye" gymnastic toning, or "relaxation with massage (and more if the mood is right)", etc. (Héas, 2004).

Meanwhile in high-level sport, male and female athletes appear more than ever to be on a single continuum. The women seem to be increasingly virile – and of course the use of hormonal doping is a factor here. The use of hormones coupled with intensive training (ultimately a form of very hard work) is gradually producing a change in gender norms, and the differences between men and women in high-level sport seem to be gradually diminishing. The real effects of this phenomenon are further exaggerated by ironic comments in the media or on the part of certain sportsmen and sportswomen.

The fact that menstruation starts later for girls involved in high-level sport is a physical indicator of the trend described: the typical age for a first period has risen from 12 to 14, then 15 and 17 years, and in some cases periods do not start at all. It is common, for example, for top female runners not to menstruate (a reflection of reduced oestrogen levels). An increasing proportion of elite sportswomen – but also of girls practising sport non-competitively – seem to be experiencing problems with their menstrual cycle, including amenorrhoea, although a link with lowered fertility or indeed infertility is not easy to prove, for other factors are involved here (diet being one) apart from intense physical activity (Rosetta, 2002; and Chapelet, 1991).

Girls who are "denied" the onset of menstruation in this way can suffer identity problems, for their experience is directly counter to the general trend: at no time in history have girls reached sexual maturity as early as they do today in the developing countries (and have done since the 1970s or 1980s). Certain girl athletes can experience real difficulties through the lack of this proof of womanhood. Meanwhile, for men, intensive exercise reduces testosterone concentrations (which can result in a return to the hormone pattern of pre-puberty). Clearly, therefore, the hormone profiles of men and women who practise sport intensively tend to become less differentiated, evolving towards a "neuter" or genderless mean.

With a few exceptions, notably tennis, women's sports at a high level of competition have become marketable only in recent years (and are still not "selling" well). Individuals in particular sports, such as tennis star Martina Navratilova, blazed the trail, concluding sponsorship contracts and, in Navratilova's case, asserting the right to her own sexuality (see below). It is also true that since the 1990s commercial partnerships in women's sport have had a higher public profile: Marie-José Pérec has been associated with Mitsubishi and Reebok, Steffi Graff with Adidas and Opel, Marie Pierce with Nike, and so on.

The value of women's individual sponsorship contracts continues, in too many cases, to be lower (sometimes as much as 50% lower) than that of equivalent contracts concluded with men. Differences in the prize money for men's and women's marathons, to take another example, are a reflection of highly convoluted thinking.[101] The arguments advanced by event organisers are not convincing: women are slower; there are fewer of them; or women's events are less profitable. Sacco has argued that the retention of this difference in the levels of financial reward is a face-saving measure (for men). That hypothesis would appear to be supported by the existence of certain difficulties in relation to the staging of large-scale women's sports events. Often women's events are blatantly in competition with the equivalent male event:

---

101. "42 kms à pieds, ça n'use pas que les souliers", extracts from an article by Francesca Sacco, Switzerland, July 2001, http://www/sos-sexisme.org/infos/42.html (consulted on 26 April 2004).

the women's Tour de France, for example, was renamed the "Grande boucle", and the race leader wears a "gold jersey" rather than a "yellow jersey", in order to avoid any risk of the male tour being overshadowed, or of financial support being adversely affected.

Nonetheless, there is general enthusiasm for women's sport, and both sport and recreational activities with a female focus have been popular in Europe since the 1980s (and in the United States since the 1970s). Women's magazines with a strong emphasis on physical activity and the body, such as *Vital* and *Biba*, have been launched and continue to sell. All publications for women now include pages on physical fitness and/or information about new types of sport and recreation – or indeed old ones: during the World Cup in France in 1998, *Marie-Claire*, for example, published a special edition offering to help women understand soccer (and soccer-loving men). For many girls and women in Europe these developments have had the effect of profoundly changing the way they think about their bodies and about sport and other forms of physical exercise (Travaillot, 1998; Héas, 2004; and Perrin, 1986).

As discussed above, the physically determined characteristics of men and women are not interchangeable: the male and the female are culturally different, just as they are naturally different ...from their ways of doing things to their ways of speaking: women's rugby cannot be the same as men's rugby, just as a male ballet dancer is not a ballerina.

> There is a crucial difference between:
> - DOING as a man does, which may well be possible;
> - and BEING like a man, which is virtually impossible (scientifically and socially), as well as unthinkable (and in most cases probably not desirable).
>
> (Based on Chodorow)

Managing not to cross the symbolic, statutory and scientific boundary between the sexes is a very tricky problem for elite sportswomen. Those who do cross it have a heavy price to pay. They can find it hard to meet partners, and may need to become emotionally self-sufficient, or in some cases they feel pressure to be overtly "masculine". Moreover, men and women cannot develop independently of one another. It has been argued that the androgynous model is a utopian one and therefore unsustainable. The fact is that societies create the gender models that seem vital to them and these are inevitably polarised. In the west (and in sport as in other spheres of life) women will tend to be admired for their appearance and men for what they do. These stereotypical perceptions remain very powerful. Sport, like society generally, seems intolerant of grey areas. Hence people who are sexually unclassifiable are rejected, except in micro-societies such as nightclubs where gender confusion is the norm and there is a strong tendency towards physical extravagance, but the members of gender-based minorities do not feel at home there beyond a certain age. Social standardisation and stigmatisation in the workplace have a powerful effect in inducing individuals to conform.

How violence in different forms excludes sportsmen as well as sportswomen: from gynophobia to homophobia

It is not only women who are affected by sexual apartheid – in what it is fair to call a form of gynophobia – but also gays, lesbians and transsexuals. The inclination of minorities oscillates between a wish to be clearly seen and a wish for total anonymity. In the high jump, Rollenberg made headlines a number of years ago by declaring his intention to take the "macho" aspect out of big sports events by becoming the "first queer at 2 metres 30". In certain sports such as handball or basketball it is estimated that the proportion of female homosexuals in some teams is over 90%.[102]

For its part the IOC issued a writ against the Gay Games to stop that event using the word "Olympic" in its title. Despite the fact that these games receive virtually no media coverage they attract large numbers of athletes: in 1982 and 1986 in San Francisco the numbers of athletes taking part were 1 300 and 3 482 respectively. The 1990 edition in Vancouver attracted 7 200 competitors and the 4th Gay Games, in New York, in 1994, involved more athletes than the Barcelona games two years previously (Griffin, 1992, p. 190). The event has grown steadily: in Amsterdam in 1998 there were 14 715 competitors (42% of them women) from five continents and the games had a budget of US$7 million.[103] In 2002 the Gay Games were held in Sydney – the same city as the "heterosexual" Olympics – and this probably helped to bring them to public attention. We have also seen two types of event (or events with two types of competitor) being staged in proximity to each other in the case of the Paralympics, which seem to have taken on a similar role to that of women's sports events in recent decades – a sort of "taster" for, or complement to, the "real" competitions.

Other events have also been organised with a view to showcasing the strength of gay and lesbian movements in sport. In France, the Fédération sportive gay et lesbienne [Gay and Lesbian Sports Federation] has been working for seventeen years to develop amateur sport for gay people, its declared aim being "recognition and integration through sport". The

---

102. Homosexuality can even become a criterion in the preliminary selection of a new player for a national women's team. Coaching staff have been known to claim that "misunderstandings" between players can be avoided if they are all "the one sort".
103. http://www.backdoor.com/castro/gaygames

federation promotes gay and lesbian sport in France, where it encourages the establishment of clubs for that purpose, and also has a European dimension as an active member of the European Gay and Lesbian Sports Federation (EGLSF), an organisation that has consultative status with the Council of Europe.[104]

Attempts like this to achieve a higher profile for gender minorities in sport run up against two related obstacles: homophobia and the low rate of "coming out" in Europe. Declaring one's homosexuality is not, in fact, common practice in Europe. There have been sustained efforts to encourage it, as in 1999 in the United Kingdom, when the Sports Minister of the day (Tony Banks), speaking in relation to homophobia in soccer, said that if a few star players were courageous enough to come out it would probably ease the situation for other players and fans.[105] Working against such a concept were, however, both the "fear of what is taboo" (Saouter, 2003) and (in the case of gay men in sport) the assumption of masculinity which (for both social and historical as well as media-related and marketing reasons) prevents athletes from revealing their true selves and forces them to live in socially ambivalent situations (Bodin and Debarbieux, 2003).

In Europe, gay and lesbian movements seem to be achieving a higher public profile and at the same time mobilising more effectively – using legitimate, legal means – against continuing homophobia. The fact that homophobia is indeed alive and well is underscored from time to time by press reports of particularly violent incidents such as the burning alive of a young gay man in northern France in January 2004. Homophobic behaviour has been defined as "any manifestation, overt or otherwise, of discrimination, exclusion or violence on the basis of homosexuality, directed against individuals, groups or practices that are homosexual or perceived as such".[106] Determining its extent is not straightforward. Studies designed to produce a better understanding of this form of rejection on the basis of people's actual or presumed sexual behaviour are ongoing. A survey of "lesbophobia", for example, makes explicit reference to sport in two of a list of sixteen areas of life in which respondents are asked to indicate whether they have experienced discrimination.[107] Researchers in Europe have begun to look at sport from this angle only recently, although there is earlier work in the field elsewhere (Griffin, 1992; Krane, 1996; Alric, 2002; and Picquart, 2004). The whole range of sexual orientation would certainly seem to be a potentially interesting dimension to explore – with reference both to the concept of respect for difference and to

---

104. www.gaysport.info
105. http://news.bbc.co.uk/1/hi/sport/344587stm (consulted on 8 November 2002).
106. www.France.qrd.org/assocs/sos/definition./php (consulted on 23 April 2004).
107. www.France.qrd.org/assocs/sos/enquetelesbophobie.php (consulted on 23 April 2004).

the observance of national and international law – in any consideration of approaches to sport.

Certain pioneering countries such as Sweden have introduced anti-discrimination programmes and legislation designed to benefit both people with disabilities and other minorities, including gays and lesbians (with the establishment of the aptly entitled "HomO" – the Ombudsman against discrimination on the basis of sexual orientation).[108]

Recently, a number of recommendations have been made and collective anti-homophobia (though not homophilic) measures taken at European level. Key texts in this regard include Resolution 1092 (1996) of the Parliamentary Assembly of the Council of Europe, on discrimination against women in the field of sport and more particularly in the Olympic Games, as well as the European Convention on Human Rights and Protocol No. 12 (Article 1) thereto. Most recently, Recommendation 1635 (2003) of the Parliamentary Assembly, adopted in November 2003, stipulated that homophobia in sport should be combated on the same grounds as racism and other forms of discrimination. The Assembly urged both sports organisations (including UEFA in European soccer) and the media to fight homophobic behaviour and language. As a result of all this, such gender-based forms of violence (both real and symbolic) are now increasingly recognised and understood for what they are.

Thus we have seen how violence, as an implicit norm, underpins both gender-based and other cultural forms of segregation in sport. By entering the male preserve of sport, female athletes (whether heterosexual or homosexual, "out" or not) run a risk of masculinisation (Mennesson, 2002; and Saouter, 2000). This applies in particular in sports such as weightlifting or track cycling that require them to develop physical strength (and thus to exercise a form of violence against themselves), and in sports where violence is an aspect of the contest (the martial arts, wrestling and "collision sports" such as boxing, rugby and American football).[109] Recent studies in France have looked at this risk for those who practise one of the forms of boxing[110] and those who play traditionally male sports such as soccer and rugby (Héas and Bodin, 2001; and Mennesson, 2002). Similar observations have been made in relation to the major sports in the United States, including American football, baseball, basketball and hockey (Griffin, 1992). This masculinisation (the mirror image of a process of feminisation that affects

---

108. http://www.sweden.se/templates/Print-CommonPageX___4722.asp (consulted on 5 December 2003).
109. The list might well be extended, for Thomas asserts (possibly ironically) that "women's sports are primarily the gentleman's arts: fencing, riding and dancing" (Thomas, 1993, p. 44).
110. In France, it is only five years ago that women and girls were first allowed to take part in boxing.

men in traditionally female sports) is a specific form of symbolic violence that has the effect of reinforcing dominant male perceptions and perpetuating conditions that militate against the integration of women athletes, particularly in traditionally male sports (Héas et al., 2004). The more physical violence and collision there is in a sport, and the greater the reliance on modern technology (as in motor sport and speedboat racing), the more women are excluded.

Generally speaking, in Europe and elsewhere, sport (or at least competitive sport) has been and remains a basic component in the male identity-building process (Coakley, 1994, p. 235) – to such an extent that some critics have compared stadiums and sports arenas to "male cultural centres" (Kidd, 1987). In this "androsocial" context, where do women athletes, as the largest minority in sport, actually fit in?

Minorities in sport are never very far from exclusion

A networking organisation for women in sport (European Women and Sport, EWS) has existed since 1991, and today covers forty-one European countries. It is concerned with women's access to education, training and positions of responsibility and aims to increase their involvement in sport at all levels and in all types of role. France has chaired the EWS since 2002 and the organisation's efforts in France are supported by an association called Fémix'sports, which combats the exclusion of women in any form, as well as all forms of violence against sportswomen (physical violence on or off the field, and verbal violence). Its aims are to foster a culture of equality between men and women, to reinforce its European network, involving southern European countries and newly networked countries, and to contribute to democracy in society.[111]

Of necessity, therefore, the reasoning behind discrimination against women in sport has changed and continues to change, partly in response to the pressures and initiatives described. Various conventions and directives, including the Convention on the Elimination of all forms of Discrimination against Women (CEDAW), point the way in this regard and provide a framework for monitoring progress. Substantial progress has been made, as is clear from studies and comparisons of regulations and legislation.

Explicit, official segregation and, to an even greater extent, overt violence are things of the past. Signs barring "women and dogs" from certain golf courses, for example, have become curiosities[112] for tourists to photograph. On the other hand, various forms of symbolic violence, involving conflict or

---
111. "8 mars 2004, femmes et sport", French Ministry of Sport, p. 13.
112. Albeit rather sick ones.

resistance over attempted reorganisation or rescheduling, for example, can serve to perpetuate the status quo in men's favour for a little longer. More insidiously, the way in which academic or supposedly academic information is communicated can sometimes create notions that strengthen resistance to change, or even encourage forms of violence such as sexual harassment or gang rape. This skewing of information is particularly significant where women are presented as the "prime" victims of (male) violence.

Of course, sociocultural differences continue, directly or indirectly, to prevent women in the lowest social categories in Europe from becoming involved in sport. In France, for example, by no means all women benefit from the changes in society that are supposed to have made it more female-friendly. Making a place for women in sport is one of the great challenges of this century. Pierre de Coubertin did not intend them to be involved in the Olympic Games. The development of gender equality in sport, the nature of women's sport and their access to positions of responsibility all mirror the situation in civil society and are accurate indicators of the social reality of this incomplete revolution (Bodin and Héas, 2002). This exclusion of women from sport – or failure to integrate them – is one form of collective violence. Unless we take a highly simplistic view of reality, we cannot say that women's freedom in general has advanced further than women's freedom in sport.

Women's situations are different, and sometimes the differences constitute major divisions. The same has to be borne in mind in considering sexual minorities, notably lesbians, as well as cultural minorities and people with disabilities. Moreover, achieving fame in sport does not automatically offer protection against stigmatisation or being made to feel like a second-class citizen. Becoming a celebrated sportswoman is not necessarily a guarantee against the spectre of masculinisation (Bodin and Héas, 2002). When they step outside their specific territories (culturally marked as female), sportswomen come under pressure to confirm their sexual identity (i.e. their gender). Some do so emphatically through traditional feminine forms of behaviour: they may put on make-up before entering the arena or stepping up to receive a medal (the French athlete Marie-José Pérec springs to mind here), or they may boast a magnificent manicure (like American Florence Griffith Joynor) or wear lacy knickers (like tennis players Arantxa Sanchez and Chris Evert-Lloyd). Studies have been carried out into the persistence of these forms of behaviour throughout the careers of certain athletes, who as they have grown older have relaxed and gradually adopted the female style that is the norm in their sport. The possibility of being "labelled" as a lesbian is a compounding factor here (Griffin, 1992; Cahn, 1995).

The contradiction between achieving recognition as a sportswoman and being devalued as a woman can sometimes lead to real sexual identity problems when female champions experience the full force of a clash between the business of fame and their own identity. The conflict is perceptible in the very language used to comment on, analyse or reward women's sport. The two athletes mentioned above were commonly known as "Marie-Jo" and "Flo-Jo" – with the boy's name "Joseph", used in its diminutive form, seeming to reinforce a perception of masculinity.[113] Less obvious perhaps, but no less significant, is the difference in expected behaviour at the presentation of medals: the obligatory kiss on the cheek is not equivalent to a handshake. Moreover, medals and trophies commonly carry the images of famous men, rather than women. The same goes for honorary titles: in 1987 and 1996 female cyclist Jeannie Longo was elected "best sportsman of the year in France". This spectre of masculinisation scarcely exists today except in sport (and in certain professions, such as the army). It is for that reason that we have chosen to concentrate on what is a blind spot in the sociology of sport, namely gender and sexual orientation as categories for stigmatisation, particularly in relation to types of behaviour that lie outside the heterosexual norm, especially overt homosexuality among athletes both male and female.

Will the losers win out in the end?

Women are always in a position of strength in the game of gender distinction, or the lack of it, because they can adopt male practices without renouncing the specificities of their gender (at least socially). The process is much less straightforward in the other direction – take, for example, the case of synchronised swimming, which in France is a sport only recently open to men. Ultimately one has to question whether any area of life is now reserved specifically for men, as women have increasingly moved into politics, business and most forms of sport and recreation, just as they have laid claim to filiation (it has gradually become possible in most European countries for children to take their mother's surname).

In fact, decision-making posts do remain largely a male preserve (in French sports clubs men occupy 90% of such posts). It is also the case that the female invasion of sport (i.e. the redressing of the balance) has led some men to up the stakes with increasingly "macho" activities such as "ultimate fighting", caged paintball and assault course events – all practices imbued with violence (or at least designed to look violent).

---

113. Without going into the symbolism of the name "Joseph" in Judaeo-Christian culture ...

Conclusion

Is there nothing more to sport in Europe than violence?

The title question is deliberately provocative and clearly needs to be answered in the light of the values that individuals see in sport as practice or spectacle, the passions that sport can arouse and the joy it can bring, as well as the good it can legitimately claim to do (in terms of education, health, citizenship and integration) – all this on condition that it is not up for grabs, at the mercy of the strongest or the richest bidder, and that it is able to develop within a framework that is clearly regulated and designed to contribute to human progress and wellbeing and the dignity of peoples.

Sport is undoubtedly capable of transmitting much that is positive, thus helping in turn to transform the society in which it has developed. There are many avenues (involving schools, communities, clubs and associations, projects, training programmes, events and leisure pursuits) through which sport can become part of a genuine blueprint for society. What remains to be done in Europe – with a view to achieving effective co-operation – is to compare different visions and cultures and a range of economic and political circumstances, and to attempt to draw from them those elements that will combine to produce a fairer, more caring model of European sport that is both mindful of the need to conserve national cultures and open to transnational development.

Paradoxically, it was violence and excess in sport that provided the initial basis for a common approach as the European nations committed themselves jointly to combating the most glaring and widespread problems, including ethical lapses, hooliganism and violence in football grounds, and doping. Pressures and difficulties thus created the conditions for new understanding, unity and a strong approach – and that is ultimately encouraging. The position that Europe has taken on these issues, at the instigation of the Council of Europe and with the support of the European Commission and European Parliament, demonstrates that new political horizons are opening up for sport, in parallel with the process of forging a new Europe.

Now that there is greater understanding of what sport can contribute, socially, educationally and culturally and in terms of health and recreation, it is regarded today in Europe as having a key part to play in Europeans' education and cultural development. The overarching aim is to use sport for the promotion of understanding among human beings, and thereby break down social barriers and promote health education.

Still to be resolved, however, is a tension that affects not only Europe but the entire world: it is the problem of the balance of strength between politics and the economy. For sport, like many of the activities that fall within what is termed the "cultural exception" (although business contests the principle), is currently under attack from two sides. On the one hand, it is an area liable to be affected by the conflict between protectionism and deregulation and, on the other hand, it requires rules that must take a range of interests and factors into account: from aspirations for independence (reflected in the rules of competition laid down by sports bodies), to the ambiguities of politics (unity or disunity, the closed ranks of various communities, different levels of nationalism and federalism) and the laws of market economics, which in principle transcend political and sport-based barriers, existing in a great "beyond" where the cardinal principles are deregulation and free competition.

At the same time, making European-level sport a reality would be a difficult undertaking without financing or media imagery.

In economic terms the task today is to assess objectively both the constraints and the advances inherent in the transformation of the sports economy. Nothing is entirely positive or entirely negative, although our investigations have focused on certain blind spots in sport and on the damage carefully concealed behind the prevailing ideology. In fact there can be no doubt that a radical separation of sport from business would result in even greater levels of discrimination. Involvement in sport would become the privilege of those with money, and sport's competitive dimension and hence its entertainment value would disappear because it needs external financing in order to survive. Yet the market cannot be allowed to be merely a means without any end in view. And herein lies the key distinction between a sports economy and a purely economic approach to sport.

If the right balance can be struck, money in sport can become an effective weapon against exclusion, discrimination and autarchy. If it is used properly in Europe – that is to say, invested more equitably and better shared among countries, federations, levels of practice, the sexes and the generations – it could guarantee solidarity in sport, which is in itself a balancing factor and helps peoples to meet, share and communicate. There is no reason to regard such a situation as unattainable in a Europe that is attempting to reconcile the interests of free trade and social protection.

With regard to media coverage and the media's incentive to invest in sport, similar conclusions can be drawn. Competition between cartels, private groups and private sector and public sector operators should be allowed to continue but the overriding concern should be to serve the greatest number of viewers. The goal should be to provide captivating coverage with improved quality and more effective distribution, and the money earned from it should be used to develop the wealth of heritage that exists in different sports in different countries, rather than continuing to focus exclusively on a few mass-audience male sports, although the universal appeal of the dominant sports cultures also needs to be reflected for the sake of the passion and joy they can communicate. The key tasks, within a more reasoned approach to sports coverage and a fairer distribution, must be to develop new sectors, to maintain core coverage and to give all Europeans access to spectator sport. Given the remarkable advances in media technology, achieving this should not be problematic except in terms of political choice.

There is no disputing that one of sport's functions today is that of mass entertainment. Whether, in that function, it is more unifying than divisive remains an open question, and we therefore have to acknowledge the importance of the media as a major factor in any fresh approach to sport. It is important that, at a very basic level, the source of this mass entertainment is not automatically equated with profit-making by a small number of people, even though as a rule (albeit a politically and socially flexible one) investment is stimulated by the prospect of significant gain. Ultimately there is thus an urgent need for clear rules to take account of all that is at stake and of the interdependent interests of European viewers and of the relevant influential bodies and operators.

In this spirit the Council of Europe has advanced on a number of fronts: organising conferences, commissioning research and holding seminars that bring together the various parties concerned, including politicians, sportspeople and academics, to analyse existing situations, observe current practice, suggest solutions and, perhaps most importantly, engage in constructive dialogue by forging contacts between representatives from different countries. The intercultural dimension of the Council of Europe's work is fundamentally important because it is by creating relationships and building networks that we are most likely to resolve problems and to foster friendships capable, in the long term, of bringing about a changed order.

There are still many stumbling blocks to be overcome, and the picture of sport in Europe that we have painted should help us to identify areas in which action is urgently needed to short-circuit the main sources of violence, be they political, economic or media-related or associated with the problems to which excess in sport can lead, namely doping, stadium violence, health damage and over-exposure.

In fact this is perhaps where the core problem lies: in the connection between a conception of sport derived from an aristocratic inner circle for whom Pierre de Coubertin himself defended a certain right to excess (de Coubertin, 1900) – a conception reflected in the worst horrors of high-level sport today – and sport for the masses, a phenomenon which, as both practice and spectacle, has gradually developed in contrast to the first model. We can only conclude that attention must be given to sport in its entirety and particularly to the relationship between the two models: elite and mass. This applies as much with regard to financing, conditions of development and shared momentum as it does with regard to balance, parity, fairness and solidarity. On this last point, however, there is considerable concern about a groundswell of change threatening to undermine the pyramid model of sport in Europe, which (for all its imperfections and all the scope for reform) ensures a minimum degree of solidarity between levels of practice, between the sexes and generations and between sports of different types.

As well as concern, though, there is hope and it can be outlined as follows.

Education – particularly in physical education (PE) and school sport – obviously represents an essential area of interest in efforts to promote awareness of sport as a healthy and balanced activity in which certain principles and rules are observed. Education offers an avenue of approach to the future of sport through the transmission of values including respect and tolerance: a future in which competition and emulation will not compromise respect for others, self-respect or respect for the rules that make any game what it is. Moreover, and quite simply, school is still the place where children and young people can discover new activities in a cultural context different from that of the family and in which they are invited to look beyond the familiar and to reach out to other people and ideas.

There are, assuredly, major differences to be taken into account within Europe: the differences, for example between French-style PE (in which the chief concern is to retain the distinction between sport and physical exercise, and between PE and sport), German PE, which effectively involves teaching sports, and Swedish PE, which focuses heavily on health-improving practices. The main concern at this level is to ensure that politicians continue to recognise the importance of physical education and resist the temptation to cut its resources, the hours allocated to it, or the number of PE staff, under the pretext of an economy drive. We have to ask ourselves what kind of sport we want to pass on to our children. Sport as practised at school continues to function as a great equaliser, for it allows certain children to discover physical and sporting activities that they would not have encountered elsewhere for reasons to do with social class.

Likewise, club-based sport has many positive aspects, not least the fact that its reliance for organisation on a tremendous input of voluntary effort demonstrates the selfless, pleasure-based impulses that underpin commitment to a sport. It is a model that has a highly educative function in counterbalancing the commercialism of spectator sport. Moreover, this committed voluntary effort – which is also what enables major events like the World Athletic Championships and the Olympic Games to continue – constitutes a fitting counterpoint to the indecently large sums of money involved. It illustrates the type of solidarity potentially possible between different levels of competition and spectacle, and between mass sport and elite sport.

The major sports events, and indeed all sports fixtures, are occasions on which people can open up towards those who are different from themselves, and learn something about others, for sport is also unrivalled as a force for bringing together and mixing different types of people and their cultures: in short for allowing them to meet and, however briefly, to share something other than mistrust. It facilitates communication and probably combats prejudice, the tendency to make value judgments and the types of belief that give rise to hatred and intolerance.

Paradoxically, deregulation in the professional sport world in Europe – with players uprooted to join teams in countries they might never even have visited previously – highlights another of sport's functions, namely that of promoting integration. Sports competitions can be excellent occasions for showcasing the extraordinarily mixed nature of European teams (although, in this respect too, situations differ). Major victories heighten a sense of fusion, helping to unite people behind the players. Although times like this – when people experience, even for a short while, a sense of belonging to a multi-coloured community and riding a tide of general goodwill – cannot last, they should be acknowledged for what they are, for they can complement and reinforce other experiences in other places and other areas of human activity. Sport can scarcely be asked to deliver something that is beyond its remit, and criticism directed at it might equally well be applied to numerous other activities in which integration has not received the attention that it might have. Sport also serves the cause of integration by making it much easier for athletes than for those in any other sort of work to make a place for themselves in society, whatever their social, ethnic or religious roots. The sports world is more ready to "forget" and one of its great strengths is the fact that some of its most eminent members come from foreign or poor backgrounds.

Sport is a celebration – although this is an external aspect of it and not an integral part of events or competitions as such. Sport brings people together, interrupting the daily routine, and it is this coming together that occasions celebration. The celebratory dimension enhances the pleasures of sport and offsets negative impressions created, for example, by spectators' misbehaviour. Happily, celebration goes hand in hand with sports events much more frequently than we might imagine, given the coverage of tragic violence, accidents and displays of hatred. Celebration is embodied in the "third half" of the game (a notion already current in some sports and one that should be encouraged in others), and in the closing ceremonies for major international events, as in the magical spectacles staged to mark the end of the Olympic Games or major world championships.

Sport also carries a message – of equal opportunity, and thus of equality between men and women. At the level of basic principle, sport excludes no one – and promises no one victory – for reasons of social status, gender or race. On the contrary, it has the capacity to relay and amplify the messages of liberation and an end to exclusion – and even contribute to their realisation. By celebrating women's victories and putting them in the public eye in countries that defend inequality between men and women, sport helps to focus the attention of the international community, providing a counterweight to the violence inherent in such discrimination, and making it less and less acceptable.

For young people, sport is the stuff of dreams. It introduces to their lives a desire to do better, to surpass themselves and prove that they can overcome obstacles through their own efforts. It can be part of the process of growing up and developing self-esteem, and it is for that reason that the role of sports stars is so important. They are presented as models and they therefore ought to behave as the young people see them – namely as heroes. In this respect, an easily implemented solution suggests itself, one which could help to combat many forms of violence – the violence affecting fans who feel themselves wronged by the outcome of a match, for example, or the "weekend violence" of children or adults who mimic the aggressive behaviour of the star players they admire. If every player who contested a referee's decision on the pitch were automatically suspended for a number of matches, fans would, in all likelihood, cease to feel that sense of being wronged.

Sport introduces the concept of observing rules which allow everyone to play the same game. It pre-supposes that the rules will be observed and this gives it a broader educational function, which is utilised not only by schools and clubs but also by leisure centres and community and social centres in towns, on housing estates and in rural areas, and even in the prison system – where, perhaps more than elsewhere, people need to rethink the way in which they relate to one another. In fact, the role of sport in prison demonstrates that, far from being merely a focus for different forms of violence, sport is also a powerful force for cohesion and a means through which people can discover and rehabilitate themselves, and modern society has not yet exhausted its full potential. Almost everywhere in Europe, the focus in prison systems is shifting from punishment to education, and sport is one of the prime tools used in the resocialising process.

All this depends – at the very least – on sport in its various forms being sufficiently widely acknowledged, on resources for sport being reviewed to achieve social, cultural, geographical and economic balance, and on the richest countries spreading those resources beyond a high-profile minority of participants.

So intimate is the connection between sport and violence that sport can sometimes be a source of violence and at other times a means of controlling it. But can sport – or indeed should sport – be superior to the rest of society? Certainly not. We probably ask more of sport than we do of other areas of life precisely because sport involves education, passion and pleasure, because it puts on a show and inspires us to dream and because it is one of the cultural building blocks of our societies. In an ideal (and probably utopian) world, sport and athletes, sports managers and sports fans would be less flawed and more restrained, and sport would thus be a totally neutral sphere of society, devoid of tension or dissension. Yet sport can do no more than mirror what our societies are, and this means that we face a real challenge. We need to build a fairer, more peaceful Europe in which justice and friendship between peoples can thrive – and can express themselves in sport.

Bibliography

Alric T., *Le sexe et le sport. Enquête sur la vie intime des dieux du stade*, Chiron, Paris, 2002

Andreff W., "L'émergence de nouveaux pays sportifs", in *Le Monde diplomatique*, September 1998a, pp. 18-19

Andreff W. (ed.), *Un nouveau secteur économique: le sport*, La Documentation française, Paris, 1998b, p. 581

Andreff W., "Economic environment of sport: A comparison between Western Europe and Hungary", in *European journal of sport management*, No. 4, 1996

Andreff W. et al., *Les enjeux économiques du sport en Europe: financement et impact économique*, Council of Europe, Dalloz, 1995

Andreff W. and Nys J.F., *Economie du sport*, PUF, Paris, 2001

Arendt H., *Le système totalitaire*, Plon, Paris, 1951, 1972 edition

Arènes J., Janvrin M.P. and Baudier F., *Baromètres Santé Jeunes 97/98*, Editions CFES, Paris, 1998

Armstrong G., Harris R. and Frankenberg R., "Football hooligans: theory and evidence", in *The sociological review*, No. 39-3, pp. 427-458, 1991

Arnaud P., "Sports et relations internationales. La nouvelle donne géopolitique. 1919-1939", in *Géopolitique*, No. 66, pp. 15-24, 1999

Arnaud P., "La méthode des modèles et l'histoire des exercices physiques", in G. Pfister, T. Niewerth and G. Steins (eds.), *Les jeux du monde, entre tradition et modernité*, Academia, Sankt Augustin, pp. 133-146, 1993

Arnaud P. and Broyer G., *La psychopédagogie des activités physiques et sportives*, Privat, Toulouse, 1985

Aubert N., *Le Culte de l'urgence. La société malade du temps*, Flammarion, Paris, 2003

Augustin J.P., "Les avatars de l'olympisme contemporain", in *Géopolitique*, No. 66, pp. 79-88, 1999

Bancel N. and Blanchard P., "L'intégration par le sport. Quelques réflexions autour d'une utopie", in *Migrance*, No. 22, pp. 50-59, 2003

Barrère-Maurisson M.A., *Partage des temps et des tâches dans les ménages*, Editions La Documentation Française, Paris, 2001

Barthes R., *Mythologies*, Paladin, London, 1973

Bassons C., *Positif*, Stock, Paris, 2000

Beaulieu M. and Perelman M., "Histoire d'un espace. Le stade.", in *Quel corps*, No. 7, pp. 31-40, 1977

Becker H.S., *Outsiders. Etudes de sociologie de la déviance*, Métailié, Paris, 1963, 1985 edition

Bénabent J., "OPA sur les champions", in *Télérama*, No. 2690, pp. 54-57, 2001

Blociszewski J., "Sous la pression technologique? Le football face au vidéoarbitrage", in *Le Monde diplomatique*, No. 33, March 1996

Bodin D., *Le hooliganisme*, PUF, Paris, 2003

Bodin D., "La déculturation du public comme facteur du hooliganisme: mythe ou réalité?", in *Staps*, No. 57, pp. 85-106, 2002

Bodin D. (ed.), *Sports et violences*, Chiron, Paris, 2001a

Bodin D., "Les problèmes posés par l'utilisation des statistiques policières et judiciaires comme source d'interprétation sociologique", in *Revue juridique et économique du sport*, No. 58, pp. 7-19, 2001b

Bodin D., *Hooliganisme: vérités et mensonges*, ESF, Paris, 1999a

Bodin D., "Le hooliganisme en France", in *Sport*, No. 165/166, pp. 38-118, 1999b

Bodin D., "Football, supporters, violence: la non-application des normes comme vecteur de la violence", in *Revue juridique et économique du sport*, No. 51, pp. 139-149, 1999c

Bodin D., "Sports et violences. Analyse des phénomènes de déviances et violences chez les supporters de football à partir d'une étude comparative du supportérisme dans le basket-ball, le football, le rugby et le volley-ball", dissertation defended in the Department of Science and Technology for Physical Education and Sports, University of Bordeaux 2, 11 December 1998

Bodin D. and Debarbieux E., "Révéler l'impensable ou la question de l'homosexualité masculine dans le sport de haut niveau", in P. Duret and D. Bodin (eds.), *Le sport en questions*, Chiron, Paris, pp. 161-172, 2003

Bodin D. and Debarbieux E., "Le sport, l'exclusion, la violence", in D. Bodin (ed.), *Sports et violences*, Chiron, Paris, pp. 13-33, 2001

Bodin D. and Héas S., *Introduction à la sociologie des sports*, Chiron, Paris, 2002

Bodin D. and Héas S., "Le dopage: entre désir d'éternité et contraintes sociales", proceedings of colloquy entitled "Le corps extrême dans les sociétés occidentales", GDR2322 Anthropologie des représentations du corps/Société d'ethnologie française, Marseilles, 17, 18 and 19 January 2001

Bodin D. and Trouilhet D., "Le contrôle social des foules sportives en France: réglementation, difficultés d'application et extension des phénomènes de violences", in D. Bodin (ed.), *Sports et violences*, Chiron, Paris, pp. 147-168, 2001

Bodin D., Robène L. and Héas S., "Les femmes hooligans: paralogisme ou réalité sociale éludée?", in *Science et motricité*, 2004a (forthcoming)

Bodin D., Robène L., Héas S. and Gendron M., "Une approche de la criminalité féminine à travers l'exemple du hooliganisme", in *Criminologie*, 2004b (forthcoming)

Bœuf J.L. and Léonard Y., *La République du Tour*, Seuil, Paris, 2003

Boniface P., "Géopolitique du football", in *Manière de voir*, No. 39, pp. 10-12, 1998

Boudon R., *Effets pervers et ordre social*, PUF, Paris, 1977

Boudon R. and Bourricaud F., *Dictionnaire critique de la sociologie*, PUF, Paris, 1982

Bourdeux C., "Par moments, la balance était mon dieu", in *Soins psychiatrie*, No. 227, pp. 18-20, 2003

Bourdieu P., *La domination masculine*, Seuil, Paris, 1998

Bourdieu P., "La domination masculine", in *Actes de la Recherche en Sciences Sociales*, No. 84, pp. 3-31,1990

Bourdieu P., *Questions de sociologie*, Editions de Minuit, Paris, 1984

Bourdieu P., *La distinction. Critique sociale du jugement*, Editions de Minuit, Paris, 1979

Bourdieu P., "Comment peut-on être sportif ?", in *Questions de sociologie*, Editions de Minuit, Paris, 1978, 1984 edition

Bourg J.F., "Le sport à l'épreuve du marché", in *Géopolitique*, No. 66, pp. 51-58, 1999

Bourg J.F., *L'argent fou du sport*, La table ronde, Paris, 1994

Bourg J.F., and Gouguet J.J., *Economie du sport*, La Découverte, Paris, 2001

Bourg J.F., and Gouguet J.J., *Analyse économique du sport*, PUF, Paris, 1998

Bredekamp H., *La naissance du football: une histoire du calcio*, Frontières, Paris, 1998

Brochier C., "Des jeunes corvéables", in *Actes de la recherche en sciences sociales*, Vol. 38, pp. 73-84, 2001

Brohm J.M., *Les meutes sportives. Critique de la domination*, L'Harmattan, Paris, 1993

Brohm J.M., *Sociologie politique du sport*, PUN, Nancy, 1992

Bromberger C., *Football, la bagatelle la plus sérieuse du monde*, Bayard, Paris, 1998

Bromberger C., "Aimez-vous les stades?", in *Manière de voir*, No. 30, pp. 37-40, 1996

Bromberger C., *Le match de football. Ethnologie d'une passion partisane à Marseille, Naples et Turin*, Maison des Sciences de l'Homme, Paris, 1995

Broussard P., *Génération supporter. Enquête sur les Ultras du football*, Robert Laffont, Paris, 1990

Bureau J., "Football, déontologie et corruption", in *Pouvoirs*, No. 101, pp. 113-119, 2002

Cahn S.K., *Coming on strong. Gender and sexuality in twentieth-century women's sport*, The Free Press, New York, 1995

Caillat M., *Sport et civilisation*, L'Harmattan, Paris, 1996

Carrier C., *L'adolescent champion: contrainte ou liberté?*, PUF, Paris, 1992

Cascua S., *Blessures du footballeur, Comprendre, prévenir, guérir et reprendre plus vite*, Amphora, Paris, 2001

Chaker A.N., *Study of national sports legislation in Europe*, Council of Europe Publishing, Strasbourg, 1999

Chamalidis M., *Splendeurs et misères des champions; l'identité masculine dans les sports de haut niveau*, VLB, Montreal, 2000

Chapelet J.L., *Le système olympique*, PUG, Grenoble, 1991

Charroin P., "Allez les verts! De l'épopée au mythe: la mobilisation du public de l'association sportive de Saint-Etienne", thesis defended in the Department of Science and Technology for Physical Education and Sports, C. Bernard Lyon I University, 1994

Chartier R. and Vigarello G., "Les trajectoires du sport: pratiques et spectacle", in *Le débat*, No. 19, pp. 35-58, 1982

Chesnais J.C., *Histoire de la violence*, Pluriel, Paris, 1981

Clarke J., "Football and working class fans", in R. Ingham et al. (eds.), *Football hooliganism*, Inter-Action, London, pp. 37-60, 1978

Clarke J., *Football hooliganism and the skinheads*, Centre for Contemporary Cultural Studies, Birmingham, 1973

Coadic L., "Tueurs de foot", in *Sport et vie*, No. 31, 1995

Coakley Jay J., *Sport and society, issues and controversies*, CV Mosby, St Louis, Missouri, 1994

Colomé G., "Conflits et identités en Catalogne", in I. Ramonet and C. De Brie (eds.) *Football et passions politiques, Le Monde diplomatique, Manière de voir*, No. 39, pp. 57-59, 1998

Colovic I., "Nationalismes dans les stades en Yougoslavie", in I. Ramonet and C. De Brie (eds.) *Football et passions politiques, Le Monde diplomatique, Manière de voir*, No. 39, pp. 54-56, 1998

Comeron M., *The prevention of violence in sport*, Council of Europe Publishing, Strasbourg, 2002

Comeron M., "Violence dans les stades de football et projet Fan Coaching au R. Standard de Liège C.", in *CM Sport: jeux et enjeux*, No. 189, pp. 118-138, 1993

Comeron M., Sécurité et violence dans les stades de football, in *Revue de droit pénal et de criminologie*, No. 9-10, pp. 829-850, 1992

Coser L., *Les fonctions du conflit social*, PUF, Paris, 1956

Coubertin (de) P., "La psychologie du sport", in *Revue des deux Mondes*, pp. 167-179, 1900

Council of Europe, *The prevention of violence in sport*, report of the Lisbon conference of 23 and 24 June 2003 on "The role of local and regional authorities in preventing violence at sports events, in particular football matches", Council of Europe Publishing, Strasbourg, 2002

Council of Europe, *The Council of Europe and sport, 1966-1998*, Vol. 1, Legal and political texts, CDDS (98) 90 Part I

Coutel C., "Le spectacle sportif à l'heure de la mondialisation", in O. Chovaux, and C. Coutel, (eds.), *Ethique et spectacle sportif*, Artois presses université, Arras, pp. 19-27, 2003

Creuzé C., "L'après sport: les sportifs sont-ils tous égaux?," in P. Duret and D. Bodin (eds.) *Le sport en questions*, Chiron, Paris, pp. 35-49, 2003

Dasque E., "La fuite des muscles", in *Télérama*, No. 2799, p. 18, 2003

Davisse A., and Louveau C., *Sport, école, société: la différence des sexes. Féminin, masculin et activités sportives*, L'Harmattan, Paris, 1998

Debarbieux E. (ed.), *L'oppression quotidienne. Recherches sur une délinquance des mineurs*, Report to IHESI, 2002 (typewritten)

Debarbieux E., *La violence en milieu scolaire: état des lieux*, ESF, Paris, 1996

Debarbieux E., "Education, exclusion, mutation", in *Le nouvel éducateur*, No. 237, pp. 3-25, 1992

Debord G.E., *La société du spectacle*, Gallimard, Paris, 1967, 1996 edition

De Brie C., "La dérive du sport de compétition", in *Le Monde diplomatique*, pp. 22-23, 1994

De Brie C., "Pour le bonheur du peuple, l'Afrique sous la coupe du football", in *Le Monde diplomatique*, No. 21,1996

De Knop P. and Elling A., *Société et sport, sport et égalité des chances*. Brussels, 2000: Fondation roi Baudoin, available on the Internet at: http://www.kbs-frb.be

Delmas A., "Sur l'entraînement physique intense chez les enfants et les adolescents", in *Bulletin de l'Académie nationale de médecine*, Vol. 165, No. 1, pp. 121-126, 1981

De Loes M., "Medical treatment and costs of sports-related Injuries in a total population", in *International journal of sports medicine*, No. 11, pp. 65-72, 1990

De Mondenard J.P., *Dopage, l'imposture des performances*, Chiron, Paris, 2000

De Silva I., "La judiciarisation du football", in *Pouvoirs*, No. 101, pp. 105-112, 2002

Devereux G., *Ethnopsychanalyse complémentariste*, Flammarion, Paris, 1972

Di Megglio A., "Enfants sportifs et traumatismes", in *Microtraumatismes et traumatismes du sport chez l'enfant*, Masson, Paris, 1999

Druon M., "Du patriotisme sportif", in *Géopolitique*, No. 66, pp. 3-5, 1999

Dubet F., *La galère: jeunes en survie*, Fayard, Paris, 1987

Dufour-Gompers R., *Dictionnaire de la violence et du crime*, Erès, Toulouse, 1992

Dugal R., "Tendances et développement récents dans la lutte contre le dopage athlétique sur le plan international", in F. Landry, M. Landry and M.Yerlès, *Sport...: The Third Millenium: Proceedings of the International Symposium,* Quebec City, Canada, pp. 487-493, 1990

Duhamel G., *Scènes de la vie future* Le Mercure de France, Paris, 1930

Dupuis B., "Le hooliganisme en Belgique. Histoire et situation actuelle", Part 1, in *Sport,* No. 143, pp. 133-157, 1993a

Dupuis B., "Le hooliganisme en Belgique. Histoire et situation actuelle", Part 2, in *Sport,* No. 144, pp. 195-226, 1993b

Duret P., *Les larmes de Marianne. Comment devient-on électeur du FN?,* Armand Colin, Paris, 2004

Duret P., *Les jeunes et l'identité masculine,* PUF, Paris, 1999

Duret P., *Anthropologie de la fraternité dans les cités,* PUF, Paris, 1996

Duret P. and Bodin D., *Le sport en questions,* Chiron, Paris 2003

Duret P. and Trabal P., *Le sport et ses affaires. Une sociologie de la justice de l'épreuve sportive,* Métailié, Paris, 2001

Durkheim E., *Les règles de la méthode sociologique,* PUF, Paris, 1895, 1997 edition [published in English as The rules of sociological method, 1895]

Durkheim E., *De la division du travail social,* PUF, Paris, 1893, 1960 edition [published in English as The division of labour, 1893]

Economic and Social Council of the French Republic, "Sport de haut niveau et argent", draft opinion submitted on behalf of the Environment Section, Rapporteur Jean-Luc Bennahmias, 15 May 2002

Ehrenberg A., "Du dépassement de soi à l'effondrement psychique; les nouvelles frontières de la drogue", in *Esprit,* No. 249, pp. 134-146, 1999

Ehrenberg A., *La fatigue d'être soi,* Odile Jacob, Paris, 1998

Ehrenberg A., *Le culte de la performance,* Pluriel, Paris, 1991

Eitzen B. S., *Fair and foul: beyond the myths and paradoxes of sport,* Rowman and Littlefield Publishers, Lanham, 1999

El Ali M., Marivain T., Le Poultier F. and Léziart Y., "Douleur et stratégies de doping chez les marathoniens", Congrès International de la SFPS, INSEP, Paris, 2000

Elias N., *La société de cour,* Flammarion, Paris, 1985 [published in English as The Court Society, 1983]

Elias N., *La dynamique de l'occident,* Agora, Paris, 1969a, French translation of 1975

Elias N., *La civilisation des mœurs,* Agora, Paris, 1969b, French translation of 1973

Elias N. and Dunning E., *Sport et civilisation. La violence maîtrisée,* Fayard, Paris, 1994 [first published in English as The quest for excitement: sport and leisure in the civilizing process, Blackwell, Oxford, 1986]

Elo M. (Finland, Socialist), *Report to the Parliamentary Assembly of the Council of Europe on young people in high-level sport,* 18 January 1996 (Doc. 7459)

Epron A. and Robène L., "La lutte bretonne, du jeu au sport traditionnel: une pratique conservée par la pratique", in L. Robène and Y. Léziart, (eds.), *L'homme en mouvement: Histoire et anthropologie des techniques sportives,* Chiron, Paris, 2004

Ernault G., "Une réussite universelle", in *Manière de voir,* No. 39, pp. 13-15, 1998

European Commission, DGX, 1996, "The European Union and sport", Europe on the Move, Brussels/Luxembourg, 1996

European Commission, DGX, "The European model of sport", 1998, available on the Internet at: http://www.sport-in europe.com/SIU/HTML/PDFfiles/EuropeanModelofSport

European Commission, DGX, "Sport and employment in Europe", final report by N. Le Roux, P. Chantelat and J. Camy, 1999, on the Internet at: http://www.ensshe.lu/pdfs/EOSEfr.pdf

European Commission, Eurobarometer special on-line survey of European Union citizens and sport [September 2003, published in November 2003], available on the Internet in pdf format

Fansten M., "Financement de la télévision publique en Europe: les termes du débat", available on the Internet: http://www.ebu.ch/union/publications/pdf/publications_dif_3_99-10.fr.pdf (consulted on 15 April 2004)

Fillieule R., *Sociologie de la délinquance,* PUF, Paris, 2001

Fohr A. and Monnin I., "La France raisonnable: alcool, tabac, vitesse: un pays à consommation modérée", in *Le Nouvel Observateur,* pp. 10-22, 1 April 2004

Fontanel J. and Bensahel L., *Reflexions sur l'économie du sport,* PUG, Grenoble, 2001

Fost N.C., "Ethical and social issues in anti-doping strategies in sport", in F. Landry, M. Landry and M. Yerlès, *Sport...: The Third Millenium: proceedings of the international symposium,* Quebec City, Canada, pp. 478-485, 1990

Foucault M., "Le souci de soi", in *Histoire de la sexualité,* Vol. 3, Gallimard, Paris, 1984

Foucault M., "La volonté de savoir", in *Histoire de la sexualité,* Vol.1, Gallimard, Paris, 1976

Foucault M., *Surveiller et punir, naissance de la prison,* Gallimard, Paris, 1975

Foucault M., *Naissance de la clinique: une archéologie du regard médical,* PUF, Paris, 1963

Galland O., "Les valeurs de la jeunesse", in *Sciences humaines,* No. 79, pp. 26-29, 1998

Garfinkel H., *Studies in ethnomethodology,* Prentice-Hall Inc., Englewood Cliffs, New Jersey, 1967

Genevois B., "Le football, la gloire fragile d'un jeu", in *Pouvoirs,* No. 101, pp. 5-14, 2002

Gernet L., *Recherches sur le développement juridique et moral en Grèce,* Leroux, Paris, 1917

Girard R., *Les origines de la culture,* Desclée de Brouwer, Paris, 2004

Girard R., *La violence et le sacré,* Pluriel, Paris, 1972

Giulianotti R., "Participant observation and research into football hooliganism: reflections on the problems of entree and everyday risks", in *Sociology of Sport Journal,* pp. 1-120, 1995

Goffman E., "Role distance" in *Encounters,* Bobbs Merrill, Indianapolis, 1961

Goldstein J.M. and Arms R.L., "Effects of observing athletic contests on hostility", in *Sociometry,* No. 34, pp. 83-90, 1971

Gouguet J.J. and Primault D., "Formation des joueurs professionnels et équilibre compétitif: l'exemple du football", in *Revue juridique et économique du sport,* No. 68, pp. 7-34, 2003

Green R.G. and Quanty M.B., "The catharsis of agression: an evaluation of hypothesis" in L. Berkowitz (ed.), *Advances in experimental social psychology,* Vol. 10, pp. 1-37, 1977

Grésy B. (ed.), *L'image des femmes dans la publicité*, report to the State Secretary for Women's Rights and Vocational Training, La Documentation française, Paris, 2002

Griffin P., "Changing the game: homophobia, sexism, and lesbians in sport", in *Quest*, No. 44 (2), pp. 251-265, 1992

Grubisa D., "Le water-polo ou la guerre par d'autres moyens", *Courrier international*, No. 660, p. 14, 2003

Guichard N., *Publicité télévisée et comportement de l'enfant*, Economica, Paris, 2000

Hargreaves J., "Sex, gender and the body in sport and leisure: has there been a civilising process?", in E. Dunning and C. Rojek (eds.) *Sport and leisure in the civilizing process: critique and counter-critique*, MacMillan, London, 1992

Haroche C., "Se gouverner, gouverner les autres: éléments d'une anthropologie des mœurs et des manières (XVI-XVIIe siècles)", in *Communication*, No. 54, pp. 51-68, 1993

Harrington J., *A preliminary report on soccer hooliganism to Mr Denis Howell*, Minister of Sport, HMSO, 1968

Héas S., *Anthropologie des relaxations: des moyens de gestion de soi entre loisirs et soins?*, L'Harmattan, Paris, 2004

Héas S., *"La relaxation comme 'médecine' de ville?"*, doctoral dissertation in Social Sciences (Sociology), supervisor D. Le Breton, University of Strasbourg 2, 1 October 1996

Héas S., "Relaxation: propédeutique d'une pratique à non risque", in *Cahiers de Sociologie Economique et Culturelle*, No. 23, pp. 111-122, 1995

Héas S., Bodin D., Amossé K. and Kerespar S., "Football féminin: C'est un jeu d'hommes", in *Cahiers du Genre*, No. 36, p. 185-204, 2004

Héas S., Bodin D. and Robène L., "Symboles et postures: les relaxations comme techniques signifiantes", in *L'Année matérialiste*, 2005 (forthcoming)

Heinich N., "Art et sport au regard d'une sociologie de la singularité", in D. Bodin and P. Duret, (eds.), *Le sport en questions*, Chiron, Paris, pp. 125-134, 2003

Héritier F., *De la violence*, Odile Jacob, Paris, 1996

Hirigoyen M.F., *Harcèlement moral*, Syros, Paris, 1998

Hobbes T., *Le Léviathan*, Sirey, Paris, 1971 [English original, Leviathan, London, 1651]

Hoch P., *Rip off the big game*, Anchor Books, New York, 1972

Hurtebise C., "Sport politique et politique du sport de la RDA", in *Géopolitique*, No. 66, pp. 35-44, 1999

IFDHBP [Paris Bar Institute of Human Rights Training], *Rapport sur les violences dans les stades et le droit*, confidential internal report, 1995

James J., "The money game", in *Time*, pp. 50-55, 5 June 2000

Jaspard M., Brown E. and Condon S., *Les violences envers les femmes en France: une enquête nationale*, La Documentation française, Paris, 2003

Jeu B., *In honorem Bernard Jeu. Le sportif, le philosophe, le dirigeant*, PUL, Lille, 1993

Jeu B., *Analyse du sport*, PUF, Paris, 1987, 1992 edition

Jeu B., *Le sport, la mort, la violence*, PUL, Lille, 1975

Jeu B., "Definition du sport", in *Diogène*, No. 80, pp. 153-167, 1972

Johnson G., *Oi ! A view from the dead end of the street*, Babylon Books, London, 1982

Jusserand J.J., *Les sports et jeux d'exercice dans l'ancienne France*, Champion, Geneva, 1901, 1986 edition

Kadritzke N., "Acheter Manchester United pour mieux vendre", in *Le Monde diplomatique*, No. 22, January 1999

Kapuscinski R., "Les médias reflètent-ils la réalité du monde?", in *Le Monde diplomatique, Manière de voir*, No. 63, pp. 50-55, 2002

Kapuscinski R., *La guerre du foot et autres guerres et aventures*, Plon, Paris, 1986, 2003 edition

Kidd B., "Sport and masculinity", in M. Kaufman, *Beyond patriarchy: Essays by men on pleasure, power and change*, Oxford University Press, New York, pp. 250-265, 1987

Krane V., "Lesbians in sport: toward acknowledgment, understanding and theory", in *Journal of sport and exercise psychology*, No. 18 (3), pp. 237-246, 1996

Lanfranchi P., "Football, cosmopolitisme et nationalisme", in *Pouvoirs*, No. 101, pp. 15-25, 2002

Lassalle J.Y., "Les responsabilités civile et pénale des auteurs de violences sportives", in *La semaine juridique édition générale*, No. 49, pp. 2223-2229, 2000

Laure P., *Le Dopage,* PUF, Paris, 1995

Laure P., Binsinger C. and Le Scanff C., "Difficultés méthodologiques lors d'enquêtes nationales sur le dopage des adolescents. A propos d'un cas", in *Science & sports,* Vol. 19, No. 2, pp. 86-90, April 2004

Le Bon G., *Psychologie des foules,* PUF, Paris, 1895, 5th quadriga edition 1995

Legros P., "Le surentraînement: bilan des recherches et perspectives", in M.J. Manidi. and I. Dafflon-Arvanitou (eds.), *Activité physique et santé. Apports des sciences humaines et sociales, Education à la santé par l'activité physique,* Masson, Paris, pp. 127-141, 2000

Lepoutre D., *Cœur de banlieue. Codes, rites et langages,* Odile Jacob, Paris, 1977, 2001 edition

Le Roux. N. and Camy J., "Etude préliminaire à la constitution d'un Observatoire Européen des Professions du Sport", report to the MJS/EZUS Convention, 1995

Le Saux L., "Ils se foot du monde!", in *Télérama,* No. 2730, pp. 152-153, 2002

Lévi-Strauss C., *Triste tropique,* Pocket, Paris, 1955, 2001 edition

Lewis R.W., "Football hooliganism in England before 1914: a critique of the Dunning thesis", in *International journal of the history of sport,* Vol. 13-3, pp. 310-339, 1996

Leymann H., *Mobbing: la persécution au travail,* Seuil, Paris, 1993, French translation of 1996

Linton R., *De l'homme,* Editions de Minuit, Paris, 1936, French translation of 1968

Lorant J., "Les bienfaits de l'exercice physique: mythe ou réalité?", in M.J. Manidi and I. Dafflon-Arvanitou (eds.), *Activité physique et santé. Apports des sciences humaines et sociales, Education à la santé par l'activité physique,* Masson, Paris, pp. 142-152, 2000

Maigret E., *Sociologie de la communication,* Armand Colin, Paris, 2003

Maitrot E., *Les scandales du sport contaminé: enquête sur les coulisses du dopage,* Flammarion, Paris, 2003

Manzella A., "La dérégulation du football par l'Europe", in *Pouvoirs,* No. 101, pp. 39-47, 2002

Marinova J., "The attitudes of adolescents to the issue of gender-based violence", in *Learning from violence: the youth dimension*, Council of Europe Publishing, Strasbourg, 2004

Marsh P., *Aggro: the Illusion of violence*, Dent, London, 1978

Martins M., "The European Convention on Spectator Violence", in J. de Quidt and E. Johnston, Report of the Conference on the Role of Local and Regional Authorities in Preventing Violence at Sports Events, in particular at Football Matches, Council of Europe, 20 October 2003 (typewritten)

Mauss M., "Essai sur le don. Forme et raison de l'échange dans les sociétés archaïques", in *Sociologie et anthropologie*, PUF, Paris, 1923, 1997 edition

Mendiague F., "L'église et les interdits religieux du jeu: hasard, passion et désordre du XVe au XVIIIe siècle", in *Staps*, No. 32, pp. 57-66, 1993

Mennesson C., "Aller aux J.O. sans être un monstre: les processus de construction de l'identité sexuée des femmes haltérophiles de haut niveau", Recherches Féministes Francophones [French-language Feminist Research], third international colloquy "Ruptures, Résistances et Utopies", Toulouse, Le Mirail University, September 2002

Merton, R.K., "Structure sociale, anomie et déviance" in *Eléments de théorie et méthode sociologique*, Plon, Paris, 1965.

Messner M., *Power at play: sport and the problem of masculinity*, Beacon Press, Boston, 1992

Messner M., Hunt D. and Dunbar M., *Boys, men, sports media*, Los Angeles, 1999; available on the Internet at: http:// www.children now.org

Miège C., *Les organisations sportives et L'Europe*, INSEP Publications, Paris, 2000

Miège C., *Le sport en Europe*, PUF, Paris, 1996

Mignon P., "La lutte contre le hooliganisme: comparaison européennes", in *Football, ombres au spectacle. Les cahiers de la sécurité intérieure*, No. 26, pp. 92-107, 1996

Mignon P., *La violence dans les stades: supporters, ultras et hooligans*, Les cahiers de l'INSEP, Paris, No. 10, 1995

Mignon P., *La société du samedi: supporters, ultras et hooligans*, Etude comparée de la Grande-Bretagne et de la France, report to the Institut des hautes études de la sécurité intérieure, 1993

Morgan W.J., *Leftist theories of sport, a critique and reconstruction*, University of Illinois Press, Urbana and Chicago, 1994

Nuytens W., "Essai de sociologie des supporters de football. Une enquête à Lens et à Lille", dissertation defended on 11 December 2000 in the Faculty of Economics and Social Science, University of Lille

Nys J.F., "L'économie du sport", lecture, *L'université de tous les savoirs* [15 April 2004]; available on the Internet at: http://www.canal-u.education.fr

Nys J.F., "Le poids économique du sport en 2001 et son évolution", in *Revue juridique et économique du sport,* No. 67, pp. 79-83, June 2003

Nys J.F., "Informations économiques", in *Revue juridique et économique du sport,* No. 65, pp. 69-75, December 2002

Palierne C., "Le sport de haut niveau: de nouvelles contraintes et leurs consequences", in P. Duret and D. Bodin (eds.), *Le sport en questions,* Chiron, Paris, pp. 51-71, 2003

Papin B., "La violence symbolique de l'institution sportive dans le processus de production de ses élites", in D. Bodin, (ed.), *Sports et violences,* Chiron, Paris, pp. 89-106, 2001

Peretti-Watel P., "Le normal et le pathologique: dépressivité et usages de drogue à l'adolescence", in *Sciences sociales et santé,* Vol. 21(3), pp. 85-114, 2003

Perrin E., *Le culte du corps,* Pierre-Fabre, Geneva, 1986

Personne J., *Le sport pour l'enfant. Ni records, ni médailles. Conseil aux parents,* L'Harmattan, Paris, 1993

Personne J., *Aucune médaille ne vaut la santé d'un enfant,* Denoël, Paris, 1987

Personne J., Commandre F. and Gounelle de Pontanelle H., report to the Académie nationale de médecine on "L'entraînement sportif intensif et précoce, et ses risques" [Early and intensive sports training and its risks], 18 October 1983, Paris

Picquart J., *Pour en finir avec l'homophobie,* Chiron, Paris, 2004

Pierrat J.L. and Riveslange J., *L'argent secret du foot,* Plon, Paris, 2002

Pociello C., *Les cultures sportives,* PUF, Paris, 1995

Pociello C., *Sports et sociétés. Approche socioculturelle des pratiques,* Vigot, Paris, 1981

Poutignat P. and Streiff-Fenart J., *Théories de l'ethnicité,* PUF, Paris, 1995

Pujol M., Freydière P.I. and Bayeux, P., "La sécurité des équipements sportifs", in *Voiron,* Pus, No. 23, 2004

Ramonet I., "Passions nationals", in I. Ramonet and C. De Brie, (eds.), "Le sport c'est la guerre", in *Le Monde diplomatique, Manière de voir*, No. 30, 1996

Ramonet I. and De Brie C. (eds.), "Football et passions politiques", in *Le Monde diplomatique, Manière de voir*, No. 39, 1998

Ramonet I. and De Brie C. (eds.), "Le sport c'est la guerre", in *Le Monde diplomatique, Manière de voir*, No. 30, 1996

Raspiengeas J.C., "Le Tour infernal" [interview with Christophe Bassons], in *Télérama*, No. 2686, pp. 78-80, 4 July 2001

Ravenel L., "Le football de haut niveau en France: espaces et territories", thesis in Geography (spatial structures and dynamics) defended on 24 October 1997 at the University of Avignon and the Pays du Vaucluse

Redeker R., *Le sport contre les peuples*, Berg International, Paris, 2002

Redhead S., *Sing when you're winning*, Pluto, London, 1987

Ricard S., "Image et son", in *Vingtième siècle*, No. 14, pp. 79-89, 1987

Robène L., "L'aménagement des terrains de jeux scolaires à Bordeaux, 1940-1944", in P. Arnaud et al. (eds.), *Le sport et les Français pendant l'occupation, 1940-1944*, L'Harmattan, Paris, pp. 85-104, 2002

Robène L., "Icare et la violence des jours", in D. Bodin (ed.), *Sports et violences*, Chiron, Paris, pp. 35-61, 2001

Rochcongar P., Bryand F., Bucher D., Ferret J.M., Eberhard D., Gerard A and Laurans J., "Etude épidémiologique du risque traumatique des footballeurs français de haut niveau", in *Science & sports*, Vol. 19, No. 2, pp. 63-68, April 2004

Roché S., *La délinquance des jeunes*, Seuil, Paris, 2001

Roché S., *La société incivile: qu'est-ce que l'insécurité?*, Seuil, Paris, 1996

Rosé J.C., "L'Odyssée du coureur de fond", 90-minute documentary, France, 1997

Rosetta L., "Fécondité féminine et activité physique intense et répétée", in *Science & sports*, Vol. 17, No. 6, pp. 269-277, 2002

Rouibi N., Colloquy on "La sécurité et la violence dans les stades lors des manifestations sportives" [Safety and violence in stadiums during sports events], French Ministry of the Interior, internal document, 1989, updated on 15 February 1994

Roumestan N., *Les supporters de football*, Anthropos, Paris, 1998

Roussel B., *Tour de vices,* Hachette, Paris, 2001

Roversi A., "Football violence in Italy", in *International review for the sociology of sport,* 26, pp. 311-331, 1991

Saouter A., "Sport et proximité corporelle: la peur du tabou", in P. Duret and D. Bodin (eds.), *Le sport en questions,* Chiron, Paris, pp. 149-159, 2003

Saouter A., *Etre rugby,* Maison des sciences de l'homme, Paris, 2000

Skogan G.W., *Disorder and decline: crime and the spiral of decay in American neighborhoods,* The Free Press, New York, 1990

Slater M.D., Henry Kimberly L., Swaim Randall C. and Anderson Lori L., "Violent media content and aggressiveness in adolescents: a downward spiral model", in *Communication research,* Vol. 30, No. 6, pp. 713-736, December 2003

Sobry C., *Socioéconomie du sport. Structures sportives et libéralisme économique,* De Boeck University, Brussels, 2003

Society of European Sport Studies, "Organization of sport in Europe": http://www.sport-in-europe.com/ [consulted on 15 April 2004]

Society of European Sport Studies, "Sport policy of the European Union": http://www.sport-in-europe.com/ [consulted on 15 April 2004]

Sporeco, "Comparaison des budgets des clubs de l'élite en sport collectif": http://www.sporeco.com [consulted on 15 April 2004]

Taylor Y., "Class, violence and sport: the case in soccer hooliganism in Britain", in H. Cantelon and R. Gruneau (eds.), *Sport, culture and the modern state,* University of Toronto Press, Toronto, pp. 39-96, 1982

Taylor Y., "Soccer consciousness and soccer hooliganism", in S. Cohen, *Images of deviance.* Hardmondsworth Penguin, London, pp. 163-164, 1973

Taylor Y., "Football mad: a speculative sociology of football hooliganism", in *The sociology of sport,* pp. 357-377, 1971

Thibault J., *Sports et éducation physique, 1870-1970,* Vrin, Paris, 1991

Thom R., "Aux frontières du pouvoir humain: le jeu", in *Modèles mathématiques de la morphogenèse,* C. Bourgeois, Paris, 1980

Thomas R., "Le sport dans l'histoire", in *Géopolitique,* No. 66, pp. 6-14, 1999

Thomas R., *Sociologie du sport,* PUF, Paris, 1993

Thomas R., *Histoire du sport,* PUF, Paris, 1992

Thuillier J.P., *Le sport dans la Rome Antique,* Errance, Paris, 1996

Tranter N.L., "The Cappielow riot and the composition and behaviour of soccer crowds in late Victorian Scotland", in *International journal of the history of sport,* Vol. 1, No. 3, pp. 125-140, 1995

Travaillot Y., *Sociologie des pratiques d'entretien du corps,* PUF, Paris, 1998

Tsoukala A., "Vers une homogénéisation des stratégies policières en Europe?", in *Les cahiers de la Sécurité intérieure,* No. 26, pp. 108-117, 1996

Tsoukala A., "Sport et violence: évolution de la politique criminelle à l'égard du hooliganisme en Angleterre et en Italie depuis 1970", doctoral dissertation in Law, University of Paris 1, 1993

Van Limbergen K., Ardant P., Carcassonne G. and Portelli H., "Aspects sociopsychologiques de l'hooliganisme: une vision criminologique", in *Pouvoirs,* No. 61, pp. 177-130, 1992

Van Limbergen K., Colaers C. and Walgrave L., "The societal and the psychosociological background of football hooliganism", in *Current psychological research and reviews,* Vol. 8, pp. 4-14, 1989

Van Praagh E. and Duché P., "L'enfant et l'adolescent", in M.J. Manidi and I. Dafflon-Arvanitou (eds.), *Activité physique et santé. Apports des sciences humaines et sociales, Education à la santé par l'activité physique,* Masson, Paris, pp. 101-106, 2000

Vassort P., *Football et politique: sociologie historique d'une domination,* Editions La Passion, Paris, 1999

Vassort P., Ollier S. and Vaugrand, H. (eds.), *L'illusion sportive: sociologie d'une idéologie totalitaire,* Institut de Recherches Sociologiques et Anthropologiques, Montpellier, 1998

Vaugrand H., *Sociologie du Sport,* L'Harmattan, Paris, 1999

Vedel T. (ed.), *Médias et violence,* Les cahiers de la sécurité intérieure, 20, Paris, 1995

Vernant J.P., Vidal-Naquet P., *Mythes et tragédies,* II, La Découverte, Paris, 1986

Vogler C. and Schwartz S. E., *The sociology of sport: an introduction,* Prentice-Hall, Englewoood Cliffs, New Jersey, 1993

Wahl A., *La balle au pied: histoire du football,* Gallimard, Paris, 1990, 1996 edition

Welzer-Lang D., "Etudier les hommes et les rapports sociaux de sexe: où sont les problèmes?", in N. Le Feuvre (ed.), "Le genre: de la catégorisation du sexe", in *UNITAM- Revue de sociologie et d'anthropologie*, No. 5, pp. 289-312, 2002

Wieviorka M., *Violence en France*, Seuil, Paris, 1999

Wieviorka M., *Le racisme, une introduction*, La Découverte, Paris, 1998

Wieviorka M., "Les skinheads", in *La France raciste*, Seuil, Paris, 1992

Williams J., "When violence overshadows the spirit of sporting competition: Italian football fans and their clubs (Commentary on paper by Zani B. and Kirchler E.)", in *Journal of community and applied social psychology*, Vol. 1, pp. 23-28, 1991

Zani B. and Kirchler E., "When violence overshadows the spirit of sporting competition: Italian football fans and their clubs", in *Journal of community and applied social psychology*, Vol. 1, pp. 5-21, 1991

Zimmerman M., "La violence dans les stades de football: le cas de l'Allemagne fédérale", in *Revue de droit pénal et de criminologie*, No. 5, p. 441-463, 1987

Sales agents for publications of the Council of Europe
Agents de vente des publications du Conseil de l'Europe

BELGIUM/BELGIQUE
La Librairie européenne SA
50, avenue A. Jonnart
B-1200 BRUXELLES 20
Tel.: (32) 2 734 0281
Fax: (32) 2 735 0860
E-mail: info@libeurop.be
http://www.libeurop.be

Jean de Lannoy
202, avenue du Roi
B-1190 BRUXELLES
Tel.: (32) 2 538 4308
Fax: (32) 2 538 0841
E-mail: jean.de.lannoy@euronet.be
http://www.jean-de-lannoy.be

CANADA
Renouf Publishing Company Limited
5369 Chemin Canotek Road
CDN-OTTAWA, Ontario, K1J 9J3
Tel.: (1) 613 745 2665
Fax: (1) 613 745 7660
E-mail: order.dept@renoufbooks.com
http://www.renoufbooks.com

**CZECH REPUBLIC/
RÉPUBLIQUE TCHÈQUE**
Suweco Cz Dovoz Tisku Praha
Ceskomoravska 21
CZ-18021 PRAHA 9
Tel.: (420) 2 660 35 364
Fax: (420) 2 683 30 42
E-mail: import@suweco.cz

DENMARK/DANEMARK
GAD Direct
Fiolstaede 31-33
DK-1171 COPENHAGEN K
Tel.: (45) 33 13 72 33
Fax: (45) 33 12 54 94
E-mail: info@gaddirect.dk

FINLAND/FINLANDE
Akateeminen Kirjakauppa
Keskuskatu 1, PO Box 218
FIN-00381 HELSINKI
Tel.: (358) 9 121 41
Fax: (358) 9 121 4450
E-mail: akatilaus@stockmann.fi
http://www.akatilaus.akateeminen.com

FRANCE
La Documentation française
(Diffusion/Vente France entière)
124, rue H. Barbusse
F-93308 AUBERVILLIERS Cedex
Tel.: (33) 01 40 15 70 00
Fax: (33) 01 40 15 68 00
E-mail: commandes.vel@ladocfrancaise.gouv.fr
http://www.ladocfrancaise.gouv.fr

Librairie Kléber (Vente Strasbourg)
Palais de l'Europe
F-67075 STRASBOURG Cedex
Fax: (33) 03 88 52 91 21
E-mail: librairie.kleber@coe.int

**GERMANY/ALLEMAGNE
AUSTRIA/AUTRICHE**
UNO Verlag
August Bebel Allee 6
D-53175 BONN
Tel.: (49) 2 28 94 90 20
Fax: (49) 2 28 94 90 222
E-mail: bestellung@uno-verlag.de
http://www.uno-verlag.de

GREECE/GRÈCE
Librairie Kauffmann
28, rue Stadiou
GR-ATHINAI 10564
Tel.: (30) 1 32 22 160
Fax: (30) 1 32 30 320
E-mail: ord@otenet.gr

HUNGARY/HONGRIE
Euro Info Service
Hungexpo Europa Kozpont ter 1
H-1101 BUDAPEST
Tel.: (361) 264 8270
Fax: (361) 264 8271
E-mail: euroinfo@euroinfo.hu
http://www.euroinfo.hu

ITALY/ITALIE
Libreria Commissionaria Sansoni
Via Duca di Calabria 1/1, CP 552
I-50125 FIRENZE
Tel.: (39) 556 4831
Fax: (39) 556 41257
E-mail: licosa@licosa.com
http://www.licosa.com

NETHERLANDS/PAYS-BAS
De Lindeboom Internationale Publikaties
PO Box 202, MA de Ruyterstraat 20 A
NL-7480 AE HAAKSBERGEN
Tel.: (31) 53 574 0004
Fax: (31) 53 572 9296
E-mail: books@delindeboom.com
http://home-1-worldonline.nl/~lindeboo/

NORWAY/NORVÈGE
Akademika, A/S Universitetsbokhandel
PO Box 84, Blindern
N-0314 OSLO
Tel.: (47) 22 85 30 30
Fax: (47) 23 12 24 20

POLAND/POLOGNE
Głowna Księgarnia Naukowa
im. B. Prusa
Krakowskie Przedmiescie 7
PL-00-068 WARSZAWA
Tel.: (48) 29 22 66
Fax: (48) 22 26 64 49
E-mail: inter@internews.com.pl
http://www.internews.com.pl

PORTUGAL
Livraria Portugal
Rua do Carmo, 70
P-1200 LISBOA
Tel.: (351) 13 47 49 82
Fax: (351) 13 47 02 64
E-mail: liv.portugal@mail.telepac.pt

SPAIN/ESPAGNE
Mundi-Prensa Libros SA
Castelló 37
E-28001 MADRID
Tel.: (34) 914 36 37 00
Fax: (34) 915 75 39 98
E-mail: libreria@mundiprensa.es
http://www.mundiprensa.com

SWITZERLAND/SUISSE
Adeco – Van Diermen
Chemin du Lacuez 41
CH-1807 BLONAY
Tel.: (41) 21 943 26 73
Fax: (41) 21 943 36 05
E-mail: info@adeco.org

UNITED KINGDOM/ROYAUME-UNI
TSO (formerly HMSO)
51 Nine Elms Lane
GB-LONDON SW8 5DR
Tel.: (44) 207 873 8372
Fax: (44) 207 873 8200
E-mail: customer.services@theso.co.uk
http://www.the-stationery-office.co.uk
http://www.itsofficial.net

**UNITED STATES and CANADA/
ÉTATS-UNIS et CANADA**
Manhattan Publishing Company
2036 Albany Post Road
CROTON-ON-HUDSON,
NY 10520, USA
Tel.: (1) 914 271 5194
Fax: (1) 914 271 5856
E-mail: Info@manhattanpublishing.com
http://www.manhattanpublishing.com

Council of Europe Publishing/Editions du Conseil de l'Europe
F-67075 Strasbourg Cedex
Tel.: (33) 03 88 41 25 81 – Fax: (33) 03 88 41 39 10 – E-mail: publishing@coe.int – Website: http://book.coe.int